T5-CQE-223

Politics in Indonesia

Politics in Asia Series
Edited by Michael Leifer
London School of Economics

ASEAN and the Security of South-East Asia
Michael Leifer

China's Policy Towards Territorial Disputes
The Case of the South China Seas
Chi-kin Lo

India and Southeast Asia
Indian Perceptions and Policies
Mohammed Ayoob

Gorbachev and Southeast Asia
Leszek Buszynski

Indonesia under Suharto
Order, Development and Pressure for Change
Michael R. J. Vatikiotis

The State and Ethnic Politics in Southeast Asia
David Brown

The Politics of Nation Building and Citizenship in Singapore
Michael Hill and Lian Kwen Fee

Communitarian Ideology and Democracy in Singapore
Beng-Huak Chua

Politics in Indonesia

Democracy, Islam and the Ideology of Tolerance

Douglas E. Ramage

London and New York

First published 1995
by Routledge
11 New Fetter Lane, London EC4P 4EE

Simultaneously published in the USA and Canada
by Routledge
29 West 35th Street, New York, NY 10001

Reprinted 1996 (twice)

Routledge is an International Thomson Publishing company

Typeset in Times Ten by
Florencetype Ltd, Stoodleigh, Devon
Printed and bound in Great Britain by
T. J. Press (Padstow) Ltd, Padstow, Cornwall

British Library Cataloguing in Publication Data
A catalogue record for this book is available from the British Library

Library of Congress Cataloguing in Publication Data
A catalogue record for this book is available from the Library of Congress

ISBN 0–415–12548–0

Contents

Foreword

Foreword

Pancasila is a set of five principles enunciated by the late President Sukarno in June 1945 in an attempt to fend off demands for an Islamic state and to reconcile the cultural diversity of the embryonic Republic of Indonesia. Divisive at first, these principles have been enthroned as the exclusive national ideology by the military-based administration of General and then President Soeharto which has been in power continuously since March 1966. For some three decades, Pancasila has been at the very heart of Indonesian political discourse, at times contentiously so when, for example, dissidents have accused President Soeharto of appropriating the concept for his narrow purposes. Initially, Douglas Ramage, the author of this volume, assumed that Pancasila was merely the uninteresting rhetoric of a government trying to legitimize its rule. Closer examination made it evident to him that Pancasila had meaning for Indonesians far beyond government propaganda. It is the dimensions and significance of that meaning which Dr Ramage addresses with great skill.

This book is a pioneering and scholarly assessment of the diversity of understanding of the longstanding core concept of Indonesian national ideology and its uses in public life. Based on extensive interviews and other primary sources within Indonesia, the author identifies, in addition to that of President Soeharto, four "voices" or views of Pancasila comprising two distinct Islamic groupings, the armed forces and the secular nationalists. Beyond explaining the diverse and adverse conceptions and uses of Pancasila, an additional significance of this volume is that the issue of political succession in Indonesia is expected to become a matter of increasingly active debate as President Soeharto approaches the end of his sixth term of office in March 1998 at the age of seventy six. In that context, this book will be essential reading for an understanding of the idiom and meaning of that debate as well as the general nature of political discourse within the Republic as its elite confronts both political change and the twenty-first century.

Michael Leifer

Preface

This book was begun several years ago with the purpose of understanding why the Indonesian government devotes an extraordinary amount of resources to the propagation of Pancasila,* the national ideology. This idea was based on observations made during numerous periods of travel and study in Indonesia over the past decade. Many visitors to Indonesia notice that references to Pancasila are everywhere – on village-square monuments, on television news, in speeches by officials reported in the press, and if one were to look, even in school textbooks. At first, like many others, I saw Pancasila as the uninteresting rhetoric of a government trying to legitimize its rule. Upon closer examination it became apparent that Pancasila has meaning for Indonesians far beyond stale government propaganda. It was also evident that Pancasila plays a central role in ongoing political debates.

METHODOLOGY AND RESEARCH NOTES

In order to gain a comprehensive understanding of Indonesian political discourse and its relation to Pancasila, a diverse range of people were interviewed. Most information in this book is based on primary sources, particularly personal, one-on-one interviews with ninety-seven people. Approximately 175 separate interviews were conducted as many people were interviewed several times. Seventy-five percent of the interviews were conducted in Indonesian; the remaining were in English. Most people interviewed are members of the "elite" – both in and out

* Pronounced "Pahn-cha-see-lah."

of government. The kinds of people interviewed for this study included the following: government ministers, high-ranking active-duty members of the armed forces (from all service branches), senior bureaucrats, Muslim intellectuals and activists including the leaders of the largest Islamic organizations in Indonesia, leaders of the three political parties, official ideologists, retired military and government officials, leading members of religious and ethnic minorities, scholars, journalists, lawyers, and human rights and democracy advocates.

The diversity of opinion in such circles is extraordinary. The difficulty in interviewing this wide range of people was in trying to discern broad areas of commonality and difference on major political issues of concern to Indonesians, and particularly in reference to perceptions of the function and meaning of the national ideology. After careful consideration of the variety of views encountered in both personal interviews and written records relating to Pancasila discourse, four general "voices" could be distinguished: those representing views that tended to be affiliated with Abdurrahman Wahid, the Chairman of the large Islamic organization, *Nahdlatul Ulama*; other Muslims associated with the Indonesian Muslim Intellectuals' Association (ICMI); the armed forces; and secular nationalists, many of whom are democracy advocates.

An important point must be emphasized regarding the content of the interview data that was obtained. Wherever possible written sources were sought to confirm or back up information gleaned from interviews. This was not always possible, however, because officials, and many members of the interviewed elite who have a stake in contemporary political outcomes, often do not write down their attitudes, beliefs and perceptions. Since this study deals with contemporary issues, there has not always been time for a written record to emerge. It is important to note that in many ways Indonesia is still an "oral" culture. Decisions by the President for example, are not always written down – they are relayed personally.

A caveat regarding the "accuracy" of various Indonesian views is also necessary. Political behavior and decisions flow from people's perceptions and statements, regardless of their accuracy. While what someone said in an interview may not be entirely "true," it is still the case that such perceptions form the reality of politics and lead to tangible political outcomes.

Interviews were generally conducted with the understanding that this material was for legitimate scholarly use and would be fully cited. However, there were times when someone would emphasize that a particular opinion or piece of information was "not-for-attribution." Those requests have been respected and so there are unnamed citations in this book. It must also be acknowledged that the candidness of members of the elite may have been limited by their own internal constraints and political agendas.

Numerous written sources were consulted in addition to interview material. Official government publications, including speeches, ideological education materials, and books were examined. Analysis of the mass media over the past decade was useful in understanding the parameters of national discourse. Finally, statements and speeches from political parties and non-governmental organizations (NGOs), including mass-based Islamic organizations such as *Nahdlatul Ulama*, were also studied.

This book uses the commonly accepted form of spelling found in Indonesian mass media or that preferred by the person in question. Thus, "Soeharto" rather than "Suharto." Many personal and proper names continue to use the old spelling. Additionally, many Indonesians, especially Javanese, do not have given and family names, as is the case of the Indonesian President. Apart from personal names, the 1972 standardization and simplification of Indonesian and Malay language is otherwise followed. All translations are by the author unless otherwise noted.

Acknowledgements

The research for this book was carried out in Indonesia from September 1991 through December 1994. The first two years of research was supported by a Fulbright Scholarship and administered in Indonesia by the American–Indonesian Exchange Foundation (AMINEF). AMINEF was always caring and attentive during nearly two years of fieldwork. I am grateful to AMINEF Directors Pamela Smith and Dahana for their support. I am especially indebted to AMINEF Program Officer Nelly Polhaupessy who was always there to guide me patiently through Indonesian and American bureaucracies and who provided invaluable advice and professional support throughout my residence in Indonesia.

Additional support was provided from 1991–1993 by the Earhart Foundation in Ann Arbor, Michigan; the Institute for the Study of World Politics in Washington D.C.; and the University of South Carolina Institute of International Studies. Assistance for research in 1994 was again provided by the Earhart Foundation for which I am grateful to David Kennedy and Antony Sullivan. The East–West Center, particularly Charles Morrison and Bruce Koppel, generously supported my efforts in 1994 to complete this book.

The Center for Strategic and International Studies (CSIS) in Jakarta has provided Indonesian institutional sponsorship and assistance in every conceivable way. I am deeply grateful to the Directors and staff of CSIS – especially Hadi Soesastro, Clara Joewono, Yusuf Wanandi, Harry Tjan Silalahi, J. Soedjati Djiwandono, and J. Kristiadi – and many other staff members who helped ensure that my stay in Indonesia was a professionally fulfilling experience.

I also thank the Australian–American Fulbright Binational Commission whose funding allowed my participation in the Conference on Indonesian Democracy at Monash University. This conference allowed me to obtain critical feedback from a wide range of scholars at an early stage of my thinking for this book. I thank Herb Feith at Monash University for his kind invitation to the Democracy Conference and his thoughtful feedback on my preliminary ideas that eventually became this book.

I would also like to acknowledge the professional and patient assistance provided to me by the Indonesian Academy of Sciences (LIPI), the Department of Immigration, and other government departments. By granting me research permission and providing all necessary documentation and residency permits, Indonesian government agencies afforded me the opportunity to live and study in their country.

I would like to thank a number of people in Indonesia, Australia, the United Kingdom, and the United States who provided commentary and criticism of various drafts or portions of this manuscript or who provided substantial assistance in other valuable ways: Muthiah Alagappa, Robert Angel, Dewi Fortuna Anwar, Richard Baker, Greg Barton, Harold Crouch, Daniel Dhakidae, Djohan Effendi, Greg Fealy, Howard Federspiel, Herb Feith, Hal Green, Karl Heider, Ariel Heryanto, Mohamad Hikam, Richard Howard, Paul Kattenburg, Aristides Katoppo, Michael Leifer, Aswab Mahasin, Mochtar Pabotinggi, Ryaas Rasyid, Adam Schwarz, Marsillam Simanjuntak, Franz Magnis-Suseno, Michael Vatikiotis, Abdurrahman Wahid and Donald Weatherbee I thank Cynthia Nakachi for her skilled secretarial assistance. Gordon Smith and Victoria Smith at Routledge were patient and encouraging at all stages of the book's production. Of course, I bear sole responsibility for the contents and analyses in this book.

Several others deserve special mention. I thank John McGlynn, Wim Soeitoe, Victor Bottini, Isla Winarto, and Eddy Rustam for helping me make Jakarta feel like home. I also thank Jed Frost and David Salman for giving me numerous respites away from Jakarta city life to relax and organize my thoughts. Long-overdue thanks also go to Jan Lingard (now at Sydney University), my first and most encouraging Indonesian language teacher. I also thank Bobby Phillips for his years of support – often given from far-distant places.

Although many individuals have contributed to this project, I would like to acknowledge a profound intellectual and personal debt of gratitude to Donald E. Weatherbee at the University of South Carolina. For ten years he has provided unfailing encouragement and wise guidance in my scholarly endeavors. I could not have had a more fitting academic role model than Donald Weatherbee. I also thank Mary Ellen Weatherbee for her kind and warm hospitality.

Three people have had an immense impact on my life and work. My parents, Donald and Joan Ramage, have always shared the excitement of my efforts and accomplishments. I could not ask for more loving and supportive parents. For the past decade, my life, as well as my years of study and immersion in Indonesia, have been immeasurably influenced and enriched by Richard S. Howard. Despite his own research and writing on Indonesia, he painstakingly critiqued both the substance and style of this book and largely set aside his own work to help me meet my deadlines. For these reasons, this book is dedicated to my parents and to Richard Howard.

Numerous other individuals (far too many to name) contributed to this book with their willingness to patiently explain all aspects of Indonesian national life. Particularly to those Indonesians who generously gave of their time in interviews and countless discussions, I extend my heartfelt appreciation and thanks.

Douglas E. Ramage
Honolulu, Hawaii
February 1995

Glossary

abangan	Nominal Muslim who also adheres to pre-Islamic spiritual beliefs.
ABRI	*Angkatan Bersenjata Republik Indonesia*, Armed Forces of the Republic of Indonesia.
aliran	Socio-cultural "streams" or patterns of social organization.
Ansor	Men's youth wing of the *Nahdlatul Ulama*.
asas tunggal	The requirement that all organizations adopt Pancasila as their official ideological foundation.
Bhinneka Tunggal Ika	Unity in diversity, Indonesia's national motto.
CIDES	Center for Information and Development Studies, ICMI's academic think-tank.
CSIS	Center for Strategic and International Studies, a policy-oriented think-tank established in 1971 with the support of key New Order strategist Ali Moertopo.
Darul Islam	An organization which fought against the central government to establish an Islamic state, 1948–1962.
dasar negara	The philosophical basis of the state.
DPR	*Dewan Perwakilan Rakyat*, 500-member People's Representative Council (effectively the lower house of parliament).
dwifungsi	The military's doctrine stipulating a dual political and security function.

Golkar	*Golongan Karya*, or "functional groups." The government political party.
haj	The pilgrimage to Mecca.
ICMI	*Ikatan Cendekiawan Muslim Indonesia*, or Indonesian Muslim Intellectuals' Association, established in 1990.
Jakarta Charter	Compromise Preamble to the Constitution of 1945 that would have stipulated that Indonesian Muslims were obliged to carry out the *syariah*. Omitted from the final draft of the Constitution.
Kiai	Title for a respected Islamic scholar.
KOPKAMTIB	The armed forces' Command to Restore Security and Order.
Konstituante	The Constituent Assembly, 1956–1959.
KPNI	Indonesian National Youth Committee.
Lemhanas	*Lembaga Pertahanan Nasional*, National Defense Institute.
Masyumi	*Majelis Syuro Muslimin Indonesia*, Consultative Council of Indonesian Muslims. One of the major Islamic political parties prior to 1960.
MPR	*Majelis Permusyawaratan Rakyat*, 1,000-member People's Consultative Assembly. Meets every five years to elect the President and Vice President.
MPRS	*Majelis Permusyawaratan Rakyat Sementara*, Provisional People's Consultative Assembly.
mubaliq	Islamic preacher.
Muhammadiyah	Modernist Indonesian Islamic organization, founded in 1912.
musyawarah and *mufakat*	consultation and consensus.
NU	*Nahdlatul Ulama*, Revival of Islamic Scholars. The largest socio-cultural Islamic organization in Indonesia, founded in 1926. Formerly a political party.
P-4	*Pedoman Penghayatan dan Pengamalan Pancasila*, the Guide to the Full Comprehension and Practice of Pancasila. A national ideological education program.

Pancasila	The Indonesian national ideology consisting of belief in God, a just and civilized humanitarianism, Indonesian national unity, Indonesian democracy through consultation and consensus, and social justice.
PDI	*Partai Demokrasi Indonesia*, Indonesian Democratic Party. A government-mandated fusion of nationalist, Protestant and Catholic political parties established in 1973.
pembangunan	The New Order's economic development program.
pesantran	Traditional Islamic boarding school.
PKI	*Partai Komunis Indonesia*, Indonesian Communist Party. Banned in 1966.
PPP	*Partai Persatuan Pembangunan*, United Development Party. A government fusion of Islamic political parties established in 1973.
pribumi	Non-Chinese Indonesians.
Qur'ān	The Holy Book of Islam.
Rois Am	Titular religious head of NU.
santri	Orthodox Muslim.
Sapta Marga	The seven-fold soldiers' oath.
SARA	*Suku, Ras, Agama, Antar Golongan*. Reference to prohibition on provoking social unrest based on ethnicity, race, religion or between classes or groups.
SESKOAD	*Sekolah Staf dan Komando Angkatan Darat*, Army Staff and Command School.
Syariah	Islamic legal code.
Syuriah	NU's supreme Islamic law council.
ulama	Muslim religious teacher, often community leaders.
umat	Community of Muslim believers.

Introduction

The ideology of [illegible]

Introduction
The ideology of tolerance

> Although no society is innocent of collective notions about itself, some countries have made more of ideology than others.
>
> For ideology, like history, is less thing than process.
>
> Carol Gluck[1]

As President Soeharto approaches the end of his sixth term in office in 1998, national debate about the future political order in Indonesia is well under way. For the remainder of the 1990s Indonesians will be debating what kind of nation Indonesia should be and what kind of political system it should have. Questions about the legitimacy of President Soeharto's government, the relationship between Islam and the state, the role of the armed forces in politics, potential for democratization, the transition to a post-Soeharto era, and the nature of economic development, will dominate political discourse.

Debates over these issues are often framed in reference to the Indonesian national ideology, Pancasila. In its simplest expression, Pancasila consists of the following five principles which are included in the Preamble to the Indonesian Constitution of 1945: belief in God, a just and civilized humanitarianism, national unity, Indonesian democracy through consultation and consensus, and social justice. Rarely do outsiders consider Indonesia's national ideology to be more than a gloss on "real" politics and worthy of in-depth study. This is unfortunate because Pancasila pervades almost every aspect of political discourse. Pancasila legitimizes political behavior of not only the government, but of regime critics as well.[2] Political debate often takes place in the framework of Pancasila because it is Pancasila that makes open debate legitimate. This study will consider the ways in which Indonesia's political, military, religious (especially Islamic), and intellectual leaders think about and use the state ideology to discuss sensitive and controversial issues of the 1990s.

Since the enunciation of Pancasila as the formal ideological basis of the Republic in 1945, it has become an indelible part of political and ideological debate. The ideology dates to the now almost sacral June 1, 1945 "Birth of Pancasila" speech by Sukarno, the leading nationalist figure at the time and President of Indonesia from 1945 to 1966.[3] The initial purpose of Pancasila was to create common ground for the establishment of an independent, unified, modern state coterminous with the former Netherlands East Indies.[4] Sukarno described a state that he hoped would appeal to all Indonesians, regardless of their religion, ethnicity or regional origins. Proposals to declare Islam as the basis of the new Republic of Indonesia were seen as divisive by secular nationalist leaders. Therefore, Pancasila was designed as a statement of universal values, brilliantly couched by Sukarno in indigenous terms, upon which all Indonesians could agree. The essential social value of Pancasila was tolerance, particularly in matters of religion. Pancasila reassured secular nationalists, both Muslims and non-Muslims, that the new state would not prioritize Islam over other religions. Instead Pancasila stipulates that while Indonesia is philosophically based on religion, the state does not endorse any particular faith. This political compromise implied that government would respect the religious diversity of its citizens.

For many Indonesians Pancasila's tolerance is represented by what Indonesia should *not* be. For example, the well-known Jesuit priest and humanitarian activist, Y.B. Mangunwijaya argues that "all nations have limits" and that in Indonesia this means that neither an Islamic nor a communist state will ever be acceptable. Mangunwijaya says that Pancasila establishes these limits by guaranteeing a state tolerant of religious diversity and inclusive of all ethnic groups.[5] Political discourse in the 1990s, however, suggests that the limits of Pancasila's tolerance are under sharp contention.

Indonesians make it clear that the government alone does not monopolize Pancasila. This study will argue that some critics of the regime – both from outside and within the government – have appropriated Pancasila as an effective tool to question Soeharto's policies and raise sensitive issues. Indonesians searching for ways to legitimately express dissent, as well as contestants for political power, have periodically opted for a strategy to legitimize their challenges to authority by mounting it from a Pancasila-based perspective. The ideology is appropriated both to negatively appraise the regime for allegedly contravening Pancasila and to inoculate criticism against the charge of being "anti-Pancasila." This study will argue that Muslim leaders, secular nationalists, and even members of the armed forces accuse Soeharto's government of contravening Pancasila, ostensibly the state's sole source of ideological legitimacy.[6] While President Soeharto and the Indonesian armed forces also depict liberal democracy as contrary to Pancasila, leading Indonesian democratizers not only reject that assertion but also maintain that Pancasila is *necessary* for future democratization.

CHANGES IN POLITICAL DISCOURSE

Pancasila remains a central element in contemporary discourse despite long-standing attempts by the government to end debate about Pancasila and to ensure that only officials have the right to determine what kind of political behavior is consistent with Pancasila. In 1985 President Soeharto's government codified into national law the requirement that all social, religious, and political organizations must adopt Pancasila as their sole ideological and philosophical basis. Organizations that refused to adopt Pancasila in their bylaws, constitutions, or charters were banned by the government. This law was adopted after heated, polemical national debate. Many organizations, especially religious groups, feared that adopting Pancasila as their *asas tunggal* [sole ideological foundation] would compromise their organizations' integrity, independence, and even replace their respective *raison d'être* with a secular state ideology.

While heated controversy surrounded this government initiative, the debate about the appropriateness of Pancasila as the basis of the state ended following the adoption of the *asas tunggal* legislation. What had happened? How could such an emotional issue, hotly debated, fade from public discourse? Was the government so successful and powerful that it was able to cut off further debate about Pancasila and the official interpretation of it? Moreover, was the *asas tunggal* legislation simply the culmination of a prolonged effort by the Soeharto government to ensure ideological conformity by way of nation-wide Pancasila propagation through highly organized and rigorously implemented education programs for all Indonesians?[7] Why, and for what purpose, does Pancasila remain a focus of national political discourse for both official and non-governmental actors? Why can we see today, fifty years after its initial enunciation by Sukarno, after twenty-five years of New Order propagation, and ten years after the government successfully forced all organizations to accept Pancasila as their sole principle, that Pancasila endures as an integral and contested part of Indonesian political life? It is because Pancasila provides legitimacy for open political discourse in an otherwise highly restrictive political system.

VOICES IN THE DISCOURSE

This study will take into account the following "voices" that are heard in Indonesian political debate today: the largest Islamic social and cultural organization, *Nahdlatul Ulama* (NU) under the leadership of its General Chairman Abdurrahman Wahid;[8] Muslim activists and scholars, particularly those associated with the government-backed Indonesian Muslim Intellectuals' Association (ICMI);[9] the Indonesian armed forces (ABRI);[10] and politically secular civilian nationalists who emphasize nationalism and democracy instead of Islam as their preferred channel for political organization. Analysis of political discourse in Indonesia today is inseparably tied to the personalities associated with each of these voices.

No study of contemporary Indonesian politics can fail to consider President Soeharto who has dominated Indonesian national life for thirty years. Soeharto's "voice" will be discussed throughout the book, particularly regarding his relationship to the Islamic community and the armed forces. It will also be argued that President Soeharto's direct participation in national Pancasila discourse is much more muted today than it was a decade ago. For example, not since the beginning of the 1980s has President Soeharto explicitly accused his critics of being "anti-Pancasila."

It is not the intention here to suggest that Abdurrahman Wahid and NU, ICMI, the armed forces, and secular nationalists are either mutually exclusive or the only determining voices in national politics. These and other voices all participate in politics with complex linkages to each other. They are also influenced by trends such as the ongoing cultural Islamization of Indonesia, the increasing appeal of ideas about democracy, the rapid industrialization of a formerly agrarian society, and international developments. The voices delineated above allow examination of broad streams of thought regarding contemporary politics and the meaning and use of Pancasila in political discourse. Two specific examples of Indonesian political debate help illustrate the prominent role of the Pancasila ideology as expressed by two "voices" in everyday politics.

A MUSLIM VOICE

On March 1, 1992 at Jakarta's Senayan Sports Stadium approximately 200,000 members of *Nahdlatul Ulama* (NU), Indonesia's largest Islamic organization (with total membership of 20–30 million), publicly celebrated its sixty-sixth anniversary. The content of the anniversary message read by the NU leadership was unusual. It was a reiteration of NU's loyalty to Pancasila. Why should such a declaration of loyalty to the state ideology warrant designation as an example of political discourse in Indonesia in the 1990s? Because it shows how the state ideology – not Islam – legitimizes NU's voice in national life. In his own explanation of the use of Pancasila in the anniversary gathering, NU's General Chairman, Abdurrahman Wahid, states that he considers Pancasila to be the best vehicle to legitimize his organization's political actions. He also argues that expressing loyalty to Pancasila is the most effective way to emphasize NU's nationalist credentials, particularly in juxtaposition to the activities of ICMI, a newly established Islamic organization. Moreover, Wahid argues that by declaring NU's devotion to Pancasila, he demonstrates his commitment to a secular democratic state.[11]

AN ARMED FORCES VOICE

Lieutenant General Harsudiyono Hartas, former powerful head of political affairs for ABRI, provides a contrasting example of the way Pancasila is used. Lieutenant General Hartas argues that the activities of the Indonesian Muslim Intellectuals' Association (ICMI) contravenes Pancasila by prioritizing Islamic politics over national interests. Hartas also contends that Western-trained human rights and democracy activists advocate ideas equally incompatible with the ideals of Indonesia as a state officially based on Pancasila ideology.[12]

What then does Pancasila mean to Indonesians? How can it be used in such contradictory ways – by Abdurrahman Wahid to both legitimate NU's political behavior and to demonstrate a commitment to a secular democratic vision of the state, and by a senior general to *de*legitimize an Islamic organization and argue that human rights and democracy advocates are contrary to Pancasila? These examples illustrate together that Pancasila is readily appropriated for various – and often contradictory – purposes by different kinds of actors.

How Pancasila resonates in different ways for members of the political, military, religious, and intellectual elite will be the focus of the following six chapters. Chapter 1 reviews the origins of discourse about Pancasila in the Sukarno period (1945–1966). It also outlines the ideological structure and political debates of the Soeharto era (1966–1995). Contemporary political arguments in Indonesia have their roots both in the initial years of independence and in the early years of the New Order. Therefore, a review of the evolving place of Pancasila in political discourse is required. Chapter 1 examines the ideological foundations of the New Order and will show how Soeharto's "Pancasila voice" is reflected in the structure of government and the political parties. While Soeharto's voice on Pancasila is less audible in the 1990s, it is not necessarily less relevant. The reasons for this are changes in the constellation of political forces and the ways in which Soeharto has sought to preserve his power base within the regime and expand his popular legitimacy. For President Soeharto and his "New Order" government, Pancasila has always been the ultimate ideology of legitimacy. It is tied to the New Order's promise to rectify the ideological, political, and the economic mistakes of the Old Order. Pancasila has also been used by the government as a potent means of proscribing political behavior in Indonesia. It has represented an effective means of delineating the permissible boundaries of political discourse and behavior for thirty years.

Chapter 2 examines Abdurrahman Wahid and *Nahdlatul Ulama*. As leader of NU since 1984, Wahid has frequently spoken out on the meaning of Pancasila for Indonesia. Although Wahid leads a vast and diverse organization, the chapter focuses primarily on his views of the relationship between Islam and the state. This is because he has successfully dominated the organization's political voice on the national stage. Furthermore, Wahid's depiction of threats to Pancasila has partially set the terms of recent political debate about the relationship of Islam to government and the appropriateness of democracy for Indonesia. He appeals for an Indonesian Islam firmly committed to a politically secular nationalist state based on Pancasila. Wahid calls for a democratic society whose necessary precondition is adherence to Pancasila as the guarantor of a non-Islamic and non-military dominated polity. Yet he argues that Soeharto's short-term political imperatives have contributed to a dangerous revival of Islamic politics which may undermine the tolerance stipulated by Pancasila. As one of Indonesia's leading proponents of secular democracy, Abdurrahman Wahid's political ideas will also be considered in the discussion of secular nationalists in Chapter 5.

Chapter 3 examines Muslim intellectuals and politicians who are associated with a major new Islamic organization, the Indonesian Muslim Intellectuals' Association (ICMI). Many of the intellectuals associated with ICMI are also members of *Muhammadiyah*, Indonesia's leading "modernist" Islamic organization.[13] Unlike the other voices analyzed in this study, ICMI does not articulate a specific interpretation or appropriation of Pancasila. For many of these intellectuals and political activists Pancasila is a non-issue. However, the single most important aspect of Pancasila for those in ICMI is that the national ideology is no longer seen as opposed to Islam. This represents a dramatic change in Islamic discourse on Pancasila. However, some activists' desire to create an "Islamic society," rather than an Islamic state, is viewed by non-Muslims, Wahid, secular nationalists, and ABRI as potentially incompatible with Pancasila. Therefore, ICMI voices are deeply relevant to national Pancasila discourse, if only as negative referents. In order to strive for an Islamic society in which politics and government policy are imbued with "Islamic values," mainstream Muslim activists have dropped their previous opposition to Soeharto and to Pancasila, and endorsed his continuance in office. This represents a political strategy to take advantage of Soeharto's perceived need for legitimacy from the *umat* [Islamic community]. ICMI activists seek to position themselves better within the bureaucracy and government to effectively promote a more Islamized society. ICMI is not dominated by a single voice to the extent NU is by Abdurrahman

Wahid and so analysis of ICMI is based on the views of a number of intellectuals active in the association.

After consideration of Islamic issues, the role of the armed forces in national political discourse is appraised in Chapter 4. The Indonesian armed forces (ABRI) are doctrinally linked to Pancasila as the self-proclaimed defenders of the national ideology. The historic role of ABRI as the only national institution with both political and security functions is justified by the military's interpretation of Pancasila as an "integralistic" ideology in which ABRI's political role is considered an indispensable part of national life. Pancasila is explained by ABRI officers as an "integralistic ideology" which rejects civilian control over the armed forces and views competitive multi-party democracy as counter to Pancasila.[14] Along with President Soeharto, ABRI also uses Pancasila to differentiate between acceptable political behavior and conduct judged incompatible with the military interpretation of Pancasila.

Politically secular civilian nationalists and democratizers are the focus of Chapter 5. Secular nationalists generally hold that political mobilization and democratization should not be tied to religious affiliation. Secular nationalists often see Pancasila as the necessary precondition of democracy and as a political compromise which guarantees minority, non-Muslim rights. This view is strongly held by Abdurrahman Wahid. While some secular nationalists are concerned that a democratically elected Islamic-majority government may limit the rights of non-Muslims and thereby be inimical to democracy, others are careful not to exaggerate such fears. Therefore, this chapter will explore the dilemma faced by secular nationalists and democracy advocates as they struggle to navigate between the armed forces, President Soeharto, and a perceived revival of Islamic politics.

Finally, the concluding chapter will suggest what consequences discourse about Pancasila has for Indonesian politics. Indonesians' perceptions that a dangerous "revival" of ideological issues has occurred in the 1990s will be evaluated. The conclusion returns to consideration of President Soeharto's Pancasila voice in the 1990s and analyzes his role in the current revival of Islamic politics. The conclusion will also indicate which voices may be most relevant to future political outcomes. The final chapter will also argue that political developments within Indonesia are internationally significant and should be considered in comparative analyses, especially those concerning the relationship between Islam and the state. Indonesia provides important examples of how Islam and a secular government have managed their relationship, as well as how a national ideology can be supportive of peaceful nation-building processes.

Chapter 1

Origins of discourse

Politics and ideology since 1945

Discourse about the meaning, interpretation, and manipulation of Pancasila has been part of the Indonesian political landscape for fifty years. When Indonesians engage in political debate in the 1990s, they often make reference to previous ideological discourse and political events in Indonesian history. The roots of contemporary arguments about the relationship of Islam to the state, the role of the armed forces in politics, and the form of democracy appropriate for Indonesia are to be found in Indonesian history since the 1940s. This chapter is organized into four sections. The first will review the origins of Pancasila and its role in politics until 1965. The second section will focus on the legitimacy imperatives of Soeharto's New Order from 1966 to 1978. The third segment will concentrate on Soeharto's efforts from 1978 to 1985 to ensure that all Indonesians and organizations accepted Pancasila. Finally, this chapter will consider the "revival" of Pancasila debates, especially concerning Islam, since 1985.

THE "BIRTH OF PANCASILA" AS BASIS OF THE STATE: 1945–1965

On March 1, 1945 the Investigating Committee for the Preparation of Indonesian Independence[1] was established under the auspices of Japanese occupation authorities to prepare for eventual independence. The Investigating Committee was composed of prominent Indonesians representing the various social, ethnic, regional, and political groups in the Japanese-occupied Netherlands East Indies. Foremost among them were secular[2] nationalist leaders including Sukarno, the first President of Indonesia, and Mohammed Hatta, later Vice President. Additionally, distinguished religious leaders representing Islam and other religions were present. The committee's most contentious task related to ideology was to establish a *dasar negara* [philosophical basis of the state] for inclusion in the new constitution. Indonesia's leaders felt compelled to specify the state's ideological or philosophical basis. The 1940s were characterized by intense ideological debates. As Adnan Buyung Nasution, one of Indonesia's leading constitutional lawyers, has aptly observed, the "spirit of the times" was influenced by the clash between fascism and democracy, the spread of communism, and the rise, especially in Asia, of nationalism and anti-colonialism.[3]

There were several major difficult-to-reconcile ideological positions advocated by the members of the Investigating Committee. Conspicuous among them were those who wished to establish Islam as the basis of the state, those who sought to establish a secular, constitutional democracy, and those who advocated what became known as a *negara integralistik* [an "integralistic state"].[4] The most emotional and confrontational debates between members of the committee concerned the proposal that Islam be adopted as the *dasar negara*. In order to bridge the strongly held positions between nationalist advocates of a secular state and those championing an Islamic state, Sukarno addressed the committee on June 1, 1945 in a now-famous speech known as "*Lahirnya* Pancasila" [The Birth of Pancasila]. Sukarno purposely set out to establish a *Weltanschauung*, or "philosophical basis" for an independent Indonesia.[5] He sought to provide an ideological foundation upon which a state coterminous with the boundaries of the former Netherlands East Indies could survive as a unified national state. This objective had also been an explicit part of the nationalist struggle since 1928 when an Indies-wide youth congress declared that a future independent republic would form "*satu bangsa, satu bahasa, dan satu tanah air*" [one people, one language, and one nation]. This pledge became a rallying cry of the independence movement. To ensure that such a diverse nation comprising hundreds of ethnic groups and most major religions would be viable, Sukarno exhorted his fellow nationalists to accept five basic tenets as the common ideals upon which the state could be built. Pancasila, a Sanskrit-derived term, literally means "five principles." The speech was clearly designed to establish a political compromise. Sukarno proposed that five principles –

nationalism or Indonesian unity, humanitarianism, Indonesian democracy through consultation and consensus, social justice, and belief in God – could form a common platform on which all competing ideologies could meet and yet not threaten the essential unity of the Republic.[6] National unity would be threatened, Sukarno implied, if one exclusive ideology, Islam in particular, were to be enshrined as the basis of the state for all citizens.[7]

Sukarno's speech summarized the ideological debate at the time and sought to find a political compromise to allow vastly differing conceptions of state ideology to coexist. A brief examination of the concepts laid out in this speech is useful to understand both the original intent of Pancasila, how it has changed over time, and why it remains a potent force for framing political debates in the 1990s.

The first principle, belief in God (*ketuhanan yang maha esa*), recognizes that the state will be based on religious belief and that every Indonesian should believe in God. This implies belief in a monotheistic religion, a concession to Muslim concerns. This principle stipulates that Indonesians should respect their fellow citizens even if they have different religious beliefs. This tenet acknowledges that the state is tolerant of diversity of religious belief and expression. Importantly, it was a proclamation that Indonesia is a "religious" state, though not based on any particular faith. In other words, even though nationalist leaders such as Sukarno and Hatta did not advocate an Islamic state, they did not call for a secular state either. The distinction between Indonesia as a "religious" state, though not "secular" or Islamic, has been frequently reiterated by President Soeharto. Indeed, "secularism" has historically been associated with "communism" in Indonesia and in recent years has also been negatively identified with liberal democracy.

The second principle is humanitarianism, (*kemanusiaan yang adil dan beradab*, literally "a just and civilized humanity") and recognizes the place of Indonesia as an equal member in the international community of nations. Sukarno also referred to this principle as "internationalism." However, because internationalism was closely associated with Sukarno's confrontational foreign policy, the New Order has dropped the international dimensions of this tenet. After 1966 the New Order sought to redirect Indonesia's energies towards domestic economic development and stability. Therefore, the use of the term "humanitarianism" has completely replaced internationalism in Pancasila terminology. This tenet represents the ideal of humanitarian behavior between all peoples, especially among Indonesian citizens. It also emphasizes tolerance and respect between all Indonesians.

Sukarno's formulation of what was initially the first principle, Indonesian national unity (*persatuan Indonesia*), stressed the imperative of maintaining the unity and integrity of Indonesia as a single state. Donald Weatherbee, in his work on Indonesian ideology under Sukarno, argues that this principle required the "submergence of regional and ethnic loyalties to an allegiance to the Indonesian state."[8] This tenet recognizes that Indonesia must be coterminous with the former Netherlands East Indies.

Pancasila's fourth principle asserts that the state should abide by a commitment to Indonesian-style democracy.[9] This principle incorporates idealized concepts of traditional village governance. These concepts are known as *musyawarah* and *mufakat* [consultation and consensus]. The ideal is that decisions are reached only after all members of a community have had an opportunity to present their opinion (consultation) and then, only after all participants unanimously agree, is a consensual, harmonious decision reached. At the national level this consultative decision-making process is to be achieved by elected representatives in the DPR [*Dewan Perwakilan Rakyat*], or the lower house of parliament. As interpreted by both Sukarno and Soeharto, this principle implicitly argues that Western forms of parliamentary or party democracy are incompatible with traditional processes of Indonesian political decision-making. It is also clear, however, from Sukarno's initial exposition of *musyawarah* and *mufakat* that his primary audience were Muslims. *Musyawarah* and *mufakat* are Islamic terms and Sukarno sought to assure those seeking an Islamic-oriented independent Indonesia that their concerns and beliefs would be accommodated in a "Pancasila" state.[10]

The fifth principle, social justice (*keadilan sosial*), posits a goal of economic and social egalitarianism and prosperity for Indonesia. Sukarno stressed that the mere existence of political democracy did not guarantee economic democracy. This principle has become extraordinarily important for the legitimacy of the New Order. The government of President Soeharto has sought to fulfill this tenet through sustained economic development and rising standards of living. That is, the state exists for the well-being of its citizens as a collectivity, not as individuals.[11] This also provides the ideological basis for an active state role in the national economy.

Islam, Pancasila, and the state

The most fundamental argument that Sukarno made was that if the new state was based on "belief in God" then it would be neither an Islamic, nor a secular state but a "religious" state. All religions, including Islam, would thereby be free to fulfill their respective religious obligations. Wahid Hasyim, head of *Nahdlatul Ulama* (NU),[12] in 1945 acknowledged the nationalists' concerns about preserving the unity of the state and agreed that for the sake of the Republic, Islam would not be granted preferential treatment. Wahid Hasyim argued that the most important question for Muslims was not "What . . . shall be the place of Islam [in the state]?" But rather, "By what means shall we assure the place of [all] religion[s] in Free Indonesia? What we need most of all at this time is the indissoluble unity of the nation."[13]

Even though Sukarno's speech was generally well received by members of the Investigating Committee as a reasonable compromise regarding the *dasar negara*, some Islamic leaders pressed Sukarno and other nationalists for an explicit recognition of Islam in both the Preamble and the body of the Constitution that was being drafted. On June 22, 1945 a new compromise was adopted. In a draft Preamble to the Constitution, the Pancasila was retained but the ordering of the principles was altered so that belief in God was placed first. Additionally, after this tenet the following words were added: "with the obligation for adherents of Islam to carry out *syariah* [Islamic law]." Islamic leaders also sought to stipulate in the Constitution that the President must be Muslim.[14] This draft Preamble became known as the Jakarta Charter. However, after the Proclamation of Independence in August 1945 the Constitution that eventually emerged did *not* contain the concessions to the Islamic position as laid out in the Jakarta Charter. There was also no requirement in the Constitution that the President must be Muslim. Mohammed Hatta succeeded in persuading the constitutional drafting committee to omit the references to Islam in the final draft of the Preamble and the Constitution. Hatta was afraid that predominantly Christian eastern Indonesia would not join the unitary Republic if the new state were to seemingly endorse Islam, even indirectly, as its *dasar negara*.[15]

Consequently, much Muslim bitterness against the governments of both Sukarno and Soeharto stem from an Islamic perception of betrayal by the nationalists.[16] However, it should not be assumed that the abandonment of the Jakarta Charter was the only cause of cleavage in ideological discourse in the new Republic. Rather, it is the case that sharp ideological debate involving Islam and other alternatives for the *dasar negara* existed before the Jakarta Charter was proposed. Indeed, it was this emotional, difficult-to-reconcile debate over the religious basis of the state that prompted the Jakarta Charter in the first place. Buyung Nasution noted that in the Investigating Committee "controversies between the proponents of the Islam state and the secular state" threatened the nascent national unity.[17] It must be stressed that although approximately 88 percent of Indonesians profess Islam as their religion, many nominal Muslims do not channel their political ambitions through Islam. For example, in what is widely regarded as the most "fair" and accurate of Indonesian elections, the 1955 parliamentary polls gave all Islamic-oriented political parties a combined total of only 43.5 percent of the vote.[18]

In order to understand some Islamic perceptions of betrayal over the omission of the Jakarta Charter, the importance of Islamic contributions to the Indonesian independence struggle should not be overlooked. Numerous Islamic cultural and economic organizations established in the early twentieth century – such as the *Sarekat Islam* [Islamic League] established in 1912, the modernist *Muhammadiyah*, also founded in 1912, and the traditionalist *Nahdlatul Ulama*, founded in 1926 – all contributed towards the creation of an Indonesian national identity.[19] Muslim Indonesians were a long-standing part of the struggle for independence.

Despite the fact that the overwhelming majority of Indonesians profess Islam as their faith, and that Muslim organizations played key roles in the independence struggle, "Indonesia is a nation of Muslims divided in their understanding of what is entailed in being an adherent to that faith," according to Fred von der Mehden.[20] That is, not all, or perhaps even most, Indonesian Muslims channel their political aspirations through Islam. Clifford Geertz has argued that Indonesians are divided into several major *aliran*, (literally "streams," and defined by Geertz as "comprehensive patterns of social integration.")[21] The most important distinctions in *aliran* are *santri* and *abangan*. *Santri* refers to devout adherents of Islam, closely attuned to daily spiritual and social behavior based on diligent reading of the Qur'ān. *Abangan* are nominal Muslims, primarily rural Javanese, for whom Islam is the latest, symbolic overlay on pre-existing Hindu, Buddhist, and Javanese religious beliefs. In terms of political affiliation, *santri* tended to follow either of the leading Muslim political parties, *Masyumi* or *Nahdlatul Ulama*, while *abangan* generally identified with the Nationalist Party (PNI) or the Indonesian Communist Party (PKI). The applicability of *santri/abangan* distinctions for understanding Islamic and/or national politics is increasingly less relevant today because of the tremendous changes in Indonesian society in the last three decades – industrialization, Islamic cultural revival, and urbanization. There remains, however, a distinction today between devout and nominal followers of Islam. Thus, Indonesian Islam is far from monolithic in its adherents' interpretation and practice of faith and in terms of how, or even whether, Indonesian Muslims express their political preferences through Islam.

Religious and political differences within the Islamic community in Indonesia are sharply evident in Pancasila discourse. For even though Christians comprise approximately 7 percent of the population, this does not explain the historic "Islam versus Pancasila" discourse in a simple "Muslim versus non-Muslim" context. None the less, an "Islam versus Pancasila" dynamic shaped much of the debate and discourse about politics in Indonesia until the mid-1980s. And in the 1990s an "Islam versus non-Islam" dynamic has emerged in political discourse. As shown in the following chapters, this dynamic has important implications for national politics.

Much of the Islam–Pancasila debate that dominated the independence preparations in 1945 re-emerged in the deliberations of the Constituent Assembly between 1956 and 1959. The Constituent Assembly (known as the *Konstituante*, elected in 1955)[22] was given the task of devising a new constitution for Indonesia.[23] Once again the question of the *dasar negara* became the most divisive portion of the debates. Some Muslim political parties and leaders in the Konstituante sought to reopen the question of the Jakarta Charter. Feelings of bitterness from some

Muslim politicians over its deletion from the Constitution's Preamble still ran high. However, by the late 1950s Pancasila no longer represented a compromise or a meeting place for all ideologies as originally envisioned by Sukarno.[24] This was because Pancasila had been increasingly utilized as an ideological tool for delegitimizing Islamic demands for state recognition of Islam. Sukarno himself explicitly used Pancasila in this fashion in a speech that generated much Islamic anxiety and anti-Pancasila sentiment. In 1953 Sukarno candidly voiced his fears of the negative implications for national unity if Muslim Indonesians pressed their demands for an Islamic state, or for constitutional or other legal provisions which would constitute formal recognition of Islam by the state.[25] Reminiscent of the concerns expressed by Mohammed Hatta in 1945, Sukarno said that he feared many parts of the young Republic would "secede" and that other parts of the former East Indies, such as West Irian would not join an Islamic Indonesia.[26]

The issue of Islamic political demands on the state were vividly illustrated in the *Darul Islam* revolts against the central government between 1948 and 1962.[27] A series of Islamic-inspired armed uprisings in West Java, South Sulawesi, and Aceh were eventually put down by the Indonesian Army. The single greatest consequence of the *Darul Islam* revolts is that the "Islamic threat" was given concrete form. The *Darul Islam* reinforced in the minds of many "Pancasilaists" in the Konstituante the manifest danger to national integrity in efforts to establish Islamic government in Indonesia. Moreover, the army's successful operations against the *Darul Islam* clearly proved to the military both the threats posed by the "extreme right" (the term officially used to refer to Islamic fundamentalism in the New Order) and the indispensability of the armed forces in defending a non-Islamic Pancasila state. The *Darul Islam* has given the military, as well as others, a pretext for their anti-Islamic politics, thinking, and behavior for over thirty years. Reflecting on the unfortunate development of military suspicions of Islam as threatening national unity, Djohan Effendi has argued that the *Darul Islam*

> added to the natural suspicion of the army that there was no fundamental difference between the Islamic parties and the *Darul Islam* armed secessionist movement. The only difference, as far as the army was concerned, was that the first struggled

to achieve an Islamic state by legal means and the second did so by means of an illegal display of force.[28]

Meanwhile, other Indonesians were increasingly advocating that Pancasila was more than simply a political compromise designed to appease both Christians and Muslims. Nasution observed that in the Konstituante there were two groups of "Pancasilaists." "The first saw Pancasila as a forum, a meeting point for all different parties and groups, a common denominator of all ideologies and streams of thought existing in Indonesia." This version was defended by the PNI (Indonesian Nationalist Party, the largest political party), the PKI (Indonesian Communist Party, which won the fourth largest share of the seats in the elections for the Konstituante in 1955) and the Protestant and Catholic parties. In other words, these groups saw Pancasila in the original terms of a political compromise.[29] According to Nasution, "the second interpretation stressed that Pancasila was the only political ideology guaranteeing national unity and suitable to the Indonesian personality, and therefore, the only appropriate basis of state for Indonesia." Nasution notes that this interpretation of Pancasila was advocated by only a few members of the Konstituante, including Professor Soepomo, the original champion of integralism. This view of Pancasila went beyond seeing it as a political compromise, but instead as the ideological expression of indigenous political culture (and hostile to both Islamic and democratic ideologies). This view of Pancasila as an all-encompassing national ideology gained favor "outside" the Konstituante, especially with President Sukarno and the armed forces.[30] Beliefs supporting Pancasila as a fully fledged ideology in its own right which was in accordance with Indonesian culture and "personality" became, in the 1980s and 1990s, a central part of the largely military-supported concept of "integralism." Integralism conceives the state and society as an organic totality in which the primary emphasis is not seen in terms of individual rights or limitations on the powers of government, but in terms of social obligations. The strongest proponent of Indonesia as an "integralistic state" in the original Investigating Committee deliberations was Professor Soepomo who stressed that integralism most accurately reflected indigenous political culture.[31] This will be examined in detail in Chapter 4.

In 1959 Sukarno, on the urging of the Commander of the Armed

Forces, General A.H. Nasution, dissolved the Konstituante and decreed the original Constitution of August 18, 1945 to be the sole legal constitution of Indonesia.[32] Sukarno declared that three years of debate in the Konstituante had failed to resolve any of the pressing ideological, political, and constitutional questions, much less write a new constitution.[33] The Pancasila remained unchanged with no Jakarta Charter-like additions, although Sukarno in a nod to Muslim concerns, did state that the Jakarta Charter influenced the "spirit" of the Constitution. The period from 1959 until the events of September 30, 1965, which implicated the Indonesian Communist Party (PKI) in a plot to overthrow the government, was a confusing and highly charged time. It was the period of so-called Guided Democracy – a period of intense three-way political maneuvering between Sukarno, the armed forces, and the PKI, the most disciplined and fastest-growing political party in the country by the early 1960s. Sukarno was the leading figure in this period as both the communists and the armed forces struggled for his support and influence.[34]

The Guided Democracy era was characterized by ongoing secessionist movements in various parts of the country and Islamic-inspired armed struggle against the central government, the *Darul Islam*. The continuance of armed threats to the nation's unity highlighted in the minds of many, especially in the armed forces, the costly political implications of ideological disagreement on the *dasar negara*. This was also the time in which the armed forces established a measure of unity over themselves, successfully crushed regional rebellions, and emerged as the leading, most disciplined, and best organized national institution apart from the PKI.

The position of Islam was also increasingly precarious as Sukarno banned the largest Islamic party, *Masyumi*, because of its alleged involvement in regional and Islamic rebellion. In the Guided Democracy period Sukarno also sought to limit the power of all political parties. In the mid-1950s Sukarno suggested that the country reject political parties because they militated against the concepts of *musyawarah* and *mufakat*, enshrined in the Pancasila.[35] In an attempt to ideologically balance the contending forces of Islam, nationalism, and communism, Sukarno advocated not just Pancasila, but also a concept known as "NASAKOM." NASAKOM referred to a forced unity of nationalism, religion, and communism. The competing political and ideological interests of the PKI, the army, and Sukarno constituted an extremely unstable political structure in the early 1960s.

The armed forces as defenders of Pancasila

The Indonesian Armed Forces were never an apolitical, Western-style institution. Born in the throes of national revolution, the military was generally not staffed by a rump colonial-trained force. Most members joined either under Japanese auspices or spontaneously after the Proclamation of Independence in August 1945 and the subsequent attempt by the Dutch and the Allies to reinstate Dutch colonial rule in Indonesia.[36] There were, however, a small number of professional Dutch-trained officers who also joined the new *Tentara Nasional Indonesia* (TNI, or Indonesian National Army). Cleavages within the ranks between the few professionally trained officers and the bulk of the officer corps, which was either recruited by the Japanese or who had joined spontaneously, marred internal military cohesiveness for years after the end of the revolutionary struggle.

However, several points must be stressed. The Indonesian Army (TNI)[37] was intensely proud of its leading role in the revolutionary struggle. Official Indonesian military history makes much of several revolutionary era events as formative in the military's thinking about its social and political roles. First, in November 1945 the TNI fiercely resisted a British-led attack on Java's second city, Surabaya. Second, in 1948 the civilian nationalist leadership of the nascent Republic was captured (or, in Indonesian military histories, "allowed itself" to be captured) in a Dutch attack against the Republic's capital in Yogyakarta, Central Java. Despite the capture of the civilian leaders, the military campaign continued as the young commander of the armed forces, the revered General Sudirman, moved his forces into rural areas to concentrate on guerilla warfare against the Dutch. Indeed, the TNI still considers the military role in the revolutionary struggle to be the paramount reason for the eventual Dutch capitulation by late 1949.[38]

Another defining experience of the TNI in the pre-1965 period was its role in suppressing a communist-led rebellion against the struggling nationalist state at the East Javanese town of Madiun in 1948. The PKI, in an act vividly remembered as treachery in Indonesian military and New Order history, rose up against the young Republic at it weakest moment, when it was in the throes of life and death struggle against the Dutch.[39]

Similarly, after the attainment of full independence the military was called upon to put down numerous revolts and rebellions. The two most serious revolts were a regional uprising known as the PRRI-Permesta Rebellion[40] and the *Darul Islam* (noted above). Successful military operations against these threats to the state, including military operations to force the Dutch withdrawal from West Irian (not relinquished by the Dutch in 1949)[41] all contributed to intense institutional feelings within the ranks, despite internal cleavages, that the Indonesian armed forces were the saviors of the nation – not just during the Revolution, but on many occasions thereafter. The role of the army in these events had a profound effect on military political thinking according to Harold Crouch: "by proving its indispensability in the crisis caused by the rebellion, the army leadership underpinned its claim to a more permanent role in the government."[42] The enemies were always understood to be the same, either communists or Muslim proponents of an Islamic state, both of whom were perceived as divisive forces. Thus, according to the military, only the army was capable of maintaining national unity and independence.

The army saw itself as the only genuine "national" institution and the development of Indonesian military ideology closely adhered to a powerful sense of the indispensability of the military for Indonesia's well-being. The military creed is contained in the almost sacral *Sapta Marga* [the seven-fold soldiers' oath] which lists the foremost duty of a soldier to "defend Pancasila." During the 1950s, the growth of the communist party, threats to the integrity of the state, and military disgust at the perceived failure of parliamentary democracy to tackle effectively the country's problems reinforced the military's perception of its legitimate political role.

The elaboration of a comprehensive military doctrine on the political and social role of the armed forces in Indonesian society is illustrated in General Nasution's concept of the "Middle Way" first enunciated in the mid-1950s. According to Harold Crouch, the "Middle Way" was a doctrine formulated by Nasution to justify military political, economic, and administrative functions. The "Middle Way" stipulated that the "army would neither seek to take over the government nor remain politically inactive."[43]

Eventually, after the rise of Soeharto's New Order, the military promulgated a fully-fledged doctrine known as the "dual function" (usually referred to as *dwifungsi*) in which the army explicitly rejects any notion of a strictly apolitical stance and asserts its right as savior of the state and defender of the Pancasila to justify a permanent political role in society. Thus, from the late 1950s to the early 1960s military perception of the most powerful civilian parties as either Islamic (*Masyumi*, for example) or communist (the PKI), set the stage for intense ideological conflict.[44] It is also important to note that the military appropriated the concept of "functional groups" (or Golkar, from *Golongan Karya*), initially promoted by Sukarno as an alternative to the political party system. Sukarno had proposed substituting party representation with "functional groups," such as peasant, labor, intellectuals and youth groups. The army, however, saw the "functional group" concept as a way to legitimize military participation in political life because it too was considered but one of society's many groups. Moreover, the army saw the functional group concept as a way to compete politically with the parties, especially the PKI. Under the New Order, Golkar has essentially become the official government-backed political party.[45]

The Indonesian army views its legitimacy as stemming from having appointed itself as the defender of the Pancasila state: a non-communist, non-Islamic, unitary state. Military-backed efforts to base the legitimacy of the New Order of President Soeharto on Pancasila were consistent with the history and ideology of the armed forces. In particular, ABRI stressed its obligation to correct the "deviations" from Pancasila that occurred under Sukarno and the parliamentary democracy period of the 1950s.

Therefore, from its very inception, Pancasila has had explicitly political functions to legitimize authority. It was used by Sukarno as the political formula to prevent Islamic demands for formal links between the state and Islam from weakening the independence struggle. The emergence of armed Islamic groups, particularly the *Darul Islam* underscored in the minds of many government officials, especially members of the armed forces, that "political" Islam was a threat to the state. Additionally, communism and liberal democracy were viewed as anti-Pancasila ideologies and remain potent negative reference points for many Indonesians, especially in ABRI.

THE NEW ORDER'S LEGITIMACY IMPERATIVES: 1965–1978

The watershed event of Indonesian political history is the coup attempt of September 30/October 1, 1965 which implicated the Communist Party in an effort to overthrow the government.[46] On that date six senior military commanders were abducted and assassinated after which a new government was proclaimed and briefly led by several relatively junior officers before being put down by Soeharto and other army forces. Although the exact parameters of PKI involvement are still unclear, the PKI was implicated in some measure in the coup attempt. The precise role of Sukarno also has yet to be fully explained. In the aftermath of this affair, Sukarno's regime was rapidly discredited. This was due to many factors, including Sukarno's unwillingness to apportion blame to the PKI for its role in the assassination of the generals by PKI-affiliated persons in the early morning hours of October 1.

The Commander of the Strategic Reserve, Lieutenant General Soeharto, emerged as the leading senior officer in the suppression of the attempted coup. Soeharto was faced with the problem of establishing legitimacy as power was gradually wrested from President Sukarno in late 1965 and early 1966. Soeharto's imperative was to establish the new regime as the legitimate, constitutional successor to the first President. From the ideological milieu of the Sukarno years the new government extracted Pancasila as the only basis of the state and hence the most appropriate formula for legitimizing its authority.[47] Soeharto and his supporters eventually styled their successor-government as the "New Order" and by 1967 had instituted fundamental reorientations of most major economic, political, and foreign policies.

The Soeharto group was forced to establish stable authority in an inordinately unstable time. From October 1965 through early 1966, Indonesia was convulsed with extraordinary violence.[48] A deep polarization among the people had developed from the late 1950s through the manipulation of the masses in the interests of, primarily, Jakarta-based elites. Intense, decades-long rivalries between Islamic, communist, and nationalist organizations and the armed forces all came to a head in a ferocious orgy of violence in the immediate wake of the coup attempt. Persons and groups suspected of communist affiliation were the prime targets of, especially, rural Islamic groups bent on taking revenge against supporters of the "atheistic" PKI who had advocated land reform (often to the detriment of the interests of Muslim landowners). Many of the attacks on suspected communist sympathizers were carried out with army backing. Often people and whole villages were the victims of grudges not necessarily connected with communism but for which accusation of "PKI!" was sufficient to warrant attack. Officials of the New Order now concede that between October 1965 and early 1966 perhaps up to 500,000 people were killed, primarily in communal violence.[49]

Both the violent aftermath of the coup attempt and the societal polarization engendered in the earlier Guided Democracy period had convinced many people and groups, not just the military, of a need to "de-politicize" society (examined in detail below). The New Order coalition initially consisted of not only the armed forces, but also student and youth groups, Muslims, intellectuals, democrats, much of the middle class, the business community, prominent media and publishing figures, and leaders of many of the political parties. The armed forces, however, were clearly the dominant force in the New Order group. This early New Order coalition successfully provided the backing to depose Sukarno in March 1966.[50]

Interpretation of the New Order's Pancasila

The New Order focused upon Pancasila and enshrined it as the ideological pillar of the regime. It now emerged as the fully-fledged ideological justification of the ruling group, no longer simply a common platform where all ideologies could meet. A decision of the Provisional Peoples' Consultative Assembly[51] (the MPRS, the nation's highest legislative body), and speeches by Soeharto and a key New Order politician, Adam Malik, illustrate the importance given to Pancasila by the New Order. Finally, the influence of the political thinking of late General Ali Moertopo, a chief New Order strategist and former principal political advisor to President Soeharto, shows how the New Order operationalized its conception of Pancasila.

In spite of the immediate problems of economic and political stabilization and security in 1966, the New Order also addressed its ideological legitimacy. In 1966 and 1967 the foundations of a government legitimized by Pancasila ideology were progressively laid. By mid-1966 the MPRS had been purged of Sukarno supporters. It was now in a position to legalize the New Order government. The MPRS issued a decision on July 5, 1966 which authorized the assumption of power by Lieutenant General Soeharto and elaborated on the "deviations" in the implementation of Pancasila and the Constitution that had occurred during the "Old Order" under Sukarno. MPRS Decision no. XX/1966 stated that the "New Order led by Lieutenant General Soeharto is based on the Constitution and the Pancasila and will carry out the goals of the Revolution." This decision explicitly recognized the lasting validity, legality, and revolutionary spirit of the Constitution and Pancasila even though, as it was pointed out, they were not properly implemented and followed under Sukarno. The consequence of deviation from Pancasila, the MPRS noted, was the communist-inspired coup attempt of September 30, 1965. The MPRS decision also gave the force of law to a triumvirate of "the people, the armed forces, and the government." The military was thus directly tied to correcting the deviations in Pancasila and the Constitution that occurred under the Old Order. Significantly, the MPRS said that the highest source of national law was the "spirit" of Pancasila which, the MPRS acknowledged, was a reflection of national character, and was given voice by Sukarno in his famous "Birth of Pancasila Speech" in 1945. Furthermore, the MPRS said that the Preamble, in which the tenets of Pancasila are stipulated, was superior to the body of the Constitution of 1945.[52]

Importantly, there was not a break with the past in a constitutional or ideological sense in that the language and terms of Pancasila and the Constitution were retained. MPRS Decision no. XX accepted the legality and validity of Sukarno's dissolution of the Konstituante in 1959, including his decree which returned Indonesia to the original Constitution of 1945. The MPRS noted that Sukarno was correct in dissolving the Konstituante and returning to the 1945 document (a decision that was strongly encouraged by the army) because the Constitution of 1950 was based on liberal, parliamentary democracy that was said to be in conflict with Indonesian values and Pancasila.[53]

On the twenty-second anniversary of the "Birth of Pancasila" in 1967 both President Soeharto and Adam Malik, then Senior Minister for political affairs and later Foreign Minister and Vice President from 1978–1983, gave speeches in which they explicitly tied the legitimacy of the New Order to the Pancasila. Furthermore, both men, but particularly Adam Malik, expressed views on the role of Pancasila as a fully-fledged ideology that simultaneously legitimized the New Order, justified deposing former President Sukarno, delegitimized both Islam (as a political force) and communism, as well as promising a better future for all Indonesians through increased national prosperity.[54]

Soeharto and Malik rejected liberal democracy as a "deviation" from the true intent of Pancasila. According to New Order thinking, Sukarno was correct to repudiate the parliamentary democracy system when he dissolved the Konstituante in favor of Guided Democracy.[55] According to the New Order, Sukarno's greatest sin against Pancasila was his encouragement of the PKI, which by definition was anti-Pancasila because communism was incompatible with the first principle, belief in God. In perhaps the clearest statement of ideological purpose of the New Order, President Soeharto rhetorically asked whether the "struggle and conviction of the New Order is nothing less than to implement Pancasila in a pure and consistent manner?"[56] These statements clearly demonstrate that there was no official interpreter of Pancasila other than the government in power. There is no independent body, such as the Supreme Court, that is charged with determining whether something is or is not consistent with Pancasila and the Constitution.

Soeharto expressed Pancasila as an all-encompassing philosophy of life, unique to Indonesia and personified by the government of the New Order. Adam Malik stated that although Pancasila was created twenty-two years earlier, only in the previous two years (since 1965) had it been given shape and substance consistent with Sukarno's original intention. Thus, even though Soeharto and the New Order deposed Sukarno, they sought legitimacy by invoking him as the creator of Pancasila. Malik noted that every major threat to the nation – the communist uprising in Madiun in 1948, the *Darul Islam*, regional separatist movements, and finally the communist-inspired coup attempt of 1965 – constituted a threat to Pancasila, and all were destroyed. Malik pointed to MPRS Decision no. XX as proof that Pancasila was indeed the supreme legal and "moral" source of law, authority, and legitimacy in Indonesia. Malik emphasized that Pancasila could not be fulfilled if there were elements in the nation that were not in accordance with the "national personality" such as "foreign ideologies" which promote Western-style opposition political parties.[57]

Soeharto's and Malik's speeches are the best examples of the ascendence of Pancasila as a fully-fledged ideology that would brook no ideological opposition. The MPRS decision, combined with Adam Malik's and President Soeharto's statement, explicitly established the legitimacy of the New Order in terms of its "pure and consistent" implementation of Pancasila. Indeed, Malik argued, Pancasila could not be separated from the New Order as, after all, Pancasila was the "starting point" of the regime. Malik declared that the New Order had therefore, a "deep conviction to serve the people and to serve the national interest based upon the philosophy of Pancasila."[58]

In addition to Sukarno's encouragement of the PKI, the New Order identified a number of other specific deviations from Pancasila that occurred under Sukarno. The principle of social justice was violated by Sukarno, according to New Order doctrine, because chaotic economic conditions of the time prevented improvement in standards of living. Adam Malik linked control of inflation and promises to improve national prosperity to the principles of Pancasila and the New Order's implementation of them.[59] The New Order has indeed emphasized *pembangunan* [economic development].

In all these formulations, the guiding, predominant role of ABRI was also emphasized.[60] Drawing on its historical experiences, two basic assumptions underscored ABRI's political thinking in the New Order. These assumptions would eventually drive away some of the early New Order supporters who initially saw the army as an agent of democratization. First, Soeharto and ABRI were convinced that Western-style parliamentary democracy with competing political parties was inappropriate for Indonesia.[61] Marsillam Simanjuntak, an early New Order supporter and now a prominent advocate of democratization, observed that many backers of the New Order who put their faith in the army as an agent of modernization and democratization were by 1968 rudely disappointed.[62] Disappointment that the New Order was not more democratic was tempered, however, by a fear among some student activists, in particular members of religious and ethnic minorities, that the establishment of a liberal, multi-party democracy would have allowed Islamic parties to prevail.[63]

The second major perception of ABRI and the new ruling group was that a state formally linked to Islam would endanger national unity. This perception was reinforced by an attempt to reintroduce the Jakarta Charter in the MPRS deliberations of 1968. For example, Yusuf Wanandi, former student activist and member of the MPRS in 1968, also argued that he felt the refusal of Islamic parties to recognize minority religious rights, as well as attempts to reintroduce the Jakarta Charter, constituted proof of threats to a state based on Pancasila-derived religious tolerance.[64] An attempt to revive the Jakarta Charter highlighted in the minds of some New Order supporters, especially among ABRI and secular-oriented civilian politicians, the feeling that having just defeated one enemy of the nationalist Pancasila state – communism – they now perceived the specter of another implacable ideological foe – Islam. Additionally, in the eyes of ABRI, a strong Islamic political coalition could present a potent civilian challenge to ABRI domination of the political landscape in the post-1965 era.

Operationalization of the New Order's Pancasila democracy

The New Order implemented its conception of Indonesian democracy by restructuring the political party system in line with its conception of Pancasila democracy. Soeharto continued the process begun by Sukarno to create a system in which political parties would not form an "opposition." Indeed, according to Ali Moertopo, former head of Special Operations (Intelligence) and key New Order political strategist,[65] parties in "opposition" were one of the major causes of political instability and turmoil in the parliamentary democracy period from 1950–1959. Not many years after the PKI was destroyed, the New Order moved against the remaining nine parties. It is important to note that the strongest Islamic party, *Masyumi* (banned under Sukarno for its perceived role in regional rebellions), was not legalized after the ascension of the New Order.

In 1973 the government forced the existing parties to combine into two groupings. An additional political organization was Golkar, the government-backed political party. As noted above, the concept of functional groups was not the creation of the New Order. Non-party, but politically organized groups composed of different segments of society (military, farmers, professionals) had been part of Sukarno's National Front strategy and had existed alongside the party system. In military thinking, functional groups took on even greater significance. Golkar became the military-backed government electoral vehicle in the New Order. Under President Soeharto Golkar has become a "direct rival against state parties rather than as a mere adjunct to them."[66]

The Islamic-based political parties were joined together under the *Partai Persatuan Pembangunan*, or PPP (United Development Party). The Protestant, Catholic, and nationalist parties formed the *Partai Demokrasi Indonesia*, or PDI. In New Order political doctrine this consolidated party system would be more amenable to the practice of Pancasila democracy including the principles of *musyawarah* and *mufakat*. This move was also in keeping with New Order political strategy designed to "de-politicize" or "de-ideologize" mass politics. It was the view of the New Order that mass-based politics, previously driven by a multi-party system in the 1950s, had encouraged political affiliation based on ethnic, regional, and especially religious affinity. The New Order's concept of the "Floating Mass" – that the masses were to be de-linked from political parties – was designed to ensure that divisive party-based politics linked to communal, religious, and ideological issues did not resurface and distract the nation from *pembangunan* [development].[67] Ali Moertopo argued that economic development could only proceed in an atmosphere of political stability. And, he argued, because political parties were identified as among the causes of the chaos and instability of the Old Order, the "consolidation" of the parties was a logical step to prevent repetition of "destabilizing" party politics.

Soeharto noted in 1982 that the "simplification" of the party system was justified because Indonesians had given their approval to the New Order, which in turn promised the people that the government would faithfully implement Pancasila. Therefore, Soeharto continued, the party restructuring was carried out because of the people's wish to follow Pancasila.[68] Moertopo argued that the 1973 consolidation of the nine existing political parties into two parties plus Golkar became the structural realization of Pancasila democracy.

The New Order paid close attention to an explicit linking of the active political and governmental participation of the armed forces to the national ideology. In order to justify ABRI's leading role in correcting the ideological errors of the Old Order,

Moertopo stated that "it is also a fact of history that the armed forces are the guardians and defenders of Pancasila from all kinds of deviation and attempts to undermine it – either by the extreme right or extreme left."[69] Moertopo explained that ABRI's concept of a dual political and military role was constitutionally justified, primarily because the Preamble (which the New Order sees as "superior" to the body of the Constitution itself) highlights the struggle for independence. And because the armed forces were an integral part of that struggle, ABRI then "has the responsibility to join in the struggle in the social, political, economic, and cultural fields in order to secure, defend and fulfill national independence."[70]

After the elimination of the PKI and Sukarno, the only challengers to the political domination by the armed forces in the New Order were the political parties, particularly the Islamic parties. Thus, the 1973 "simplification" of the party system can be seen as a way, using Pancasila as justification and explanation, of restricting political opposition by specifying what Pancasila means in terms of permissible political organizations and behavior.

The characteristics and developments in this early New Order period have implications for the study of political discourse in the 1990s. First, the destruction of communism left Islam as the major political alternative to the military-backed Pancasila state. Political Islam clearly felt the New Order's creation was due in a large part to its support. Yet much of the construction of New Order "Pancasila democracy" has been designed to severely dilute the appeal of Islamic – and all other – political parties. Today, many Islamic figures speak of the "trauma" and "bitterness" Islam experienced in Indonesia in the late 1960s.[71] It is important to distinguish between the different streams of political Islam. The "modernist" party, *Masyumi*, was not legalized after Soeharto's rise to power. It tends to be politicians associated with the old *Masyumi* party who express feelings of trauma and bitterness towards the New Order. The other major Islamic party, *Nahdlatul Ulama* (NU), Sidney Jones observes, "represented a more amenable form of Islam than the more outspoken *Masyumi*." However, NU's participation – particularly through its youth arm the *Ansor* – in the destruction of the PKI "had [also] led it to expect more rewards from Sukarno's successor than it received." Even though NU was the "more amenable" Islamic party, its strong showing in the elections of 1971 and its willingness to "harshly criticize New Order policies" highlighted for the regime a potential challenge from Islam to the ABRI-dominated political landscape.[72]

Second, there existed a powerful feeling within the New Order that Islamic political parties and politicians tried to revive the notion of an Islamic state, or at a minimum, tried formally to link the new government to Islam. Perceptions of this sort had a particularly strong impact on ABRI, secular-oriented civilian politicians, and religious and ethnic minorities who feared that in the wake of the destruction of the PKI Islam was left as a powerful political alternative. It is also the case that the New Order exaggerated "threats" from Islam. Every Islamic figure interviewed for this study said that they believed that Islamic "extremism" was always exaggerated in order to bolster New Order regime legitimacy by portraying Islam as a threat to national unity. Even retired ABRI officers conceded that the government and military depiction of an Islamic threat had "gone too far."

Third, as noted above, there was a strong conviction on the part of New Order strategists, exemplified by Ali Moertopo, that economic development must take precedence over politics. Towards that end the nation had to be "de-politicized" and "de-ideologized," according to Moertopo. New Order strategists argued that because politics had been based on religious, ethnic, regional, and class affiliations, society had become dangerously polarized and divided. Pancasila was seen as the formulaic expression of a non-ideological, "tolerant" state to which all parties must conform. It is important to recognize that Pancasila in the New Order became an effective tool to de-legitimize political challengers, legitimize the new government, *and* to convey genuine desires for a less-confrontational, religiously, and culturally tolerant society.

EDUCATION, LEGISLATION, DISSENT, AND ACQUIESCENCE: 1978–1985

Although the forced merger of the parties in 1973 is an example of the government's overt reliance on the national ideology to create its vision of Pancasila democracy and legitimize its actions, it was not until 1978 that the government undertook an ideological offensive designed to further specify the parameters and controls on political discourse in Indonesia. On March 22, 1978 the MPR (Peoples' Consultative Assembly)[73] approved a decree entitled "The Guide to the Full Comprehension and Practice of Pancasila" (known in Indonesia as P-4).[74] This decree was given particular prominence in that it was attached to the MPR's guidelines for the next five-year plan.[75] With P-4 began the nationwide propagation of Pancasila through rigorously implemented ideological education courses.[76]

During the 1978 deliberations in the MPR on the proposed P-4 legislation, the NU faction of the PPP walked out of the Assembly in protest.[77] Sidney Jones argued that NU was the "last mass-based organization in the country with political aspirations" and as such was "worrisome" to the regime because of "its refusal in 1971 to conform to the New Order ideals of political behavior" and later in 1981, NU "refused to endorse Soeharto for a third term or confer on him the title of 'Father of Development.'"[78] In other words, NU was still acting like an independent political party. Such behavior made NU an easy target for accusations by the regime of being "anti-Pancasila" as was made clear in a speech by President Soeharto in 1980 when he attacked the NU walkout in such terms.

On March 27 and April 16, 1980, President Soeharto issued stern warnings against those who he said still failed to accept Pancasila. In the first speech, at the armed forces' Commanders' Call in Pekanbaru, Soeharto noted that prior to the New Order Pancasila had been grievously threatened by the existence of other ideologies such as Marxism, Leninism, communism, socialism, nationalism, and religion. Furthermore, Soeharto asserted that some organizations continued to uphold ideologies other than Pancasila and therefore it was imperative that the armed forces support groups that truly defend and adhere to Pancasila. Soeharto strongly implied that ABRI itself was not supportive of Pancasila to the fullest possible degree if it sought to back a political party other than Golkar. Prior to these speeches, the Minister of Defense and Security, General Mohammed Yusuf, had reiterated an ABRI belief that the armed forces should stand "above" politics. According to David Jenkins, Soeharto and his allies in ABRI felt that if the military was "neutral" in the elections then the Islamic party PPP might beat Golkar. As framed by Soeharto in these speeches, Islam was clearly depicted as a threat to Pancasila so therefore ABRI neutrality was, in effect, endangering Pancasila.[79]

Soeharto also warned against any attempts to alter either the Pancasila or the Constitution of 1945. He mentioned the "walk-out" (although he did not mention NU by name) during the Pancasila education legislation deliberations (P-4) in 1978 as an example of anti-Pancasila behavior and proof that not all social-political forces yet fully accepted Pancasila as the basis of the state.[80] Jenkins argued that the NU action

> was proof, in Soeharto's eyes, that there were elements within the Islamic political movement which were not to be trusted. More than anything else, the Pekanbaru speech expressed Soeharto's underlying concern, his near obsession, that there were groups seeking to change Pancasila.[81]

However, as will be shown below, ABRI is also extremely concerned that some groups today are seeking to change Pancasila.

Two weeks later, in his remarks at the anniversary ceremony of an ABRI commando unit (the Indonesian "Red Berets") President Soeharto explicitly linked attempts to destroy him with attacks on Pancasila. He said, "they forget that soldiers will rise up to defend the Pancasila and the Constitution of 1945 if they are successful in destroying me."[82] In this speech Soeharto lashed out at criticism of his wife's business activities and emotionally rejected rumors about his personal life. The President linked such rumors to those who would destroy him and sought to replace Pancasila. Members of the MPR, particularly from the PPP, declared that they considered Soeharto's harsh criticism of "anti-Pancasila" elements to be directed at the Islamic party coalition.[83] It is essential to keep in mind how Soeharto was perceived in the early 1980s as being "obsessed" with Pancasila and alleged threats to the ideology from Islam. How then can the conspicuous *rapprochement* between the President and Islam in the 1990s be explained? Has Soeharto's obsession with Pancasila changed? Soeharto's relationship with the Islamic movement will be a analyzed in greater detail in later chapters.

These two sets of remarks created the impetus for an extra-ordinary dissent and revival of heated debate about Pancasila. A group of fifty prominent retired military officers, former party leaders, and academics (the so-called "Petition of Fifty") attacked Soeharto in an open "statement of concern" sent to the DPR (House of Representatives). The statement said that Soeharto had used the "excuse" of threats to Pancasila for his own political purposes. The signatories further stated that Pancasila was never intended to be used as a political threat against perceived political opponents. The statement criticized Soeharto for attempting to "personify" Pancasila so that each rumor about him would be interpreted as an anti-Pancasila attitude. The statement of concern was signed by leading retired officers, including former Soeharto allies such as Major General Dharsono (Secretary General of ASEAN), two former Prime Ministers, and the popular former Governor of Jakarta, Major General (retired) Ali Sadikin.[84]

Members of the Petition of Fifty were eventually blacklisted by the regime and some lost their jobs and were prohibited for a time from travel abroad.[85] However, the Petition of Fifty highlighted issues that were taken up by many critics of the regime, especially from the NU faction in the PPP. The Petition also raised concerns within military circles about the political role of the armed forces and its relationship to Soeharto. Issues raised by the Petition remain part of the discourse today, and similar arguments are even raised (in private) by ABRI officers.[86] Soeharto's anti-Pancasila speeches and the outcry they provoked, exemplified by the Petition's statement of concern, dominated political discourse for most of 1980 and up until the MPR elections in 1982.[87]

The ideologically contentious early 1980s were also marked by concerns and accusations that Soeharto's conception of Pancasila was deeply informed by his adherence to Javanese cultural and religious beliefs.[88] The concern was that if Pancasila – as a "national" ideology – was increasingly "Javanized" then it would lose its adhesive value in a diverse society (only about 45 percent of Indonesians are Javanese).[89] Orthodox Muslims in particular were concerned that Soeharto perceived Pancasila as representative of pre-Islamic Javanese religion. The best single example of how Soeharto's conception of Pancasila is informed by Javanese culture is found in his remarks before the KPNI (Indonesian National Youth Committee) on July 19, 1982. In these extraordinary remarks Soeharto delves into Javanese spirituality and religious beliefs to explain the essential tolerance and appropriateness of Pancasila for Indonesia. All religions, Soeharto explained, "are basically like this." In a long exegesis on Javanese *ilmu kasunyatan* [highest wisdom], Soeharto conceded that "some of the things I have said will be difficult to follow if you are not

Javanese like I am. But everything we have now [spiritual knowledge and the Pancasila] is an inheritance from our forefathers, Javanese or not."[90] Devout Muslim concern about Soeharto's alleged "Javanization" of Pancasila is raised because this fear has disappeared from the Pancasila discourse in recent years and has been replaced by concerns that Soeharto is instead allowing the "Islamization" of Pancasila.[91]

Pancasila as the "sole foundation"

The final and most controversial New Order Pancasila initiative was the promulgation of legislation to ensure that all mass-based organizations in the country accepted Pancasila as their sole philosophical foundation. In two speeches, one on Independence Day in 1982 and the other in July 1983, President Soeharto laid out the rationale for the government's desire to ensure Pancasila conformity. In the first speech Soeharto warned of the existence of alternative ideologies, apart from Pancasila, that were still promoted in Indonesia. Therefore, he proposed that "all sociopolitical groups, especially the political parties, accept Pancasila as their *asas tunggal* [sole foundation]."[92]

Dissent against the *asas tunggal* legislation came from a number of sources, particularly Islamic organizations and leaders. Perhaps the strongest statement of dissent is the open letter from Sjafruddin Prawiranegara, a prominent Muslim leader and former Prime Minister, to President Soeharto on July 7, 1983 when the legislation was still in its formative stages. Sjafruddin interpreted the bill as an instrument for government control of Islamic organizations. He asked, "Why only now has the Islamic foundation [of organizations] to be replaced by the Pancasila? What crime has any Muslim organization committed?"[93]

President Soeharto's second set of remarks has been interpreted as a reaction to the bitter criticism from Sjafruddin.[94] In July 1983 Soeharto reiterated his intention to ensure that all organizations, especially political parties, adopt Pancasila as their *asas tunggal* in a speech to senior ABRI leaders. Soeharto argued that the unconditional acceptance of Pancasila was essential for continued national stability and unity. He said that even though the New Order had been based on Pancasila for many years, there were still people and groups that refused to accept Pancasila or that saw it as "dangerous."[95] The continued existence of societal elements that are still reluctant to accept Pancasila, argued Soeharto, meant that the government must continue its propagation and popular promotion of the ideology. Furthermore, Soeharto emphasized ABRI's role as the defender of Pancasila as the *asas tunggal.*

This legislation, proposed in 1982 and formally adopted in 1985, stipulated that all social organizations must adopt Pancasila as their sole ideological foundation. In practice, this meant that regardless of an organization's original purpose – religious, professional, or political – only Pancasila could be adopted as its sole basis.[96] William Liddle explained why *asas tunggal* was so important:

> The government perceived Islam as the only social force not yet brought to heel, not yet fully willing to accept the government's notion of where authority ultimately resides. Acceptance of the state doctrine of Pancasila by the Muslims symbolizes this recognition. It also legitimizes the government's growing control of their organizational life.[97]

Indeed, in May 1982 the then Vice President Adam Malik explicitly identified political Islam as the main target of the government:

> We ought to steer away from debates on ideology and religion. . . . In the campaign [for the DPR in May 1982] I stressed the dangers of dividing and polarizing ourselves along religious lines. Whether by design or not, the Islamic party exploited popular religious feelings to the full. This is wrong and can be very counter-productive, an artificial way of dividing the people.[98]

At the time of the DPR's tabling of Soeharto-initiated legislation to extend Pancasila ideological education in 1978, it was widely perceived that Pancasila was being used by the government to undermine the influence of the Islamic parties. The *Nahdlatul Ulama* perceived that the regime was attempting to elevate Pancasila above the Constitution itself and to have it replace religion as the spiritual guide in daily life.[99] At this time NU, as part of the PPP, was acting like a fairly independent opposition political party that would not go quietly in the New Order creation of "Pancasila democracy." The process was further intensified in 1982–1985 with the promulgation of the *asas tunggal* legislation. Susumu Awanohara referred to the early 1980s *asas tunggal* initiative as part of Soeharto's "de-Islamizing" of the Islamic parties.[100]

It is important to note that great fear and apprehension over the political implications of *asas tunggal* were not confined to Islamic groups. Christians also worried that the *asas tunggal* was a government strategy to create a secular ideology, or "civil religion." The Minister of Religion at the time, Munawir Sjadzali, recalled that one Christian pastor had told him that even "should the sky itself fall in," he "would not accept the *asas tunggal*."[101]

The perception within part of the Islamic community that the state was using Pancasila as an ideological tool to proscribe political Islam reached its peak in violent riots in North Jakarta's Tanjung Priok port neighborhoods in September 1984.[102] According to the official government version of events, after a clash between neighborhood Islamic leaders and local military police in Tanjung Priok, extremist Muslim preachers incited an attack on a police post. The rioters explicitly attacked the Pancasila as a civil religion and an affront to Islam. General Benny Moerdani, the armed forces commander at the time, said that eighteen people were killed.[103] Abdurrahman Wahid, however, maintains that hundreds of people were killed in the rioting.[104] Susumu Awanohara reported that

> the bloody rioting . . . revealed, among other things, the serious polarization of opinion which has resulted from the Indonesian government's insistence that all social – including religious – organizations must adopt the state ideology, Pancasila, as their only ideological foundation.[105]

The Tanjung Priok rioting was followed in October 1984 by a series of bombings – attributed by the government to anti-Pancasila Islamic extremists – in downtown Jakarta.[106] Members of the Petition of Fifty, including retired Major General H.R. Dharsono, were arrested and tried on subversion (anti-Pancasila) charges for inciting the Priok riots and the Jakarta bombings.[107]

Abdurrahman Wahid, the Chairman of NU since 1984, lamented that Tanjung Priok was an avoidable tragedy. Wahid argued that the cause of the violence originated with the extreme and misguided actions of a small group of Muslims who themselves were unhappy with the direction of the Islamic movement as a whole in Indonesia and therefore sought to depict the government as the "scapegoat" and as anti-Islamic. However, Wahid argued that such actions did great harm to the *umat* [the Islamic community] by unfortunately associating Islam in general with extremism and anti-Pancasila behavior. Those who incited the riot, wrote Wahid, falsely depicted "Islam and Pancasila as two opposing enemies, in which one must eliminate the other." Such attitudes, Wahid said, simply added to suspicion of Islamic activities by other religions and the authorities.[108]

Acquiescence

Ultimately, despite the ideological polarization over Pancasila, the government was successful in promulgating the *asas tunggal* legislation. By 1985–1986 all major social, political, and religious organizations had formally adopted Pancasila as their sole philosophical foundation. For example, the NU adopted Pancasila as its *asas tunggal* on the basis of a compromise with the government which recognized that the ideology would be considered a "philosophy" (and hence a creation of man) which could never supplant religion which is the word of God. Organizations that had not accepted Pancasila as their *asas tunggal*, such as the PII (Indonesian Islamic Students' Organization), were disbanded by the government.

Several critical questions are suggested by the preceding review of political discourse about Pancasila in the New Order. Does the successful promulgation of Pancasila during the New Order – the consolidation of the parties in 1973, the nation-wide propagation of Pancasila through P-4 after 1978, the silencing of the attack on Soeharto's use of Pancasila by the Petition of Fifty in 1980, and finally the adoption of *asas tunggal* in 1985 – represent the final ideological victory of the New Order? That is, has Soeharto succeeded, in spite of widely and publicly argued opposing views, in so tightly and effectively controlling political discourse that no interpretations and uses of Pancasila other than his own are of relevance by the mid-1980s? Moreover, are the politically secular philosophical principles of the state no longer under serious contention, especially by Islam? Has the *asas tunggal* debate, with a government victory, finally settled the questions of the legitimacy and permanence of Pancasila as the *dasar negara* and the legitimizer of the New Order? I will return to these questions in the Conclusion as they can only be addressed after consideration of what happened to political discourse framed by Pancasila in the years after *asas tunggal* and after the regime's apparently successful domination of debate.

However, before turning to the body of the study, the general political and economic context of Indonesia since 1985 must be considered briefly. In this way the significance and meaning of political debate for the remainder of the 1990s can be more fully understood.

INDONESIA IN THE 1990s

Indonesian politics in the post-1985 *asas tunggal* era is characterized by developments in the following five areas: political economy, state ideology, leadership, Islam, and challenges to the regime.

Political economy

Indonesian politics in the 1990s must be viewed against a background of impressive economic development. Pragmatic economic policies for the past twenty-five years, particularly since the collapse of the world oil market in the early 1980s, have paid off. Indonesia has deregulated its economy, freed up the banking sector, and assiduously promoted non-oil exports.[109] The World Bank, in a widely cited September 1993 report (*The East Asian Miracle*), identified Indonesia as a "high-performing East-Asian economy" and predicted that it will enter the ranks of middle-income nations by the turn of the century. The New Order's promise in the mid-1960s of a vastly increased GNP and per capita income has in fact been realized. Living standards have dramatically improved.[110]

The legitimacy of Soeharto's New Order rests, in part, upon a successful program of economic development. Soeharto has managed to "deliver" on his promise of better lives for most Indonesians. It is the fulfillment of this promise – laid out by Ali Moertopo, Soeharto, and others twenty-five years ago – that forms the backbone of New Order legitimacy. The New Order has always been able to compare its success favorably with the economic wreckage under Sukarno. The terrible economic background of Sukarno's rule provided a hospitable context for ideological appeals for legitimacy based on the promise to correct deviations in Sukarno's implementation of Pancasila. After all, the New

Order argued, the consequences of those deviations were chaotic economic conditions and political instability. There are voices in Indonesia today that also call for corrections in the implementation of Pancasila and which criticize the current *pembangunan* [economic development] program as anti-Pancasila. For example, Sri Bintang Pamungkas, a vocal PPP politician and leading member of the Indonesian Muslim Intellectuals' Association (ICMI), argues that Pancasila's "social justice" tenet is violated by inequitable distribution of the benefits of development.[111] However, such criticisms today are set against a political economy characterized by rapid growth and industrialization. Thus, the success or failure of appeals to ideology – and especially to Pancasila as legitimizer of criticism of the government – are made in a radically different economic environment than at the beginning of the New Order.

State ideology

Formal, permissible politics in Indonesia today are officially characterized by ideological conformity. All politics are said to be based on Pancasila. Islam as a political movement is not officially allowed to present an ideological alternative to Pancasila based on religion in the form of organized opposition to the New Order regime. The "Islamic" party, the PPP, never regained the appeal that Muslim parties had in the pre-1973 period. In fact, for reasons that will be explored below, many Muslims decided in the 1980s that the best way to channel their political aspirations was through the government party, Golkar. A conspicuous development by the late 1980s is that President Soeharto rarely identifies Islamic extremism *per se* as a threat to Pancasila, himself, the nation, or the government. On the contrary, and perhaps the most striking dynamic of the post-*asas tunggal* era, is the mutual cooptation that has occurred between Soeharto and the Islamic community. As a result, there appear to be no manifest ideological threats to the New Order from either the "left" (communism), or from the "right" (fundamentalist Islam).

Ideological discourse in recent years is also influenced by a new development: the enunciation by the government of Pancasila as an "open ideology." In 1984 President Soeharto said that Pançasila was to be considered "open" in its implementation and practice. One leading political scientist and former deputy head of the state ideological propagation agency, the late Alfian, argued that because of earlier threats to Pancasila the ideology was often only used to show what it was not, rather than what is. Since the mid-1980s, Alfian argued, "we are trying to give Pancasila meaning, because it is an 'open ideology.' "[112] This is an unusual statement from an official of a government that has always claimed plenty of "meaning" for Pancasila.

Pancasila as an "open ideology" is a significant element in understanding the recent New Order discourse on Pancasila. Soeharto's conception of Pancasila as an open ideology illustrates that he is conscious of the political implications of the use and function of Pancasila in the national discourse. That is, Soeharto always distinguishes between harmless appropriation of Pancasila by others and appropriation of Pancasila that is potentially connected to "action" that may challenge the power or prerogative of the presidency. For example, Nurcholish Madjid, one of Indonesia's most renowned Islamic scholars, interprets the "open ideology" language of the President to mean that Islamic values are compatible with Pancasila and that the *umat* should not juxtapose Pancasila against religious faith. This kind of appropriation of Pancasila as an open ideology is acceptable. However, if there is an attempted appropriation of Pancasila with the purpose of explicitly attacking the government, such as the original statement of the Petition of Fifty, this is not tolerated.

Despite of the development of Pancasila as an open ideology and the formal acceptance of Pancasila as the "sole foundation" of all organizations, the government continues to perceive threats to Pancasila in this ostensibly "no-threat" ideological environment. Since the late 1980s members of the government, especially from ABRI, perceive new kinds of threats, particularly in the realm of democracy and human rights. Finally, there is the re-emergence, largely in ABRI circles, of "integralism" and an ABRI attempt to redefine Pancasila as an "integralistic ideology." Professor Franz Magnis Suseno, a widely respected scholar at the Jesuit Driyakara College of Philosophy in Jakarta, suggests that the reason for the re-emergence of integralism was due to regime, particularly ABRI, self-perceptions that they no longer monopolized Pancasila discourse. ABRI revival of integralism was also occurring at a time when Islam – the traditional negative reference point in ABRI conceptions of itself as defender of Pancasila – was being openly coopted by Soeharto. Discernable pressure for openness and democratization also began building in the late 1980s, perhaps adding to ABRI anxiety.[113] The political implications of ABRI's Pancasila discourse is examined in Chapter 4.

Leadership

Since 1988 Indonesian politics has been increasingly dominated by uncertainty over presidential succession. The overriding political issue for many Indonesians concerns who and what will follow aging President Soeharto. Succession debate so far has been effectively dominated by Soeharto himself. He has consistently and successfully kept the discussion off-balance and seemingly to his advantage. He is still the dominant single political figure in Indonesia. Yet, aside from the presidency, political and military leadership has already peacefully passed to a new generation. In fact, President Soeharto is the only member of the original 1945 generation of leaders still in office. This is a significant development. Indonesia is not ruled by a gerontocracy – there has been a continual regeneration of leadership in all fields. The most recent Cabinet selections in March 1993 reflect renewal in many senior Cabinet positions, including Soeharto's long-serving chief economic advisors.[114]

Important shifts are occurring in the constellation and alliances in the political leadership, however. Although Soeharto remains pre-eminent, he is no longer fully supported by ABRI. This was particularly apparent in 1988 when the military campaigned (unsuccessfully) against Soeharto's vice-presidential choice. ABRI was more successful in 1993 when it engineered a *fait accompli* in which Soeharto was forced to accept the military's commander, General Try Sutrisno, as his Vice President. Moreover, there is a perception within ABRI circles that the political interests of Soeharto no longer closely adhere to ABRI's perception of its own institutional and national interests. There is also a growing ABRI undercurrent of dissatisfaction with Soeharto. Interviews with a wide range of military leaders confirm that there is a barely concealed impatience with Soeharto. He is widely perceived among ABRI as "having stayed too long." However, these perceptions do not necessarily mean that the armed forces will in any way seek to forcefully replace the President or that Soeharto himself has forsaken ABRI backing. It should also be noted that the political-economic position of ABRI has changed. That is, as the economy has boomed, ABRI has not been the primary beneficiary. Large civilian conglomerates, many associated with the children and extended family of President Soeharto, have successfully acquired most new contracts and businesses.[115] ABRI no longer possesses the economic resources that it once enjoyed.[116]

Islam

The 1990s have seen a continuing cultural revival of Islam in Indonesia. Indeed, Islam in many ways has been enjoying an intellectual and broad-based cultural renaissance for at least two decades. In the Islamic political sphere, one of the most striking developments is the apparent abandonment of any expressions of Islamic discomfort with Pancasila. Some Islamic politicians, who in earlier years had been opposed to Soeharto and worried about his use of Pancasila as an anti-Islamic tool, now praise his government as having done more for Islam than they had ever hoped, even during the period of open Islamic political parties.[117]

The other most significant development in Islam is the emergence of *Nahdlatul Ulama* as the most dynamic Muslim organization which, under the leadership of Abdurrahman Wahid, has become the most important "non-political" political actor.[118] Wahid, implicitly using the NU mass base as his support, is at the forefront of championing democratization in Indonesia by arguing that Islam and democracy are mutually compatible. There is also the extraordinary development – especially considering the history of Islamic contention over Pancasila – of Wahid as leader of an Islamic organization accusing the regime of abandoning or misusing Pancasila. Wahid has also repeatedly raised the problem of "threats to Pancasila." The contrast to the image of "Islam versus Pancasila" in earlier years could not be more striking. Prominent Islamic thinkers such as Nurcholish Madjid continue to rethink and reinterpret Islam in an Indonesian context.[119] Nurcholish, Abdurrahman Wahid and others represent a new generation of provocative Islamic scholars who depict Islam in an inclusive, democratic, Indonesian context where there is no imperative for an Islamic state.[120]

Accompanying the socio-cultural changes in Islam, the relationship between government and Islam has changed dramatically since 1985. President Soeharto openly sponsored the establishment of ICMI, a major new Islamic organization. Among others, ICMI has also attracted the participation of Muslim activists, scholars, and politicians who had been opposed to Soeharto in previous years. Developments associated with ICMI and NU hint at the return to mass-based Islamic politics in Indonesia. The ICMI phenomenon and its relationship to contemporary politics and political discourse will be examined in depth.

Challenges and paradox

In the past several years two distinct challenges to government domination of Pancasila and its discourse have emerged: from Islam (though in a very different "Pancasila-ized" context), and from a host of issues including democratization and human rights. These issues serve to maintain the government perception of threats to Pancasila. Within the regime there are also important changes in the Pancasila discourse, particularly concerning ABRI's ideological threat perceptions and the military's relationship with Soeharto.

The general developments and trends of the 1980s and 1990s suggest the appearance of two major paradoxes of Soeharto's late New Order. First, although there is growing economic development and prosperity, it is accompanied by elite political anxiety that "economic growth could be threatened by internal power struggles linked to the politics of succession."[121] Second, although the Islamic movement is increasingly characterized by inclusive, progressive, and indeed, "revolutionary" thinking on the relationship of Islam to the state, Islam in Indonesia in recent years is also characterized by a small, yet discernable tide of rising intolerance and stridency at a cultural, and possibly political, level.

This chapter provided an overview of the key areas of political discourse framed by Pancasila under both Sukarno and Soeharto. Because one of the most extraordinary developments in recent years is the appropriation of Pancasila by NU's Abdurrahman Wahid, it is fitting that analysis of Indonesian voices in the 1990s begins with him.

Chapter 2

Abdurrahman Wahid and *Nahdlatul Ulama*

> Without it – Pancasila – we will cease to be a state.
>
> Pancasila is a set of principles and it will live forever. It is the idea of the state that we should have, that we strive for. And this Pancasila I'll defend with my own life. Regardless of its being castrated by the armed forces or its being manipulated by the Muslims, misused by both.
>
> Abdurrahman Wahid[1]

Carol Gluck, writing about Meiji ideology in Japan, has observed that "ideology does not march disembodied through time, . . . it has names and faces."[2] Abdurrahman Wahid, the General Chairman of *Nahdlatul Ulama*, is one of the most prominent "names and faces" of Indonesia's ideological discourse in the 1990s. Wahid is leader of NU, the largest and most influential Indonesian Islamic organization with a membership of 20–30 million. Wahid is not only leader of NU (the largest non-governmental Islamic organization in the world), but he is also a provocative religious and political thinker and a leading proponent of secular democracy in Indonesia.[3] Additionally, Wahid is a figure of considerable international stature, having been honored with a Ramon Magsaysay Award in 1993 (Asia's equivelent of a Nobel Prize) and, since late 1994, he has served as a member of the Presidential Board of the prestigious World Council on Religion and Peace.[4] Yet Wahid's voice in Indonesia is also prominent because of other, more personal, factors. He is a member of one of Indonesia's most famous families which has been involved in nationalist and Islamic movements for more than seventy years. Wahid himself is a man of tremendous personal charisma and intelligence. His voice finds ready outlets in the national media because he is easily accessible to journalists and is known for his "newsworthy" commentary. Thus, his chairmanship of NU, advocacy of democracy, international recognition, family background, and personal qualities combine to account for his central role in Indonesian political debates.

Institutionally, Wahid's contributions to national ideological discourse emanate from both his position as chief representative of his mass-based organization, NU, and since 1991 as the leader of Forum Democracy, a group of intellectuals committed to democratization of Indonesian society.[5] Because of his Islamic *and* secular democratic leadership positions, Wahid will figure conspicuously in this chapter as well as in the consideration of Forum Democracy as a prime example of a secular nationalist organization in Chapter 5.

Most importantly, Abdurrahman Wahid deserves particular attention because his ideas have had major influence on recent political debate. Wahid's ability to set the agenda of national discourse may not ultimately have direct bearing on Indonesia's political future. None the less, his arguments about Islam, politics, democracy, and their relationship to Pancasila have a central and fundamental role in contemporary Indonesia. Importantly, what Wahid says has had the effect of prompting reactions – sometimes defensive – from other political actors.[6]

While Wahid is Chairman of NU, it is not the case that his views are always synonymous with the organization. There are many prominent NU leaders among the *kiai* [Islamic scholars and community leaders] and a number of senior NU figures, including Wahid's uncle Yusuf Hasyim, who openly oppose many of Wahid's initiatives and statements. Given the size, diversity, and contentiousness of the organization, it is not surprising that some observers wonder if Wahid is "representing himself, not NU."[7] Indeed, there is no way that one person could reflect the political and ideological aspirations of so many. Yet Wahid has been selected three times (1984, 1989, and 1994) to head the organization. In general, the NU's leadership selection process does represent the aspirations of its membership.[8] It is therefore appropriate to conclude that Wahid, while not always understood by NU members, has consistently been supported more than any other figure as the organization's leader and spokesman.[9]

Wahid's NU support continues despite the fact that he generates intense controversy both within NU and on the level of national politics. For example, in mid-1994 NU was deeply divided over how to reassert its influence within the PPP, the nominal Islamic party. Matori Abdul Djalil, a leading NU member who was previously Secretary General of PPP, was supported by Wahid to become the new Chairman of the party. This was opposed by two senior NU figures, Yusuf Hasyim and Idham Chalid. Although Matori did not become PPP Chairman, Wahid's obvious support for him seemed not to have significantly damaged his standing within NU.[10] Similarly, in October 1994 Wahid travelled to Israel and upon his return home recommended that the Indonesian government open diplomatic relations with Israel. This provoked a furore in the Indonesian Muslim community, particularly among those Indonesians who have used Islam as a political vehicle and for whom Israel is a convenient foil. Moreover, while abroad, Wahid reportedly referred to Indonesia as an "authoritarian" state, prompting government displeasure. Again, despite the controversy Wahid generated, including significant opposition within NU to his re-election, he none the less was re-elected as NU Chairman for a third five-year term at the twenty-ninth NU congress in December 1994.[11]

It must also be recognized that Wahid's contribution to national discourse is worthy of serious consideration apart from his role as NU chairman. His institutional bases and family history aside, Wahid's ideas are a major intellectual force. Greg Barton has observed that

> the thought of Abdurrahman is little examined by outside commentators and the clear impression is left that he is considered important because of his connections, his grass roots networking and his political acumen, not primarily because of his ideas. Seldom do external scholars study, let alone consider important, his ideas, and yet it may be that at the end of the day that it is seen that it was his thought that was the most important contribution of all.[12]

None of this means that Abdurrahman Wahid's – and through him NU's – participation in national discourse is, objectively, the most politically relevant. Wahid's voice, while among the loudest, may not carry the most political weight. A key purpose of this chapter, and in the study's conclusion, is to analyze and evaluate the influence of Wahid's voice on Indonesian politics.

It is extremely unusual to hear a prominent public figure like Wahid speak about Pancasila in terms that go beyond ritual usage and strike at the core of Indonesian politics and society. That Wahid's voice on Pancasila should stand out is somewhat anomalous, because in Indonesia of the 1990s there is frequent, almost daily, mention of Pancasila in the national news media and in official speeches. Pancasila is invoked by officials in an almost sacral, obligatory fashion. It has become part of the government mantra and citizens rarely see any connection between the invocation of Pancasila and the particular issue at hand. Several years ago the government had taken to identifying so many things as "Pancasilaist" (press, democracy, economy, etc.) that it became a joke that there was even "Pancasila football" (the national sport). Many Indonesians speak of feeling "*jenuh*," or being "fed up" with the constant bombardment of government Pancasila "propaganda." Some have become cynical about the use and meaning of the national ideology. Mochtar Lubis, one of Indonesia's distinguished writers and social commentators, remarked that he is "fed up" with Pancasila because of the way it has been used to justify everything.[13] Indeed, even Indonesia's foremost government "ideologist" (and former Foreign Minister) Roeslan Abdulgani, who was instrumental in the propagation of Pancasila under both presidents Sukarno and Soeharto, wrote that all Indonesian people feel "saturated" with Pancasila because of its unnecessarily heavy-handed promotion.[14] Yet Abdurrahman Wahid's contribution to the discourse on Pancasila is different. Wahid is not "fed up" with Pancasila. Rather, he challenges regime domination of the meaning and political relevance of Pancasila in a conspicuous fashion. And he connects his use and interpretation of the ideology to political ideas and concrete political behavior in ways rarely seen in Indonesia today.

What exactly does Wahid say about Pancasila and why? This chapter will examine the content of his ideas and indicate why he has partially defined Pancasila discourse in Indonesia in recent years. The ways in which Pancasila functions to fulfill the political goals of Wahid and NU will be examined in detail. Before consideration of Wahid's contributions to political discourse in detail, a brief biographical sketch is necessary to understand his prominence in the Islamic movement in Indonesia. This will be followed by analysis of the Rapat Akbar, the NU's 66th Anniversary Rally held in Jakarta on March 1, 1992.

Interviews with Wahid, his supporters, and his critics indicate the prominent position of Pancasila as a political tool for expressing key values and ideas about Indonesian politics and government. An examination of "threats to Pancasila" as envisioned by Wahid will illustrate another side of political discourse. Wahid considers Pancasila to be a living political compromise which allows all Indonesians to live together in a national, unitary, non-Islamic state. Yet Wahid sees numerous threats to his conception of Pancasila as a tolerant basis for the creation of a civil democratic society, particularly within the Islamic community itself. He also identifies threats to Pancasila from the armed forces. Indeed, Wahid's concerns are often more nationalist than they are explicitly "Islamic." This chapter, however, focuses primarily on Wahid's voice as it is expressed through *Nahdlatul Ulama* or his actions associated with NU, whereas Wahid's secular democratic vision of society will be fully considered in Chapter 5.

Biographical sketch of Abdurrahman Wahid

Abdurrahman Wahid leads Indonesia's largest Islamic mass-based socio-cultural organization, widely described as "traditionalist" and "rural-based."[15] Yet Abdurrahman Wahid is also the foremost leader of the urban-centered, modern, liberal-oriented democratization movement in Indonesia. Adam Schwarz, a former *Far Eastern Economic Review* correspondent in Jakarta, sees Wahid as a man of many contradictions and paradoxes. Schwarz's description of Wahid nicely captures his complexity and controversial nature:

> Wahid leads a "traditional, conservative, rural-based socio-cultural organization of some 25–30 million Muslim Indonesians. But he himself is modern in outlook, liberal in approach, and very much an urban intellectual. In a land of decision by consensus [*musyawarah* and *mufakat*], Wahid, an unabashed individualist, leads by inspiration. In a culture that rewards acquiescence to authority, Wahid speaks his mind. In a society ruled along authoritarian lines, Wahid argues for democracy. At a time of nascent Islamic revivalism, Wahid, the single most influential Muslim leader in the land, warns the government against helping Muslims too much."[16]

Recognition of his prominence outside Indonesia has earned Wahid the prestigious Ramon Magsaysay Award for community leadership. However, the man that the Magsaysay Foundation, Asia's equivalent of the Nobel Committee, recognized for "guiding Southeast Asia's largest Muslim organization as a force for religious tolerance, fair economic development, and democracy," is derided by others.[17] For example, political scientist Amir Santoso observes that for many people in ICMI, an organization strongly criticized by Wahid, questions about him are framed in terms of "how to Islamize Abdurrahman?" Another leading scholar critical of Wahid notes that people, including some in ICMI, regard him as a "collaborator" of Christians and the "non-Islamic groups." Ismail Sunny, Professor of Law at the University of Indonesia, bluntly attacked Wahid for suggesting that a non-Muslim would be acceptable as President of Indonesia.[18] Adi Sasono, a leading figure in the NGO movement in Indonesia and senior member of ICMI, says that Soeharto is more Islamic than Wahid.[19] The subtext of such derisive statements is that a perception exists that Wahid's concerns about minority rights, equal treatment of non-Muslims, and support for secular government mean he is not sufficiently Islamic. Yet Mochtar Buchori, a well-known intellectual and Rector of the *Muhammadiyah* Teachers Training College in Jakarta, argues that it is precisely Wahid's ability to interact with other religions and his recognition of the equality of all religions that are his greatest strengths. Buchori sees that Wahid

> never feels more Islamic [than others] and he never judges the "Muslimness" of other Muslims.

Moreover, Wahid

> sincerely accepts [non-Muslims] as his equals. He never considers people of other religions less worthy. He is a true believer in Pancasila.[20]

Among his followers Wahid is revered. A popular Muslim *mubaliq* [preacher] in central Java calls Wahid "an extraordinary man, a great man of vision."[21] Wahid frequently relates remarks made to him by *Kiai* Muntaha, an NU spiritual leader in the small central Javanese town of Wonosobo. According to Wahid, Muntaha says that although he disagrees with Wahid's outspoken liberalism, he nevertheless regards him as both NU's and the nation's "bridge to the future."[22] In a similar vein, Professor Franz Magnis Suseno observes that because of Wahid's unique ability to appeal to almost all Indonesians – devout Muslims, religious minorities, democracy advocates, *and* the armed forces – he is able to "bridge" the differences in Indonesian society and help move the nation towards a future democratic civil society.[23]

The diverse opinions Indonesians have of Wahid are matched by contradictions and paradoxes in his personal life.[24] Born in 1940 he now leads the organization founded by his grandfather, Hasyim Asyari, and later led by his father, Wahid Hasyim, a nationalist figure and Minister of Religion under Sukarno. He was educated both in traditional Islamic boarding schools (*pesantran*) and in modern universities in Cairo and Baghdad. By all accounts he read widely in politics, philosophy, and religion in numerous foreign languages as a youth. He is fluent in English, Arabic, and Dutch (and reads French and German), as well as his own Javanese and Indonesian. Wahid has a unique ability to move fluently among the intellectual and government elites of Jakarta, New York, or Tokyo and, in the words of his brother, among Indonesia's "*orang awam*" and "*orang muslim kaki lima*."[25] He is equally comfortable discussing liberalism and the philosophical origins of the American Revolution or nuanced points of Islamic theology and scholarship.

Islamic theological background to Wahid's discourse

Most importantly, for the purposes of understanding Wahid's participation in contemporary discourse, he should be seen as representative of a revolutionary generation of Islamic thinkers in Indonesia. Greg Barton argues that the thought of Wahid, along with "Djohan Effendi, Nurcholish Madjid, and the late Ahmad Wahib[26] is sufficiently coherent and complete to be called a school of thought in its own right." Barton identifies these thinkers as "neo-modernists" and argues that this school of Islamic thought has "been instrumental in the creation of a new intellectual/political position in [Indonesian] Islamic thought." One of the defining consequences of these neo-modernists is a "commitment to pluralism and the core values of democracy." Moreover, these pluralistic values have been "woven into the very fabric of [Islamic] faith as ... the core values of Islam itself." Barton concludes that for these reasons Wahid and other neo-modernist Muslims are "in the vanguard of democratic reform."[27]

Abdurrahman Wahid's interpretation and frequent reference to Pancasila in the 1990s is tied to his role as a leading exponent of neo-modernist Islam which is fully supportive of democratic pluralism. Wahid has long argued that Muslims should embrace Pancasila.[28] As will be argued below, Wahid conceives of Pancasila as the precondition for democratization *and* the healthy spiritual development of Islam in a national context. This is a position that contrasts with many of the "modernists" who seek to "Islamize" Indonesia. It is particularly different from the Islam versus Pancasila dichotomy of the Konstituante and the Independence Preparatory Committee deliberations.

Nationalist foundations of NU

One way to understand Wahid's and NU's role in contemporary discourse is to see NU as both a nationalist organization *and* an Islamic organization. This is important because some Muslims have conceived Pancasila as a secular ideology which is incompatible with Islam. The nationalist factor is equally the case with Wahid himself, who has become both a national secular political figure as well as remaining head of NU, a religious organization. As noted in the previous chapter, NU's leader in 1945, Wahid Hasyim (Abdurrahman Wahid's father), agreed to support a nationalist, non-Islamic state. NU was also a key early supporter of the New Order. In the minds of its members, NU is as firmly grounded in nationalist credentials as are the armed forces. Achmad Buchori Masruri, the head of NU's Central Java provincial branch, outlines the standard NU position on nationalism as well as the reasons for NU's acceptance of and affinity for Pancasila. Buchori contends there is no imperative in Islamic teaching for the establishment of an Islamic state. That is why, he argues, at the beginning of the Republic the NU Chairman, Wahid Hasyim, could easily accept a state not explicitly based on Islam.[29] Buchori illustrates the NU nationalist position when he argues that Indonesia is a state based on consensus and compromise and that compromise is inherent in Pancasila. And the compromise – a religious state, but not one based exclusively on Islam, is "fully in keeping with the Prophet Muhammad's natural tolerance of Jesus and other people of the Book." Pancasila, Buchori concludes, is a "political recipe for all Indonesians to live together in the state."[30]

Wahid too frequently stresses NU's nationalist credentials. For example, in a major speech to the NU membership in 1992, Wahid recalls that NU acceptance and indeed its embracing of Pancasila made perfect sense for several reasons.[31] He explains that in 1945 Sukarno sought the advice of NU leadership, including his father who helped Sukarno devise the five principles of Pancasila. There is no doubt that Wahid has a sentimental attachment to Pancasila derived from his pride that his father helped create the basis of the state together with Sukarno. Furthermore, Wahid argues that there is no contradiction between Islam and nationalism and that Islam can thrive spiritually in a nationalist state that is not formally based on Islam.[32] This outlook, Wahid argues, makes the Indonesian armed forces (ABRI) and non-Muslims sympathetic and appreciative of NU's inclusive stance:[33]

> NU adheres to a conception of nationalism that is *in accordance with the Pancasila* and the Constitution of 1945. NU has become the pioneer in ideological affairs. This is the case even though throughout the entire Islamic world there is still a problem between nationalism and Islam. All the Saudi writers consider nationalism a form of secularism. They do not yet understand that nationalism such as in Indonesia is not secular, but rather respects the role of religion.[34]

Wahid does not have to look to Saudi Arabia for Islamic rejection of a nationalist perspective. For example, Imaduddin Abdul Rahim, one of the founding members of ICMI, argues that nationalism cannot be the unifying basis of Indonesia. He contends that only Islam, the belief of "90 percent of the people," can serve as the moral basis for the state.[35]

In 1983 *Nahdlatul Ulama* became the first major Islamic organization to agree to the Soeharto government's *asas tunggal* stipulation and accept Pancasila as part of its constitutional charter.[36] It is necessary to recall the extraordinary contentiousness of this time. President Soeharto's attempt to monopolize Pancasila discourse by insisting on the sole right to interpret and operationalize it through New Order political structures was best illustrated by his initiatives between 1973 and 1983. The 1973 emasculation of the competitive political party system reduced the number of parties to three, one of which was ostensibly "Islamic" (the PPP) and included NU as a faction member. Soeharto's plans for the "de-politicization" of politics were directed at de-linking religion, especially Islam, from party affiliation and behavior. This constituted a genuine "Pancasila democracy" in the political thinking and planning of New Order strategists, particularly Ali Moertopo. As noted in Chapter 1, however, the desire to prevent a return to political violence and contentiousness based on "primordial" loyalties was a widely shared goal in the immediate post-Sukarno era.

It was in the highly polarized political climate after the Tanjung Priok riots and bombings in Jakarta that NU held its 27th National Congress in December 1984 at Situbondo in East Java.[37] A year earlier at an NU conference in 1983 the organization had stated its intention to accept Pancasila for reasons based on the nationalist heritage of NU. NU's Islamic scholars concluded that there was no need to establish an Islamic state and that Pancasila was compatible with the principles of Islam.[38] At the 1984 Congress NU formally proclaimed that Indonesia is a state based on Pancasila and the Constitution of 1945 which is the "final form of state" that will govern the Indonesian archipelago.[39] The acceptance of Pancasila by NU was, as noted by former Minister of Religion Munawir Sjadzali, a "brilliant compromise." This compromise was formulated by the late NU leader Achmad Siddiq, who together with Wahid formed the duumvirate responsible for the transformation and revitalization of NU as a base for a pluralist, neo-modernist Islam. Siddiq argued (as he had in 1957) that NU could accept Pancasila as its *asas tunggal* because it was a "philosophy created by human beings, whereas Islam was a revelation."[40] Munawir acknowledges the government's debt to NU as he says that this was the compromise language that was subsequently used to convince other religions that the New Order's Pancasila initiative was neither a form of "secularization" nor a civil religion.[41] In a concession to the religions, Soeharto himself noted that Pancasila was never intended as replacement of religion. Indeed, when President Soeharto addressed the 28th NU Congress in 1989 he acknowledged that NU was the first to accept the *asas tunggal*. Moreover, according to Martin van Bruinessen, the speech by Soeharto showed that "two decades of mutual mistrust between the government and NU had definitively ended."[42]

Withdrawal from politics?

There were two momentous political decisions taken by NU in 1983 and 1984: the adoption of Pancasila as *asas tunggal* and, equally significant, a decision to withdraw from active participation in politics. NU formulated this decision in a statement known as "*Kembali Ke Khittah* 1926", or "Return to the Commitment of 1926."[43] NU was originally established as a purely socio-cultural organization primarily concerned with educational and spiritual well-being of the *umat*. It participated as an independent political party from 1952 to 1973 and then until 1983 as a faction within the PPP (the New Order's forced fusion of pre-1973 Islamic political parties). For many reasons, particularly cleavages within the Islamic movement, and manipulation of Islamic politics and parties by the Soeharto government, as well as internal organizational disputes over doctrine and politics, a progressive NU faction won control of the organization at its 1984 Congress. There the progressives, led by Abdurrahman Wahid and Achmad Siddiq succeeded in convincing the membership that NU should withdraw from formal participation in party politics and return to its original 1926 charter as a purely socio-cultural organization. It would redirect its energies away from national politics towards educational, cultural, spiritual, and economic activities designed to improve the situation of the *umat*. Greg Barton traces NU's decision to leave formal politics to a recognition that "party-political activity in the name of Islam was both counter productive for the *umat*, and, inasmuch as such activity gives rise to sectarianism, is unhealthy for society at large." Moreover, Barton adds,

> By the mid 1970s Abdurrahman and his colleagues were expressing the conviction that the interests of the *umat*, and of broader society, would be better served by the *umat* turning away from party-political activity and embracing the non-sectarian state philosophy of Pancasila, fifteen years before it became popular, or even acceptable, to express such thought.[44]

Abdurrahman Wahid explains that the decision to withdraw from politics was based not only on a desire to focus on social, educational, and religious goals, but also on political factors which Wahid says stemmed directly from the New Order's de-politization strategy. Wahid argues that because of the unrelenting government proscription of Islamic politics and use of Pancasila to restrict the legitimate political behavior of parties in the 1970s and early 1980s, NU decided to "leave politics." Wahid said that if NU allowed itself to stay in the formal, government-sanctioned political structure then it would be increasingly compromised and unable to protect its institutional interests or the interests of the *umat*. NU would also be unable to contribute to national discourse on development and politics with a distinctive, independent voice. Wahid argues that formal political institutions allowed by the government were set up to support the New Order's development program and simply served to proscribe independent political behavior outside government control. Thus, in order to avoid government control and manipulation, NU decided to "leave politics." NU's decision to leave politics was a response to the de-politicization efforts of the government which included a monopoly on Pancasila. Wahid explained it in the following way:

> So the idea was that in order to resist the government's interpretation of Pancasila as the all-embodying, all-dominating ideology, an alternative view of Pancasila should be developed. And that vision of Pancasila could only be developed outside politics.[45]

NU felt ideologically imprisoned in the authoritative structure of the "Pancasila democracy" created by the New Order. It was widely perceived that Soeharto had reserved the right to define and interpret what constituted political behavior compatible with Pancasila. While Wahid and NU emphasized Pancasila as the inclusive, non-sectarian state ideology, they rejected Soeharto's monopolization of the interpretation and application of Pancasila.

NU's withdrawal from the PPP to return solely to non-political activity, and its endorsement of Pancasila and the Republic of Indonesia based on the 1945 Constitution, had two major political results. First, the acceptance of Pancasila bolstered the Soeharto regime's long-term goal of ensuring ideological Pancasila conformity. Second, NU's withdrawal from party politics resulted in many PPP supporters streaming towards Golkar in the elections of the 1980s.[46] Yet Abdurrahman Wahid has made it clear that NU withdrew from politics in order to participate *more* effectively in politics.[47] In essence, this was NU's response to Ali Moertopo's and the New Order's restraints on organizational activity. NU saw that continued participation in the restrictive New Order political structure would render NU completely useless. NU's freedom of "political" movement was heightened outside the formal structure of the New Order, thus allowing it to more effectively participate "in" politics during the last decade. The most obvious example of this strategy is NU's appropriation of Pancasila which has served to inoculate the organization against accusations of being anti-Pancasila.

The *Rapat Akbar*, March 1, 1992

On March 1, 1992 *Nahdlatul Ulama* commemorated its sixty-sixth anniversary by holding a mass rally (the Rapat Akbar[48] at the Senayan Sports Stadium in Jakarta. According to the Jakarta press, between 150,000 and 200,000 people attended the rally.[49] This was the largest non-governmental mass rally held for twenty-five years.[50] The ostensible purpose of the Rapat Akbar was to celebrate the organization's anniversary by publicly reiterating NU loyalty to Pancasila. Several things are curious in this. Why would the nation's largest mass-based Islamic organization commemorate its anniversary by pledging loyalty to the state ideology? NU had already in 1983 taken the major decision at its National Conference in Sitobundo, East Java to accept Pancasila as its formal ideological basis.

It is important to note that Wahid consulted few people when devising the agenda of the Rapat Akbar. It is unlikely that the thousands of NU members who attended did so solely in order to pledge loyalty to Pancasila. None the less, it is Wahid's explanation of the political purposes of the *Ikrar* [the declaration on Pancasila read at the stadium] that speaks directly to the interpretation and appropriation of Pancasila.

During the Rapat Akbar, NU issued a powerful endorsement of Pancasila and the Constitution.[51] Why did Abdurrahman Wahid feel the need to again stress NU's support for Pancasila at a time when this was not a burning political issue? There are several reasons for Wahid's and NU's public reiteration of loyalty to Pancasila. First, Wahid was searching for a way to avoid approving of President Soeharto for a fifth five-year term in office. Wahid argues that because NU was no longer a "political" organization, endorsement of the President was inappropriate. He contends that NU avoided an explicit endorsement of Soeharto by limiting itself to public reiteration of loyalty to Pancasila. Moreover, in his quest for a more democratic society, Wahid argues that supporting Soeharto for another five-year term was contrary to genuine democratic choice which should be expressed through free and fair political competition.

Second, Wahid was deeply distressed by the formation of the new government-sponsored Islamic organization, the Indonesian Muslim Intellectuals' Association (ICMI). He was anxious to demonstrate that the *umat* was still united behind him and supportive of his vision of an inclusive, democratic Islam. ICMI, Wahid believes, legitimizes Islamic exclusivism and erodes social tolerance for non-Muslim Indonesians. Wahid wished to show that NU supported a nascent democratization process and would not be coopted by the government in the manner of Muslim intellectuals who had recently thrown their weight behind the government-backed ICMI.

Third, Wahid perceived a rising tide of sectarianism and fundamentalism in Indonesia and so he wanted to depict in the NU rally a pluralistic, non-sectarian Islam which recognized Pancasila as the religiously neutral basis of the state. Wahid perceived that sectarianism threatened one of the most positive aspects of New Order society: the severing of direct links between one's religion or ethnicity and how one participates in politics. Wahid believed that the New Order formula for de-linking religion and other "primordial" affinities from mass politics was under grave threat.

Fourth, there was an internal NU purpose to the Rapat Akbar. Wahid sought to demonstrate that his control and support of NU could be objectively demonstrated by a rally of up to two million NU members.[52] Divisions within NU were heightened in 1991 after Wahid's formation of Forum Democracy, a group of intellectuals dedicated to democratizing Indonesia. Some NU leaders were worried that Wahid's activities on behalf of democratization would damage NU by too closely associating it with democratic critics of the regime. Therefore, according to one observer, Wahid was anxious to "prove he was still in charge as the General Chairman of NU" and that he intended the rally as a "direct response to his critics inside the NU."[53]

Pressure to endorse Soeharto and support for democracy

From late 1991 to early 1992 there was considerable indirect pressure on NU to endorse Soeharto for another term in office. Other major Islamic organizations had already done so, particularly *Muhammadiyah*. Yet, as a way to avoid endorsing Soeharto and thereby prevent further rifts within the NU membership,[54] NU instead pledged loyalty to Pancasila and the Constitution. Wahid also sought to preserve NU's future freedom of movement on the succession question and therefore wanted to avoid being locked into a statement of public support for Soeharto. It was difficult for the government to prohibit a mass meeting which sought to endorse the ideological pillars of the regime. Thus, NU did not look like it was opposing Soeharto because it supported the pillars of the state, something Soeharto has always called for. Yet the Rapat Akbar was also Wahid's vehicle for criticizing the government for acting in an undemocratic and "anti-Pancasila" fashion.[55]

Wahid said that if NU were to succumb to pressure to endorse Soeharto, this would have two "catastrophic" consequences. First, such an decision would "create dissension within NU because it is a political act." Because NU was no longer a political organization, it had no business formally supporting political leaders. Furthermore, Wahid pointed out that the NU membership was divided over perceptions of Soeharto. Some members argued that the President should not be supported because he was "not Islamic enough" while others argued that NU should not tolerate what they perceived as Soeharto's manipulation of Islam, of "pre-empting NU's role" as a major representative of the *umat*. Although Wahid acknowledges that NU still acts "politically," he contends that if NU got involved in the business of political endorsements then it would lose its power and influence in Indonesian national life. Now, Wahid stresses,

> NU is in a very good position as the anchor of politics in Indonesia; PPP, PDI, and Golkar all need us, the armed forces needs us; nearly everybody needs us because of our mass base, which we utilize very prudently.

Wahid concludes that NU must at all costs avoid an endorsement of Soeharto because it would exacerbate internal NU dissension and wreck NU's unique position as a "political anchor."[56] That is,

Wahid tried to avoid a situation where NU would be identified as supporting another Soeharto term, an act which would damage NU's freedom of political movement. Such a development, Wahid implies, would also have made a mockery of NU's withdrawal from formal politics a decade earlier. Yet, if NU instead endorses the Constitution of 1945 and the permanence and justness of Pancasila, then the organization takes the "high road," according to Wahid. Wahid says that NU's endorsement of Pancasila shows a commitment to constitutional process, and Wahid does not agree that the government has a special right to judge the "Pancasila-ness" of others.[57]

Wahid interprets the holding of the Rapat Akbar and the NU's refusal to use the rally to endorse Soeharto as evidence that NU is acting as an "agent of change":

> By refusing to endorse Soeharto openly, we withhold support to this unbalanced system of governing. By supporting Pancasila and the Constitution we can say that NU is trying to smooth the transition from the current system based on cronyism, and the destruction of the country in the long run, and the robbing of our natural resources for the benefit of a few.[58]

Wahid sees NU's refusal to support Soeharto as a sophisticated and safe way of encouraging political change. Even though the government tried to condition the issuance of permission for the massive Jakarta rally on NU's endorsement of Soeharto, it was none the less difficult, and eventually impossible, to refuse permission for a mass rally whose message the government would otherwise like to hear: reiteration of support for Pancasila and a public commitment to constitutional principles. Wahid explicitly sees that NU's commitment to Pancasila and the Constitution was a way of saying "we are for Pancasila, for the Constitution, but we say that you [the government and Soeharto] are not doing enough for the Constitution."[59] By using Pancasila as the message of the Rapat Akbar, Abdurrahman Wahid says that this protects NU from criticism:

> We have said to the people, to history, to our friends, to my followers, that we work for an idealized form of government based on Pancasila which we have yet to establish. So we are loyal to an idealized form of state which will embrace the real, the true, spirit of Pancasila.[60]

The New Order claims it is the very embodiment of Pancasila, while Wahid argues that the "true" spirit of Pancasila is a

> just government, a government which protects freedom of expression, movement, association, a government that guarantees equality before the law. This is not the case with the current government, . . . because the current government does not take into account the necessity of the democratic aspect of governing.

Wahid argues the New Order government is only concerned with using Pancasila to bolster its "legitimacy" and avoid fostering a more just or democratic society.[61]

Aswab Mahasin, a leading intellectual,[62] has argued that Wahid was forced into a corner by the impending question of Soeharto's re-election and ultimate succession. Mahasin suggests that the Rapat Akbar allowed Wahid and NU to avoid being involved in polarizing politics by skillfully focusing on the overriding importance of the Constitution and Pancasila.[63]

There was an additional, more urgent message in the Pancasila strategy of the Rapat Akbar. Wahid sees that Pancasila represents an essential political compromise by stating that Islam should not be the formal basis of the state. In a religiously and ethnically diverse nation, Pancasila is the ideological expression of tolerance and commitment to inclusive behavior and politics. Wahid contends that Pancasila and its stress on religious and ethnic tolerance is a necessary precondition to the development of a genuine democracy in Indonesia. Wahid frequently argues that democracy will fail in an environment of religious strife and intolerance. Wahid has strongly reiterated this point on numerous occasions since the 1992 Rapat Akbar. For example, in remarks to the December 1994 NU Congress Wahid implored NU members to support a "nationalist outlook" in which all Indonesians, regardless of religion, are treated the same under the law.[64]

Wahid was alarmed at what he perceived to be a trend towards "re-confessionalization" of politics and a decline in religious tolerance. In this context, Wahid has focused on the new Islamic organization, ICMI, founded in December 1990, as representative of a major threat to his vision of a religiously tolerant Pancasila society (upon which a genuine democracy can be built). The full range of perspectives in the ICMI voice in the discourse will be examined in the following chapter. The following section considers

Wahid's views of ICMI and how these views relate to contemporary discourse and Pancasila.

ICMI and Wahid's perception of threats to Pancasila

One of Wahid's purposes for holding the massive Rapat Akbar was to depict NU as supportive of an inclusive, democratic Islam that fully accepts the religiously neutral interpretation of Pancasila. Wahid sought to positively portray NU in contrast to ICMI. However, before describing in detail Abdurrahman Wahid's objections to ICMI and how his discourse relates to ICMI, additional background to Wahid's view of Islam and the state is necessary.

As Chairman of NU Wahid describes his "job" as one of primarily looking after the well-being of the *umat*.[65] However, he also criticizes the government for doing "too much" for the Muslims.[66] Detailed consideration of this apparent contradiction is essential in order to grasp Wahid's conception of what kind of nation Indonesia should be. Wahid argues that Indonesia's national unity is based on a living political compromise – the Pancasila ideology – an agreement of the Muslims to live in a state which would never be based on formal recognition of Islam as objectively "better" or more deserving of government support than other religions. Such a development would threaten national unity. Wahid (as did other NU leaders before him, especially his father and the late Achmad Siddiq as well as the Muslim intellectuals Djohan Effendi and Nurcholish Madjid) sees that in Pancasila, Indonesians, including Indonesian Muslims, have gotten the best possible deal: the freedom to follow their religion by their own volition in a religious, though not an Islamic state. Wahid argues this is politically realistic in the light of Indonesia's religious diversity. Moreover, according to Wahid and NU scholars, it is fully consistent with Islamic religious doctrine which does not recognize an absolute imperative for the establishment of an Islamic state. Again, at the December 1994 NU Congress Wahid strongly reiterated that the power of the government should never be used on behalf of particular religions *or* against any religion.[67]

Against this background there is the political competition throughout Indonesian history in which Islamic-oriented parties were deeply involved. While Wahid and others fundamentally agree with de-linking "primordial" affiliations from day-to-day politics, they do not agree with the restrictive political structure established by the New Order and the long-standing depiction of Islam by the government as an enemy of Pancasila and the state. Therefore, it is rather extraordinary that by the mid- to late 1980s President Soeharto actively began courting Indonesian Muslims to enhance his Islamic credentials. This has been widely interpreted as an attempt by Soeharto to diversify his own power base as it became apparent by 1988 that the armed forces were no longer automatically behind him. In an environment of shifting constellations of power and support in elite politics, Soeharto looked to the *umat* to enhance his legitimacy. At the same time, some members of the Islamic community, distressed over the powerful role of the Catholic commander of ABRI, Benny Moerdani, began to look to Soeharto for support against the armed forces which were perceived to be more hostile to Islam than Soeharto.

In 1990, Soeharto made the much publicized *haj* [pilgrimage] to Mecca for the first time. As if to stress the significance of this occasion, political scientist Soedjati Djiwandono observes that this was the first time a reigning "Javanese king" had made the *haj*.[68] Among many Muslims it was interpreted as a sign of piety and a normal step in one's life journey – particularly for an aged man such as Soeharto.[69] Yet for a master politician like Soeharto, even personal spiritual journeys have political implications. Among elite circles, Soeharto's *haj* was widely seen as a step towards political reconciliation with Islam. Additionally, there were legislative and programmatic aspects to this reconciliation and courtship such as the 1989 religious education law and the 1990 law on religious courts' judicial authority (all examined in the following chapter).

Finally, in December 1990 President Soeharto gave his official consent to the establishment of a major new Islamic organization: *Ikatan Cendekiawan Muslim Indonesia* [Indonesian Muslim Intellectuals' Association, or ICMI].[70] This was an extraordinary event. The association grouped together government officials and leading Islamic intellectuals, including many who had been bitterly critical of Soeharto's New Order and its treatment of Islam in previous years. Noticeably absent from prominent intellectuals who joined the new organization was Abdurrahman Wahid. Wahid's fundamental disagreement with ICMI is that it represents manipulation of Islam to support the government. It also shows that Islamic activists are allowing themselves to be manipulated by Soeharto in order to advance their own goal of Islamizing government and society. For Wahid, such a development constitutes an abandonment of Pancasila's principle of religious tolerance and national unity. ICMI supporters, however, contend that the new organization is the most appropriate and effective means for serving the well-being of the *umat* as well as for seeking greater democratization in Indonesia. ICMI members also argue that the organization can be an effective means of advocating the "de-militarization" of Indonesian politics.[71]

Wahid's apprehension regarding ICMI is also based on fundamental disagreement over the meaning of an Islamic society. A number of prominent intellectuals in ICMI advocate the establishment in Indonesia of an "Islamic society." An Islamic society is one in which government policy, programs, and law are imbued with Islamic values. Wahid argues that intellectuals who advocate an Islamic society are, in reality, still seeking to establish an Islamic state in Indonesia.[72] Wahid outlines his opposition to those who call for an Islamic society in the following way:

> That's why I quarrel with Amien Rais [a political scientist, Chairman of *Muhammadiyah* and an ICMI leader] who would like to establish an Islamic society. For me an Islamic society in Indonesia is treason against the Constitution because it will make non-Muslims second-class citizens. But an "*Indonesian* society" where the Muslims are strong – and strong means functioning well – then I think that is good.[73]

ICMI is dangerous, according to Wahid, not because of the mere existence of a new Islamic organization, but due to the

> simple fact that their behavior [members of ICMI] and the behavior of Soeharto in using ICMI for his own – non-Islamic – goals "re-confessionalizes" politics. ICMI returns Islam and religion to the political arena after two decades of efforts to de-confessionalize politics.[74]

Moreover, Wahid argues, the strategy of Islamic activists in ICMI, which is to "take advantage of being used by Soeharto, will increase ABRI anxiety and reignite ABRI fears of Islamic fundamentalism." ABRI, Wahid repeatedly states, is deeply suspicious of ICMI and perceives it as manipulation by Soeharto to strengthen his position *vis-à-vis* the armed forces.[75] Wahid argues that the activities, statements, and simple presence of "naive" Islamic activists in ICMI, may provoke ABRI action against the Islamic community. Wahid worries that ICMI will give ABRI the excuse to "clamp down" again on Islam. An ABRI-perceived "Islamic threat to Pancasila" will be manipulated by the armed forces to highlight threats to Pancasila and hence to reinforce the image of ABRI as the bulwark against the "extreme right" and defender of the tolerant Pancasila state.[76] Wahid adds that if ABRI persecutes Islamic activists for pursuing a political agenda incompatible with the inclusive, tolerant nature of Pancasila, then this heavy-handed response will encourage fundamentalism or "sectarianism" to grow. Wahid argues that "if ABRI is relied upon to defend Pancasila against those who would seek an Islamic Indonesia then we end up using an undemocratic force [ABRI] in a counter-productive way."[77] So, Wahid argues, ICMI's urging of greater Islamization of government and society may have the unintended consequence of setting back democratization efforts by giving the armed forces an excuse to further restrict all forms of independent political activity, Islamic or otherwise.

Sectarianism and New Order society

Wahid refers to the de-linking of mass-based politics from religion as "de-confessionalized" politics. It is similar to what the New Order has called the "de-politicization" or "de-ideologization" of politics. As noted in the previous chapter, there was a widely shared perception in the mid-1960s that something had gone terribly wrong, and this culminated in the communal and religiously based violence of 1965–1966. Wahid seeks to avoid a return to a political system in which people channel their political aspirations through organizations which appeal solely on a "confessional" basis. Yet Wahid along with many others argue that de-confessionalization does not necessitate the current restrictive and authoritarian political structure which the New Order calls "Pancasila democracy."[78]

Wahid says the purpose of the Rapat Akbar was to show that NU exemplified an Indonesian Islam that was accepting of non-Muslims and Indonesians of Chinese descent by its adherence to Pancasila. By arguing strongly for Pancasila, Wahid hoped to show all Indonesians that NU rejected the attempts of some Muslims to blame Indonesia's or the Islamic community's problems on non-Muslims. Wahid relates that he has been deeply disturbed by the emergence of anti-Chinese and anti-Christian discourse since 1990. Wahid asserts that some of the persons responsible for starting an anti-Christian dynamic in public discourse are now prominently associated with ICMI. Wahid fears that ICMI, as a government-sponsored organization, legitimizes intolerant voices, and Wahid believes it is the "duty" of NU to demonstrate an alternative, tolerant vision of Islam and society.[79]

Wahid's letter to Soeharto

As it turned out, Abdurrahman Wahid was bitterly disappointed with the results of his Pancasila strategy taken during the Rapat Akbar in Jakarta on March 1, 1992. The rally did not attract the initially hoped-for one to two million members. On March 2 Wahid sent a letter to President Soeharto containing a "Report on the 68th Anniversary Mass Meeting of NU."[80] Wahid states in the letter that the internal goals of NU were successfully achieved in the Rapat Akbar. These included the ceremonial celebration of NU's founding at a national level; the firm expression of NU's commitment to Pancasila and the Constitution of 1945; the expression of a clear path for the NU membership to ensure the success and safety of both the 1992 general elections and the coming General Assembly of the MPR; and the demonstration of NU unity and solidarity after a long period of internal challenges.[81]

However, Wahid also reported to Soeharto that the "external" goals of the rally were not achieved. First and foremost, Wahid wrote that the NU executive board was unable to obtain endorsement for its vision of an Indonesian Islam characterized by openness and pluralism. Wahid noted that

> if we follow the contemporary discussions and debates in mosques and other Islamic councils, it is clear that the issues of sectarianism, such as fear of something called the "Christianization movement" and the like [are prominent in society today].

According to Wahid, the consequence of the emergence of fears of "Christianization" and sectarianism, and the failure of NU through its rally to firmly suppress them "will be the emergence of ignorant attitudes *emphasizing differences which endanger our national integrity.*"[82] Wahid reasoned that NU would have only been able to firmly establish grassroots legitimacy for a tolerant, inclusive Islam if a much larger number of its members – the hoped-for one to two million – had attended the Rapat Akbar. Only with such a huge public endorsement, argued Wahid, would the "modern, pluralistic" character of Indonesian Islam be "conclusively endorsed." Wahid further pointed out that government security forces had forcibly prevented hundreds of thousands of NU members from coming to Jakarta from other areas of Java. Therefore, he argued, the government was to blame for the failure of NU's attempted mass public endorsement of Pancasila and the Constitution as the vehicles for an open, pluralistic society. Wahid also said that NU, as a non-governmental organization, tried its best to establish legitimacy for a positive, nationalist-oriented religious perspective in Indonesia. Because the government impeded this attempt, Wahid wrote that it was no longer the responsibility or the burden of NU to help guide the nation along a tolerant pluralist path and that the government alone must deal with the problem of rising sectarianism and religious intolerance.

Wahid concluded his letter to Soeharto by predicting that if the government failed to ensure the establishment of NU's goals for the successful nurturing of harmonious, open-minded religious life, then those who do not accept this vision of Indonesia would present a significant threat to the "perpetuity of Pancasila and the Republic of Indonesia." Wahid closed by saying that Indonesia's political future may end up resembling Algeria; that is, there may be an attempt to establish an Islamic state in place of the current Indonesian state which will also threaten the continuation of national economic development.[83] In private, Wahid elaborated on the meaning of the Algerian analogy. He sees that some Muslims, particularly those now associated with ICMI, appear to support both the democratization and de-militarization of Indonesian national politics. This, Wahid claims, is disingenuous. He says that what such activists really seek is to manipulate Islam using an ostensibly democratic process to set up an Islamic state in which (because the rights of non-Muslims would then be implicitly devalued) democracy would be demeaned and, indeed, short-lived.[84] Matori Abdul Djalil, an NU stalwart and former Secretary General of the PPP, strongly concurs with Wahid's analysis. Matori argues that

> Whenever man acts as the agent of God, then there will be no democracy and theocracy will corrupt. If one group of people say they get legitimacy to govern from God, then they will use God as an instrument against others. And this is fundamentally undemocratic.[85]

Wahid's critique of ICMI boils down to what he sees as essentially a "Trojan Horse" theory.[86] That is, Wahid sees that many of the Islamic activists involved in ICMI have accepted Pancasila simply as a tactic to enter the government and Islamize politics from within. The ideal vehicle for the Islamization of government is ICMI as a government-sponsored, bureaucratically staffed and supported entity. According to Wahid, ICMI support for Soeharto will be rewarded with the appointment of Muslim advocates of an Islamic society to senior bureaucratic positions.[87] However, the failure of many ICMI activists to be appointed to the Cabinet announced on March 17, 1993 indicates shortcomings of the Trojan Horse scenario. In spite of the failure of such an approach, as evidenced by the Cabinet line-up that did not include ICMI activists, Wahid continues to view ICMI efforts (successful or not) to Islamize government as a dangerous and polarizing attempt to "re-confessionalize" national life.[88]

Wahid's arguments as encapsulated in the Rapat Akbar, his letter to President Soeharto, and in his private explanations of these events seem to have resonated throughout Indonesian political life. The issues he raises in a complicated web of interrelatedness (Islam, nationalism, democracy, the role of the armed forces) are given form in Wahid's conception of Pancasila as a precondition for democratic and religiously tolerant national life. Wahid and his supporters clearly see NU as an inclusive Islamic organization dedicated to a non-sectarian civil society, a view clearly bolstered by Wahid's re-election as NU Chairman in December 1994 despite strong criticism from both ICMI and parts of the regime. However, many of these views are criticized, supported, and/or manipulated by ABRI, ICMI, and other intellectuals and politicians in an increasingly polarized national discourse.

It was suggested in Chapter 1 that the endorsement of Pancasila by Muslim organizations in the early 1980s should have been pleasing to the Soeharto regime. The largest Islamic organization in the country, NU, reiterated in 1992 what it had said in 1983 –

a firm endorsement of Indonesia as *Negara Pancasila* (the Pancasila state). But it should not be surprising that Soeharto was not satisfied with NU's anniversary gathering in which NU pledged loyalty to Pancasila and the Constitution.[89] Indeed, Soeharto may have been perfectly aware of Wahid's tactics, as Aswab Mahasin has suggested. Yet, despite the numerous and highly nuanced political objectives (including avoidance of endorsing Soeharto) that Wahid sought to achieve by holding the Rapat Akbar and reiterating unconditional loyalty to part of the New Order's basic political foundation, such a declaration by NU should have been welcomed by the regime. After all, NU's Pancasila message of March 1, 1992 is also a powerful endorsement of the ideals of New Order. It stands for much that Soeharto has said he wants from mass organizations, especially from Muslims. Yet Soeharto clearly does *not* want independent political activity from Islamic or any other organizations.[90]

Soeharto may no longer have simply wanted affirmation of loyalty to the state's basic principles. As he has aged in office, according to the Petition of Fifty's original statement of concern, President Soeharto may have come to personally appropriate Pancasila and see that his rule, his government, and Pancasila are one and the same. Therefore, when Wahid refused to allow his organization to endorse Soeharto for another term in office, Soeharto was not pleased, even though ideologically and politically NU's Pancasila statement at the Rapat Akbar was supportive of the New Order's goal to de-link religion from political behavior. Wahid, on the other hand, sees that he is giving the maximum to Soeharto in pledging NU loyalty to the basis of the state in a massive public forum. Yet Wahid feels he was obstructed by the government in this endeavor.[91]

The NU Pancasila message at the Rapat Akbar represents one of the best and most explicit examples of the regime's loosening control over the use and interpretation of Pancasila. It shows how a major social-cultural organization has appropriated Pancasila to inoculate itself and advance its own vision of Indonesian society. Regime ideologists have sought to ensure that the Soeharto version of Pancasila ideologically blankets society through nation-wide Pancasila education courses. Soeharto has sought to ensure that his version of Pancasila was accepted by all Indonesians, and thereby guarantee the maintenance of the New Order's "Pancasila democracy." Yet he succeeded only too well – Pancasila's legitimacy function is so all-encompassing that people and their organizations can successfully appropriate it for uses that the government does not control.

It is very difficult for the government to delegitimize an organization such as NU which takes as its starting point the Pancasila and the Constitution itself. Moreover, the NU case represents a genuinely different view of a Pancasila state. That is, the voice of Abdurrahman Wahid's NU says that in order to realize a state based on the five principles expressed in Pancasila, and for such values to have functional meaning in Indonesia, then Pancasila must not used by the government solely to legitimize the current authoritarian system of politics. Wahid argues that the root cause of the emergence of sectarian and Islamic politics is both the political system created by the New Order itself and the personal political imperatives of Soeharto. Although supportive of the idea of "de-confessionalized" politics, Wahid argues that because the political system is so tightly controlled and because individuals cannot find outlets for their critical voices in the government-sanctioned parties, people are forced to rely on religion to participate in politics.

Moreover, the regime must not manipulate the Islamic community in ways which may re-politicize Islam in a divisive fashion, as Wahid perceives is the case regarding the creation of ICMI, simply to bolster the short-term political fortunes of Soeharto. This is fundamentally different from the nature of debate about the meaning of Pancasila in earlier decades. Never before has an Islamic organization or a nationalist Islamic leader with the stature of Abdurrahman Wahid so explicitly used Pancasila as the vehicle for a political message. The NU message regarding the implementation of Pancasila as enunciated by Wahid is complex and multi-layered, involving concerns about Islam, democratization, Soeharto's legitimacy, and the role of the armed forces in politics.

It is essential to recognize that Wahid's desire for a "de-confessionalized" polity with Pancasila as its tolerant, non-Islamic glue grows out of a shared desire with the New Order to avoid repeating disastrous periods in Indonesian history.[92] The disastrous political history that Wahid seeks to avoid is the 1950s and 1960s when political conflict was manifested along religious, regional and ethnic lines. For NU, Pancasila is used to advance its own political agenda, to protect itself against government perceptions of anti-regime behavior, *and* to ensure that Indonesia is a "de-confessionalized" polity. Indeed, by withholding endorsement of Soeharto in 1992, NU implicitly used Pancasila to de-legitimize the Soeharto government. For Abdurrahman Wahid, Pancasila represents a "noble compromise" which allows all Indonesians to participate in a "de-confessionalized" political system.[93]

The growing accommodation between Soeharto and elements of the Islamic movement in ICMI are seen by Wahid as jeopardizing the "de-confessionalized" polity that will prevent the repetition of history.[94] Importantly, it must also be recognized that NU's use of Pancasila and the complex political maneuvering and appropriation of state ideology by Wahid also constitute re-politicization of Islam. It is clear that Wahid is an intensely "political" figure and that NU continues to engage in politics. However, Wahid argues that his and NU's politics are not based on any imperative to establish an Islamic state or to formalize the relationship between Islam and the government. Moreover, NU as an institution and through Wahid as its leader, is supportive of Pancasila as a religiously neutral ideology necessary for maintenance of national unity. This view contrasts sharply with that of some Islamic activists who see no special role for Pancasila in Indonesian politics and who argue that Islam, not Pancasila, is the unifying ideology of the state.[95]

Many ABRI officers also share Wahid's concern over the re-emergence of "Islamic" politics. For both Wahid and ABRI, concern is focused on ICMI. However, a potential fear among democrats, and those seeking a political future in which the military role in Indonesian politics is reduced, is that nationalists and religious and ethnic minorities will see the armed forces as the guarantor of a non-Islamic state. Wahid argues that NU is ideally situated to bridge the gaps and reconcile the misperceptions between the Islamic movement, non-Muslims, and the armed forces. This is because, Wahid argues, ABRI "accepts NU as the legitimate representative of the *umat*." Indeed, senior ABRI officers confirm that they do recognize NU as a nationalist organization committed to the religious tolerance implicit in Pancasila and opposed to an Islamic state.[96] Wahid and other NU leaders contend that it is NU's loyalty to Pancasila that "guarantees NU's nationalist credentials." Wahid asserts that "the armed forces understand NU as a positive factor ideologically and that NU is safe on Pancasila."[97]

"A very narrow path"

The core of Wahid's dilemma as he sees it is that he wants Islam, with NU as a prominent element in the Islamic movement, to be a force for peaceful change and transition towards a democratic, tolerant society. Yet the emergence of ICMI and manipulation of Islam for political support by Soeharto, and the potential for Islam – because of ICMI – being persecuted again by ABRI for being "anti-Pancasila," makes the journey to Wahid's preferred political future difficult. Wahid summed up his dilemma in the following way:

> So it's clear that we have to handle this thing [ICMI] very carefully. On one side we should not allow Islam to be used in the wrong way by those fellow Muslims who would like to evolve an Islamic society here. On the other hand, we would have to avert the use of excessive force against them in an undemocratic way. This way it's a very narrow path for us . . . [and] because the military, in acting harshly in an undemocratic fashion to defend Pancasila, in essence, castrates Pancasila.[98]

Wahid is trying to look to a political future of greater democratization, less military influence, and no Islamic fundamentalism. Wahid harbors deep fears that democratization will provide Indonesians with the opportunity to "choose Islam" which in turn may play into the hands of both Islamic radicals and the armed forces which reject both democracy and Islamic politics. This is his Algeria analogy. According to Wahid, the democratic option may be exercised only once – and then a fundamentally undemocratic state may emerge from a democratic process. In the interests of a "de-confessionalized" state many Indonesians, and perhaps Wahid as well, may opt for an ABRI-dominated non-democratic state that at least protects religious, ethnic, and regional minority rights in the interest of national unity rather than democratization in which re-confessionalized political Islam may win at the ballot box. For NU and Abdurrahman Wahid, Pancasila is first and foremost an ideology of "de-confessionalization," national unity, and tolerance.

Wahid strongly argues that precisely because the armed forces accept Pancasila's stipulation of respect for all citizens regardless of religion or ethnicity, ABRI has also accepted the foundation of a liberal, democratic society. Even though the armed forces still reject liberal democracy, Wahid believes that the "logic of liberalism is already there in ABRI's stance on Pancasila." Therefore, the chances for eventual democratization are greater through eventual compromise between ABRI, NU and others who share the inclusive vision of Pancasila rather than through a process of "democratization through Islamization."[99] Wahid is quick to add that democracy needs much more than Pancasila. Wahid's fuller prescription for democratization will be analyzed through his leadership of Forum Democracy in Chapter 5.

Many of Wahid's concerns about Pancasila have become the terms of reference for wider political debate on a complex range of issues involving the relationship between Islam and government, democratization, national development, and the role of the armed forces in politics. It is Wahid's terms that, in part, delineate the discourse about Pancasila in the 1990s. Wahid has focused on "Pancasila" as the way to attempt to influence the substance of national political debate. In many ways Pancasila has become Wahid's preferred political and ideological vehicle for the expression of his – and NU's – ideas and political messages.

Wahid has also used Pancasila as a tool to improve his standing both within the Islamic movement and to appeal to all Indonesians. Indeed, many Indonesian observers see the Rapat Akbar and use of Pancasila there as clear attempts by Wahid to shore up his position as pre-eminent leader of the *umat* in spite of the emergence of ICMI, now the beneficiary of government attention. Even though Wahid bitterly referred to the Rapat Akbar as a failure in many respects, the significance of Wahid's role in the Rapat Akbar was editorialized in the *Jakarta Post* as proof that "nobody can take him lightly." The *Post* editorial argued that the Rapat Akbar demonstrated Wahid's and NU's relevance in contemporary politics:

> The ease with which Wahid has "summoned" his thousands of followers despite the authorities' earlier objections undoubtedly has catapulted him into a new perspective. Nobody can play him down. Sunday's gathering demonstrated NU's potential and confirmed its place in this country's politics.[100]

What the editorial failed to mention was that the rally went ahead primarily because it became impossible for the regime to prohibit NU's public expression of loyalty to the basic legitimizing tenet of the New Order. However, Abdurrahman Wahid and

Nahdlatul Ulama constitute only one part of the Islamic contribution to contemporary discourse. Wahid's concerns are influenced and provoked by others in the Islamic movement, especially Muslim activists associated with ICMI. Therefore, the following chapter will consider the "ICMI voice" in the ongoing Pancasila discourse.

Chapter 3

The Indonesian Muslim Intellectuals' Association (ICMI)

> The scariest thing is to be accused of being an enemy of Pancasila.
>
> Amien Rais[1]

> It is difficult to organize the masses for purposes of democratization and de-militarization if we don't use the reason of religion.
>
> Adi Sasono[2]

The establishment of the Indonesian Muslim Intellectuals' Association (ICMI) in December 1990 is one of the most consequential political events of recent years. ICMI's creation has had a profound impact on political and ideological discourse in the 1990s.

Unlike NU, the "ICMI voice" is not dominated by one distinctive person or perspective. It is a loosely organized, newly established association represented by numerous people. The head of ICMI is the controversial Minister of Technology, B.J. Habibie, a close confidant of President Soeharto. ICMI is heavily staffed and run by government bureaucrats, many of whom have been close associates of Habibie. Although Habibie's role in ICMI will be considered, his contribution to political discourse is not always the most significant in terms of ICMI's impact on ideological and political discourse. In fact, many of the non-bureaucratic members of ICMI, many who are well-known Muslim intellectuals, activists, and NGO figures, do not consider Habibie to be wholly representative of the organization. Some members of ICMI even question Habibie's piety.[3] Such divisions between ICMI's Muslim "activists" and its government bureaucrat members is due, in part, to the fact that activists need official association with the regime so that they can legitimately carry out their Islamizing activities.

Furthermore, the conspicuous presence of notable Islamic scholars and activists tends to dominate elite perceptions of the organization. Therefore, analysis of ICMI's role in national political and ideological discourse will focus on those voices that are generally associated with ICMI both by ICMI's non-bureaucratic activist leaders themselves and by members of ABRI, secular nationalists, and Abdurrahman Wahid and NU. This chapter is divided into three sections. The first section examines the political significance of ICMI, its main component groups, and why it deserves detailed analysis. The second section outlines the political and religious context of ICMI's establishment. It examines the impact of three developments – the cultural revival of Islam, the changing relationship of President Soeharto to the Islamic community, and the divisions in the Islamic movement concerning the relationship of Islam and the state. The third section examines the political strategies and objectives of ICMI and evaluates their implications for national politics.

ICMI members can be roughly divided into three groups: Muslim theologians and scholars, Islamic activists and politicians, and government bureaucrats. Scholars and theologians were initially most prominently represented by Nurcholish Madjid and Dawam Rahardjo, who are (together with Abdurrahman Wahid outside ICMI) perhaps the most "revolutionary" Islamic thinkers and scholars in Indonesia since the 1970s.[4] Nurcholish, while originally approving of ICMI, is not dependent upon it for participating in scholarly or national discourse. He should not be viewed as a key member of ICMI although he has been more amenable to it than Abdurrahman Wahid. Nurcholish heads his own Islamic institute, Yayasan Paramadina, in Jakarta and since 1994 has distanced himself from ICMI and criticized it for becoming "too political."[5]

The Islamic activists and politicians form the most vocal component group of ICMI. These include many people associated with *Muhammadiyah*, including followers of the late Mohammed Natsir, the former Prime Minister and leader of *Masyumi*, the modernist Islamic party banned in the early 1960s (and not revived under the New Order). Activists include leaders of NGOs and former dissidents (some jailed under the New Order), including people previously opposed to Soeharto, Pancasila and *asas tunggal* [the 1985 law which required all organizations to adopt Pancasila as their sole philosophical foundation]. Politicians also include some current members of the PPP, including the party's Chairman, Ismail Hasan Metareum. Members of this "activist" group considered in greatest detail include Amien Rais, Dawam Rahardjo, Sri Bintang Pamungkas, Adi Sasono, Nasir Tamara, Din Syamsuddin, and Imaduddin Abdul Rahim. A number of these figures are also simultaneously scholars and activists.

Finally, because ICMI is a government-sponsored organization under the patronage of Minister Habibie and President Soeharto, many bureaucrats have joined. These include such figures as Wardiman Djojonegoro, the Minister of Education and Culture, and the Minister of Transportation, Haryanto Dhanutirto. Soetjipto Wirosardjono, formerly a high-ranking civil servant in the Bureau of Statistics, has also been an active ICMI member. Additionally, the views of former Minister of Religious Affairs, Munawir Sjadzali, will be examined. The majority of attention in this chapter will be focused on the second group, the ICMI activists and politicians who dominate elite perceptions of ICMI.

ICMI's establishment is one of the most striking political phenomena in the New Order. One of the founding members of ICMI, Nasir Tamara, now a senior editor for the daily *Republika*, recalled that he told his colleagues in December 1990 that "ICMI is among the most important developments in Indonesia since the founding of the *Sarekat Dagang Islam* [Islamic Traders' Association]" in 1912.[6] There are four reasons for accentuating the significance of ICMI in this study of contemporary Indonesian politics.

First, ICMI members view their organization as giving "voice" to Islam. This is according to Imaduddin Abdul Rahim, one of the most prominent intellectuals in ICMI and an inspiration behind its establishment.[7] Imaduddin also proclaims that "before we had no voice, now we do." Some ICMI figures, such as Nasir Tamara, speak explicitly of ICMI providing a new voice in national discourse. Tamara also observes that ICMI "allows a nationalist discourse about whether Islam can participate as a main actor or as only an observer in politics." Moreover, he argues that ICMI is significant because it gives Islam the chance to respond to its political opponents. Tamara sees ICMI as giving opportunity to an Islam which "is tired of being smeared by others."[8] Specifically, Tamara views that with ICMI as a strong voice of Islam, "no longer will Abdurrahman Wahid monopolize the discourse about Islam" in

Indonesia. Before ICMI's establishment, he argues, it was only NU or *Muhammadiyah* and a few well-known Muslims (such as Wahid and Nurcholish Madjid) who dominated Islamic discourse. ICMI gives voice to a whole new group of people.

Second, ICMI is politically significant as a concrete manifestation of change in President Soeharto's attitude and approach to Islam in Indonesia. Soeharto appears more prepared to accommodate Muslim interests in recent years. This is because of both Islamic acceptance of *asas tunggal* and the fact that Soeharto needs Islamic support to compensate for decreased backing from the armed forces. Finally, there is an important personal dimension. Soeharto may genuinely feel closer to religion. Many Indonesians allow that it is natural as a person ages for him or her to become more religiously devout. However, all the President's actions are political, regardless of their initial motivation, spiritual or otherwise.

Third, ICMI's establishment and sponsorship by the government is because the New Order, and especially Soeharto himself, perceives that it "won" against political Islam. After the successful enactment of Pancasila as the *asas tunggal*, according to former Minister of Religious Affairs, Munawir Sjadzali, the "psychological and political problem of an Islamic state" no longer exists. This, he allows, is a major change and it is a "victory," not for Soeharto or the New Order but for "the nation." Munawir explains that because the state no longer feels threatened, it is only natural "by virtue of democratic principles" that Islam should get more attention from the government including official endorsement for ICMI's creation.[9]

Fourth, ICMI is important because it attempts to speak to (and for) the new urban, increasingly middle-class, educated Muslims who are the beneficiaries of *pembangunan* [the New Order's program of economic development].[10] However, because ICMI is highly politicized, dependent upon Habibie and Soeharto, and internally divided, its appeal to the middle classes is limited. Considering the highly polarized views of ICMI, membership may be as much a liability as a benefit. None the less, for some of its followers, ICMI represents a modern Islamic organization that accommodates the interests of Muslims who consider the old *aliran* [socio-cultural based "streams" or groups in Indonesian society, in this case *santri* and *abangan*] inappropriate for distinguishing between Muslims.[11]

However, before examining in detail the voices of ICMI and their role in the Pancasila discourse, cultural and political developments within the Islamic community and the Indonesian polity during the past decade must be further examined. Moreover, this section will account for the crucial changing relationship between Soeharto and the Islamic movement.

CONTEXT OF ICMI'S ESTABLISHMENT

Apart from the government-mandated fusion of Islamic political parties that became the PPP (or United Development Party in 1973), ICMI is the only major Islamic organization established during the New Order. Moreover, it is the first time that President Soeharto has directly supported the creation of such an association. In August 1993 Soeharto became the official chief "patron" of ICMI. In order to understand why this has come about, three concurrent developments must be considered. The first includes both the cultural revival of Islam and closely related political decisions not to problematize Pancasila made by Muslim figures, many of whom are now associated with ICMI. The second general set of conditions and developments revolves around the perceptions of President Soeharto and his changing political needs *vis-à-vis* Islam and the armed forces. Third, attention must be devoted to the split in the Islamic movement evident by the late 1980s, particularly in terms of Abdurrahman Wahid's growing disenchantment with government steps to accommodate Islamic interests.

Cultural revival and political decisions

As noted in the previous chapter, Indonesia has been enjoying an Islamic cultural revival over the past two decades. This cultural revival has been paralleled by the strict proscription of explicit Islamic political activity in the New Order. Prohibition of political organization in the New Order on the basis of religious, ethnic, racial, or class affiliations is a key element in the regime's conception of a Pancasila democracy. However, many view the cultural, spiritual, and educational flowering of Indonesian Islam as partly a consequence of Muslim energies directed away from Islamic politics.[12]

In place of Islamic striving for the formalization of links between the government and Islam (which had been a core issue for a minority in the Islamic movement for decades), a striving for the creation of a "*Masyarakat Islam*" or "Islamic society" gained prominence within the Muslim community in the 1980s. Nurcholish Madjid best explains the concept of Islamic society. Nurcholish argues that Muslims realize that Indonesia *is* increasingly an Islamic society and that "from 1985 [Muslims] began to find out even Pancasila could accommodate their religious interests" in the context of an Islamic society. Nurcholish argues that Pancasila was beside the point and that Indonesia was increasingly becoming an Islamic society:

> We begin with something very symbolic, like doing the Friday prayers, not only in the offices, but in the banks, in hotels, everywhere – that begins in the mid-1980s. Then there is such a gesture from all politicians to say, very symbolically, "*assalamu'alaikum*" [Arabic greeting for "may peace be with you"]. More and more Islamic nomenclatures are used. And despite its superficiality, symbolism is very important, especially to those people who don't question much about the system *because they cannot question*, so instead symbolism functions very well.[13]

Nurcholish's statement that people cannot question the system is indicative of the "success" of the New Order in eliminating critical voices from public discourse. Nurcholish argues that because Muslims could not turn to political activity in the New Order, they naturally expressed their faith culturally and symbolically.

Nurcholish Madjid concludes that the healthy development of an Islamic society in Indonesia is seen by the new generation of educated, primarily urban-based Muslims to be perfectly compatible with Pancasila. The difference in the 1980s and 1990s is also that Muslims wish to see a government that reflects the values of Islam. Nurcholish argues this is a "natural" development and should be considered in "exactly the sense that the United States is a Christian society imbued with Judeo-Christian values." He argues that this does not imply lack of recognition of the many other faiths and values in society – in America or Indonesia – but rather it is a form of "cultural and historical realism" that cannot be denied. In Indonesia of the 1980s and 1990s, Nurcholish observes, young people say that Islam, being the religion of the largest number of the community, is expected to supply the community with ethical values; that is, the foundation of the social interactions within the state of Indonesia. I always argue that this is a kind of social and cultural realism. Its unrealistic culturally to deny the possible role of the Muslims, especially because of their [advances in] education.[14]

Consequently, according to Nurcholish Madjid, educated, politically mature Indonesian Muslims are seeking the best ways to find "positive roles in society" in the post-*asas tunggal* era. "And therefore they come to organized activities," Nurcholish added. The explosion of interest in ICMI, both in government and from part of the Islamic community as a whole, should not be surprising when considered in the context of the needs and ambitions of Indonesian Muslims who have learned how to accommodate their faith in the Pancasila state, according to Nurcholish.

Abdurrahman Wahid basically concurs with Nurcholish Madjid's analysis on the broad sociological trends in Indonesian Islam. Wahid too, agrees that Muslims have realized that Pancasila in no way impinges upon Muslims' voluntary adherence to their faith. However, Wahid is deeply suspicious of the concept of an "Islamic society." As indicated in Chapter 2, Wahid believes that Islamic society is a code word for a persistent ambition to create an Islamic state. It is not Nurcholish *per se* who worries Wahid. The two men are personally close and intellectually similar in their desire to accommodate Islam within the Indonesian national context. Wahid believes that ICMI, as Nurcholish may conceive it, is relatively benign. Yet it is the manipulation of the *umat* and the creation of ICMI by Soeharto to serve his political objectives that is most disturbing to Wahid.

In the 1970s Nurcholish Madjid urged Muslims to understand that there is no Islamic theological imperative to establish an Islamic state. This argument caused an emotional uproar among a minority group of Muslims who insisted that the establishment of an Islamic state was the logical conclusion of Islamic teachings. However, in the 1980s and 1990s, Nurcholish contends that his argument (that there is no imperative to create an Islamic state) spread widely in society, and that all but a very few Indonesian Muslims have abandoned efforts to establish an Islamic state. Moreover, he argues, the educational maturation of the Islamic community, especially among urban Muslims, is representative of acceptance of new thinking about Islam and the state.

As demonstrated by the surge in votes for Golkar after the withdrawal of NU from the PPP in the 1980s, many Muslim Indonesians have channelled their political aspirations through the government-backed party. Islam was still seeking a way to act politically in the New Order. In the post-*asas tunggal* era, according to Din Syamsuddin, the head of *Muhammadiyah*'s youth organization, there has in fact been a "re-politicization of Islam" which cannot be divorced from Islamic cultural revival. Syamsuddin sees the 1985 passage of the *asas tunggal* as the "peak" of New Order "Pancasila-ization" efforts. After 1985 there emerged an "attractive group of Islamic intellectuals" exemplified by Abdurrahman Wahid and Nurcholish Madjid. Additionally, according to Syamsuddin, the government felt less threatened by Islam after all Islamic organizations accepted Pancasila.[15] These perspectives from the Islamic movement also confirm Munawir Sjadzali's explanation that Soeharto's *rapprochement* with Islam was genuinely influenced by Muslims' acceptance of *asas tunggal*.

The abandonment of Muslim concerns about Pancasila is the result of two different, though mutually complementary developments. Nurcholish argues that expansion of access to higher education, especially overseas, allows Muslims to begin to "catch up" and reduce the educational gaps between Muslims and non-Muslims that were the result of discriminatory Dutch policies. According to Nurcholish, "Muslims cease to ask whether this [Pancasila] is valid or not. It is valid, but how do we interpret it?" Muslims are more confident and self-assured and they see that Pancasila does not need to be problematized.[16] Amir Santoso, Chair of the Political Science Department at the University of Indonesia and the head of the social and cultural section of ICMI, argues that the abandonment of opposition to Pancasila was possible because it became apparent that Pancasila through the *asas tunggal* did not become a civil religion or seek to secularize the state.[17] Indeed, President Soeharto states in his autobiography that it was never his intention to secularize the state because Pancasila stipulates that Indonesia must be a religious state.[18] Thus, changes in social conditions "allowed" Muslims to move beyond Pancasila. On the other hand, there were also explicit political decisions made to abandon opposition to Pancasila or discussion of the Jakarta Charter.[19]

Political aspirations, however, simply do not disappear. As we have seen, even though NU took itself out of politics, it was done so that NU could, in reality, participate more effectively in national politics. Amien Rais, a political scientist and leading ICMI figure, argues that by 1985 many Muslims decided that opposition to Pancasila was a losing political issue for Indonesian Islam.[20] Muslims began to see that their perceptions of problems in Indonesian society lay not with *asas tunggal* and Pancasila, but with specific policies and programs. Therefore, the question for Amien Rais and others was how to influence policy. For some, rather than attacking Pancasila, the solution was to seek the Islamization of society using the power of the state. Rather than oppose the government, which was a losing strategy in the New Order, the only alternative was to enter government and to influence policy from within.

In addition to the cultural and educational conditions extant in Indonesian Islamic society by the 1980s, there was the political dynamic of an unrelenting New Order offensive against any form of independent Islamic political opposition to the government. Indeed, Islamic political activity that was in no way connected to Pancasila, such as NU's behavior as a sometimes oppositionist party in the 1970s, was depicted as anti-Pancasila. Although Muslim politics were unacceptable to the New Order, the government built thousands of mosques and organized the transport of tens of thousands of Indonesians on the *haj* every year. Indeed, it has appeared to many observers that government treatment of Islam in the New Order is reminiscent of the policies advocated by Snouck Hurgronje, the famous Dutch advisor to the colonial regime who argued that Islam as a cultural and spiritual force was to be encouraged and nurtured while political manifestations of faith were to be suppressed.[21] Therefore, as President Soeharto's changing relationship with Islam is considered, it is important to remember that the Islamic revival in the 1980s occurred in a context in which political Islam was severely proscribed.

Soeharto's changing relationship with Islam

The former Minister of Religious Affairs, Munawir Sjadzali (1983–1993) observed that the Muslim "acceptance of Pancasila had a profound impact on President Soeharto." Munawir sees that "before *asas tunggal* Muslims were viewed suspiciously by the government" but not after 1985. While Munawir says that fundamentalism in Indonesia was always a minority view, he stresses that especially after *asas tunggal* there is "no more danger at all from fundamentalism."[22] It is this perception of the change in Indonesian Islam – in terms of its unequivocal abandonment of what Soeharto saw as "fundamentalism" – through the acceptance of Pancasila as the *asas tunggal* that permitted Soeharto to "do more for Islam." According to Munawir, President Soeharto's obsession with ensuring that Pancasila was accepted by all was satisfied after 1985.

Munawir Sjadzali's explanation of why Soeharto pushed so hard for the *asas tunggal* and then quickly adopted programs and legislation favorable to the Islamic community is worth discussing at length in order to understand his relationship with ICMI today.[23] Munawir argues that for Soeharto, *asas tunggal* was never narrowly conceived as a political weapon or as a "reaction to something." This contrasts sharply with former Prime Minister Sjafruddin's open letter to Soeharto in 1984 in which he accused the President of using Pancasila "against" the Islamic community. Munawir relates how in the early 1980s Soeharto was aware of an impending generational change in national leadership. Soeharto, according to Munawir, felt the nation had remained unified partly because of the shared experiences, values, and fellow feelings born out of the "1945 generation" and its revolutionary participation. "Feelings of shared experience," according to Munawir, helped hold the country together in Soeharto's view. But Soeharto feared that the successor generations did not share such bonds. According to Munawir, Soeharto thought that if the remaining problems concerning continuing dissension over Pancasila (which in Soeharto's eyes was proven by the disagreements over the implementation of the Pancasila education programs) were not resolved before the generational transfer of power, then unsolved questions about the philosophical foundation of the state would remain.[24] The ultimate purpose of the *asas tunggal* in Munawir's words, was "to be sure there would be no Islamic state, and that neither a theocratic nor secular state would emerge in the future." Munawir contends that the promulgation of legislation favorable to the Islamic community in the late 1980s and early 1990s (outlined below) could not have happened before Muslims' acceptance of *asas tunggal*.[25]

Munawir's explanation of Soeharto's feelings and perceptions are consistent with Soeharto's views as expressed in his autobiography and explained by others. This explanation firmly places Soeharto as a nationalist first, and a religious man second. However, according Harry Tjan Silalahi, a political observer and former Secretary General of the Catholic Party in the 1960s, it is difficult to separate the political from spiritual motivations to account for Soeharto's actions.[26] That is, ICMI activists who feel they can Islamize the state from within (views that are explored below) may underestimate Soeharto's obsession with Pancasila and his reasons for "doing more for Islam" in recent years.

A second element in the change in Soeharto's approach towards Islam concerns what many Indonesians see as his deepening spiritual commitment to the faith in the last several years. While some of the Jakarta elite consider Soeharto's *haj* to Mecca in 1991 a political ploy to enlist Muslim support for his re-election in 1993, Mohtar Mas'oed at Gajah Mada University in Yogyakarta argues that the "vast majority of ordinary Muslims, the *orang awam* [the common people], recognize Soeharto as an increasingly 'good' Muslim and cite his *haj* as proof."[27] Nurcholish Madjid confirms Munawir's assertion that Soeharto has always had a commitment to Islam which he is "able" to fulfill now because he perceives that all Muslims have genuinely accepted Pancasila.[28]

The issues reviewed above – the Islamic cultural revival, Muslim recognition that *asas tunggal* did not impinge upon religion, Soeharto's perception of "victory" over Islamic politics, the profound personal impact acceptance of *asas tunggal* had on Soeharto, and finally the more public manifestation of the President's religiosity must all be considered in the context of a perceptible change in the relationship between ABRI and the President. The increasing divergence of ABRI views from those of Soeharto is most evident in the 1988 and 1993 vice-presidential selection processes. Soeharto's 1988 choice, Sudharmono, met unconcealed, though ineffective, opposition from ABRI. Indeed, it was especially after open ABRI opposition to Sudharmono[29] that Soeharto most assiduously courted the Islamic community, initially both *Nahdlatul Ulama* and *Muhammadiyah* and other Muslim groups.[30] ABRI was more successful in 1993 when the military choice for the vice presidency, General Try Sutrisno, was selected.

After the establishment of ICMI many Muslim leaders and politicians were increasingly satisfied with Soeharto's attention to the concerns of the *umat*. There was an apparent growing *rapprochement* between many Islamic activists, a number of whom would become prominent members of ICMI, and the Soeharto government. Yet ICMI's appearance, which coincided with a deterioration in Wahid's relationship with Soeharto and the government at a time of generally growing satisfaction both in the *umat* and among other Muslim leaders, reflects a long-standing split in the Indonesian Islamic movement. As noted in preceding chapters, Wahid and his supporters in NU were always in basic agreement with the broad political objectives of the New Order to de-link primordial affiliations based on religion, race, ethnicity, and class (the so-called "SARA" issues) from politics.

Two pieces of legislation initiated by Soeharto and the controversial banning of a newspaper in 1989 and 1990 highlight the growing differences in the public discourse about Islam, government, and Pancasila. Law no. 7 passed by the DPR in 1989 concerned "religious court law." It was not so much new law, but a clarification and reaffirmation of the independence and equality of religious (Islamic) courts of law (that deal with family, divorce, and inheritance matters) with civil courts. Law no. 2, 1989 on the national education system affirmed the continuance of religious education in public schools and recognized religious education as a formal subsystem to the national education system. It stipulated that religious instruction was to be compulsory in all public schools and universities. The religious education law was technically neutral with regard to faith – it would allow religious instruction in all faiths in government schools. However, Wahid argued that it would, in fact, give Muslim fundamentalists the opportunity to propagate Islam in a much more intensive and politically relevant fashion than other faiths. Therefore, Wahid concluded, the law favored Muslims and would be used by *dakwah* [fundamentalist] groups to promote narrow "Muslim-only" concepts in the school system.[31] Minister of Religious Affairs, Munawir Sjadzali, later argued that even when Indonesia had Muslim political parties they had not been successful in promulgation of such legislation favorable to the Islamic community.[32]

These two laws highlight controversies in political discourse because they generated deep anxiety among both non-Muslims and others, including Wahid. That is, at the same time as Soeharto stepped up his display of good intentions towards the *umat* by supporting these two pieces of legislation, Abdurrahman Wahid began to argue that the government should be careful not to move too far in the direction of Islam. In 1989 and 1990, on the eve of the establishment of ICMI, there was a distinct change in the nature of NU's relationship with Soeharto. Wahid sensed that government legislative moves smacked of manipulation of the *umat* for political purposes.[33] After NU's acceptance of Pancasila and *asas tunggal*, former Minister of Religious Affairs, Munawir Sjadzali, said that in the Cabinet and government "all doors were open to NU and Abdurrahman Wahid." However, particularly since the "*Monitor* Affair" (described below) and events in the 1990s, Wahid has had much less access to government officials.[34] Ironically, at the time of increasing government attention to Muslims, Wahid and the regime were increasingly unhappy with each other.

Abdurrahman Wahid argued against the two laws because he contended that there should be only one law code for all Indonesian citizens.[35] The human rights lawyer Adnan Buyung Nasution (himself a Muslim) agrees with Wahid that the Islamic courts and education legislation are inappropriate. Nasution argues that all Indonesians should be equal before the law based on the sole criterion of "sameness of citizenship," not religious faith.[36] Moreover, some non-Muslim intellectuals voiced considerable apprehension over these laws. Prominent Catholic and Protestant intellectuals argued that these Islam-specific laws heightened fears that a desire to Islamize government and law still exists, even though everyone formally accepts Pancasila and no longer advocates special mention of Islam in the Constitution or Pancasila (the Jakarta Charter, for example).[37]

The "*Monitor* Affair"

In October 1990 the "*Monitor* Affair" crystallized differences in the Islamic community and between Wahid and those who by December 1990 had joined ICMI. It was also a powerful illustration of religious and political tension extant in Indonesian society. In mid-October the weekly (and extremely popular) tabloid *Monitor* published the results of a readers' poll of most-admired public figures. President Soeharto was placed first, the prophet Muhammad eleventh. Much of the Muslim community was outraged. Some were baffled as to how a newspaper could conceive much less publish a poll which compared the Prophet of God to worldly figures. For these Muslims, this was an illustration of extreme insensitivity towards Islamic beliefs. The outrage was heightened by the fact that *Monitor* was part of the Catholic-owned Gramedia publishing group, which also publishes Jakarta's paper of record, *Kompas*. Amien Rais, soon to become a leading member of ICMI's board of experts, said that by publishing such a poll, "*Monitor* dealt a blow that severely insulted the Islamic community and at the same time destroyed government efforts to establish religious harmony."[38] Even Nurcholish Madjid criticized the tabloid and its non-Muslim editor, Arswendo Atmowiloto, by saying that publication of the poll constituted "SARA" (SARA is the Indonesian acronym for the forbidden set of highly emotive issues involving ethnicity, religion, race and class). Nurcholish Madjid argued that *Monitor* should be permanently banned. The resolution of the issue included the permanent withdrawal of *Monitor*'s publishing license and the arrest, trial and conviction of Arswendo on charges of insulting Islam. Arswendo Atmowiloto served four years of a five-year prison sentence and was released in 1994.[39]

The "*Monitor* Affair" highlighted one of the disturbing paradoxes of contemporary Indonesian society: the simultaneous emergence of thoughtful, tolerant, "revolutionary" new thinking on Islam – pluralism and democracy – coupled with increasing social intolerance and sectarianism. Abdurrahman Wahid was the only major Muslim leader to argue for calm in the "*Monitor* Affair." He said that in spite of whatever one may feel concerning how the Prophet Muhammad was depicted in *Monitor*'s poll, the right to publish cannot be infringed. If Muslims are insulted, Wahid argued, they should simply boycott the tabloid. Under no circumstances, Wahid declared, could he accept the banning and revocation of the fundamental right to free speech and publication of anyone, by anyone, in any place.[40] Wahid argued that the "*Monitor* Affair" confirmed for him the ominous trend towards the "re-confessionalization" of politics. He argues that certain Islamic groups and individuals exaggerated the issue and used Arswendo Atmowiloto as a scapegoat to promote their political agenda which emphasized exaggerating fears of "Christianization." Wahid contends they forced the government to cave in to religious pressure that resulted in a fundamentally undemocratic result: the banning of the paper and imprisonment of its editor. Although Wahid speaks respectfully of Nurcholish Madjid (indeed, many of their positions are extremely close), he bitterly criticizes Nurcholish's endorsement of the banning of *Monitor*.

By 1990 the following developments merged at about the same time. The Islamic cultural revival occurred within the Islamic movement which no longer problematized Pancasila as the sole ideological basis of the state. Soeharto recognized *asas tunggal* as a success and became less suspicious of political Islam, seeing it more as an ally than a political threat. Soeharto's relationship with ABRI had also become increasingly strained and contributed to his accommodation with Islam. Furthermore, a conspicuous split developed in the Islamic movement based on divergent views of Soeharto's *rapprochement* with Islam. These developments contributed to the political environment at the time of Soeharto's sponsorship of ICMI in December 1990. Moreover, the "*Monitor* Affair" and the Islamic courts and education legislation added to a perception by non-Muslims and politically secular Muslims that Indonesia was being Islamized. Furthermore, Abdurrahman Wahid and NU's growing distance from the government and their perceived danger of the deepening accommodation between Islam and the state helped set the stage for an increasingly acute debate over the meaning and implementation of Pancasila ideology in the 1990s.

THE ICMI VOICE IN NATIONAL DISCOURSE

ICMI has added new and dynamic voices to the national political discourse. In the short time since its December 1990 inauguration, ICMI has established formal outlets for its political views: an academic think-tank, CIDES (Center for Information and Development Studies) and a daily newspaper, *Republika*.[41] However, ICMI has been embroiled in controversy since its founding. This is due to two reasons. First, Abdurrahman Wahid, leader of NU and the most powerful single Islamic leader in the nation, did not join. Second, the Indonesian armed forces are alarmed by this new organization.

The ICMI contribution to political discourse is not explicitly ideological or, with a few important exceptions, about Pancasila at all. This is very different from Wahid's, Soeharto's, or ABRI's

Pancasila-related participation in national politics. However, it may be that the political and programmatic agenda being advanced by some of the most vocal and visible members of ICMI is deeply ideological. That is, according to ICMI critics (Wahid in NU, ABRI, some secular nationalists, and voices from within the government bureaucracy), the ICMI agenda as conceived by some members of the organization may indeed be about realizing an Islamic state. What matters most in analysis here is perception. Virtually no one explicitly seeks to turn Indonesia into an Islamic state. Nurcholish Madjid is at the forefront of new thinking in Islam that seeks to de-link Islamic aspirations for an Islamic state from the Indonesian context. Instead, what Nurcholish seeks is a healthy "Islamic society." Abdurrahman Wahid and others, however, argue that Islamic society means essentially the same thing as an Islamic state and as such it would mean the contravention of the core religious tolerance implicit in Pancasila.[42]

ICMI membership comprises a diverse group of intellectuals with strongly differing opinions. For example, as will be shown below, some members of ICMI do conceive of a future political system in which Islam provides moral and political guidance. This is a vision that other Indonesians find profoundly disturbing. There is a perception that ICMI activists wish to circumvent Pancasila and formalize links between Islam and the government. The consequence of such a development, argue ICMI critics, would be the contravention of Pancasila as the formulaic expression of a religiously tolerant society.

The purpose of ICMI (or, "What does ICMI really want?")

Munawir Sjadzali argued in a widely publicized speech in mid-1992 that Muslims' interests are better served in the absence of Islamic political parties.[43] In this speech he noted that President Soeharto's sponsorship of ICMI was proof that Muslims are well served in the Pancasila democracy without having to channel their political aspirations through explicitly Islamic parties. Nothing like ICMI or the other benefits that have accrued to Islam in the New Order were ever even close to being attained during the period of Islamic political parties, Munawir asserted. Yet some of the prominent voices in the ICMI discourse do claim that ICMI is a nascent Islamic political party. To what then has President Soeharto lent his imprimatur? The aspiration for Islamic parties persists, particularly among some ICMI activists. It appears that these aspirations are partly given voice through ICMI.

What then does ICMI want? Or rather, what is the purpose of ICMI according to some of its most prominent members and leaders? What is ICMI's contribution to contemporary political discourse and how is this connected to Pancasila? Is an ICMI voice articulating an alternative ideological and political vision for Indonesia? Or is it simply a politically benign organization that reflects the natural sociological trends of a more sophisticated and better-educated *umat*, as suggested by Nurcholish Madjid? Are Islamic activists and politicians using ICMI, a government-backed organization led by one of Soeharto's closest advisors, Minister of Technology B.J. Habibie, to give themselves a voice that may not be the intention of the organization's protectors and sponsors (Soeharto and Habibie)? And what are the implications of these contributions to the discourse?

If the purpose of ICMI is "to establish the new *Masyumi*," as stated by one senior ICMI organizer, then the political implications may be profound.[44] This is an illustration of the suspected agenda of ICMI that worries some Indonesians and contributes to the high level of tension regarding ICMI since its establishment. That is, if Munawir Sjadzali and President Soeharto established ICMI with no intention of encouraging a revival of Islamic party politics (which is the case), then it appears that members of the organization do not share that benign official vision. Moreover, by identifying ICMI as "the new *Masyumi*," ICMI "activist" members have raised "red flags" for many other participants in the discourse. Djohan Effendi notes that *Masyumi*'s stance in the 1950s, especially in the Konstituante, tended to see Pancasila juxtaposed against Islam. This "narrow-minded stand by the Islamic parties, particularly *Masyumi*," argues Djohan Effendi, "was a very unwise policy, one that resulted in political prejudice being directed to Islamic movements and organizations in general."[45] The implications of thinking in ICMI that it is a nascent political party are not so much that a party like *Masyumi* might in fact emerge, but rather in the impact such wishes have on the character of ideological discourse and the political behavior of other members of the elite.

ICMI leaders identify three basic purposes of the organization: first, to help Muslims educationally, culturally, and economically; second, to unify the Indonesian Islamic movement and to break away from historic splits (for example, "modernist" *Muhammadiyah* versus "traditionalist" NU); and third, to implement a number of specific political objectives.

The first general purpose is also the most politically benign and is what the government – and perhaps Habibie himself – has in mind regarding ICMI's function. This is the educative, economic, and cultural approach. For example, Soetjipto Wirosardjono argues that Muslims generally have poorer access to high-quality education and that ICMI intends to direct attention and resources to improving schools and higher education. A non-profit educational foundation to further this goal, *Yayasan Abdi Bangsa*, has been established. ICMI provides university scholarships for Muslim students and initiated small-scale credit schemes for slum-dwellers.[46] In order to improve educational standards and opportunities for the mass of poor Muslims, Soetjipto says that ICMI encourages special attention by the government towards such disadvantaged groups. Imaduddin Abdul Rahim, a founder of ICMI, and Sri Bintang Pamungkas, a leading member of ICMI and PPP member of the DPR, both argue that the purpose of ICMI is to "help Muslims who are uneducated, poor, and backward."[47] In other words, in this benign, non-political characterization, ICMI acts like an ordinary NGO. Similarly, Dewi Fortuna Anwar at CIDES describes ICMI as a "lobbying group" with no pretensions as a political party.[48]

Second, many ICMI leaders argue that a central purpose of the organization is to unify the Islamic movements in Indonesia. Both Adi Sasono and Nasir Tamara argue that old conceptions of Indonesian Islam divided along *aliran* no longer apply. *Santri* and *abangan* do not adequately represent the diversity and variety of perspectives in contemporary Indonesian Islam. Similarly, the historic "*Nahdlatul Ulama–Muhammadiyah*" dichotomy is also less helpful.[49] Nasir Tamara says that a purpose of ICMI is to act as a place where "all Muslims can meet," while Adi Sasono asserts that many members of NU also belong to ICMI. Therefore, ICMI is a meeting place for Muslims who no longer feel comfortable in the old groupings. ICMI, Tamara observes, is representative of "an Islam that is moderate, modern, and industrialized." It is a way to connect all streams of Islam in Indonesia. Additionally, senior ICMI leaders from the bureaucracy, such as Soetjipto Wirosardjono, also contend that ICMI's purpose is to "make Islam one, to reach a consensus in Islam."[50]

By using ICMI as a "moderate, modern" association of all Muslims, Soetjipto argues, ICMI can prove that "Islam is not a threat." He feels that because of the actions of a few extremists in the past all Muslims were discredited. As a result of this misperception, Soetjipto observes, many "Muslims are still locked out of the state and denied positions commensurate with their abilities." ICMI hopes to lessen this perceived threat. The question naturally arises whether ICMI can project a moderate image and unify the *umat* without the participation of Abdurrahman Wahid and other prominent Muslim intellectuals such as Nurcholish Madjid (who has distanced himself from ICMI), Djohan Effendi, Aswab Mahasin, and Emha Ainun Nadjib.[51] Soetjipto Wirosardjono, formerly close to Wahid, argues that "although Wahid is very, very influential, he is not NU."[52] Nasir Tamara also argues that one of the purposes of ICMI is to end the monopolization of the nationalist discourse about Islam by Abdurrahman Wahid, Nurcholish Madjid, and other well-known figures.[53]

Political objectives

The third basic set of purposes of ICMI according to its activist members is explicitly political or has direct political or political-economic implications. These involve desires to establish ICMI as a mass-based organization, or a political party; to call for the de-militarization of Indonesian politics; to seek democratization; and to create a system of "proportionalization" in which Muslims are represented in government (the Cabinet, the MPR and DPR, and so on) in accordance with their percentage of the general population (88 percent). Additionally, ICMI members speak of changing the character of political discourse in Indonesia, of coopting the government, and finally, of achieving a diverse set of personal and emotional objectives. Members of ICMI note the need to assuage the "bitterness" and "trauma" they experienced at the hands of the early New Order. One ICMI member even allowed that although he did not agree with this approach, others in ICMI viewed the organization in "revenge-taking" terms, especially *vis-à-vis* "non-Muslim" groups that some perceive to have been responsible for the lock-out of political Islam and the de-politicization of Muslim parties in the early 1970s.[54] Each of these political objectives will be considered.

Prominent government officials and bureaucrats associated with ICMI steadfastly deny that ICMI has any political purpose. For example, the General Chairman of ICMI, Minister Habibie, firmly rejects the notion that ICMI is a political organization, Islamic or otherwise: "ICMI is not a political organization and it doesn't belong to any political group. It was established only to fight ignorance and poverty among Muslims."[55] To the contrary, senior ABRI officers, Wahid, democratization advocates, and other bureaucrats firmly believe that ICMI is, in part, Habibie's personal political machine that he is using to strategically position himself for the post-Soeharto era.[56] Even though ICMI is officially non-political, as frequently stated by its government sponsors, ICMI members see the organization in political terms. There is a sharp discontinuity between official public statements of ICMI goals and private commentary. The most conspicuous difference between what Munawir Sjadzali and other former and current government ministers see as the purpose of ICMI involves whether or not it is perceived as a nascent political party.

ICMI as a political party?

Some ICMI activist members consider their organization to be a nascent Islamic political party. "The purpose of ICMI is to establish the new *Masyumi*!" according to one prominent member.[57] On the record, however, a different ICMI leader, Sri Bintang Pamungkas of the PPP, asserts that he would "like to create an Islamic party" and that such a party is not forbidden based on law and the Constitution.[58] Amir Santoso of the University of Indonesia argues that the purpose of ICMI "is to gain control of political resources."[59]

The respected scholar Aswab Mahasin describes himself as a "non-active" member of ICMI and his lack of active support for ICMI is lamented by some ICMI activists. Mahasin argues that his "inactive" status is precisely because ICMI has become a "pseudo-political party" and behaves "like a political machine."[60] Clearly, it is not only Abdurrahman Wahid who has reservations about ICMI. As a "political machine" ICMI is intimately involved with the government and allows itself to be used by Soeharto for his own political needs (*vis-à-vis* ABRI, for example). Such a tacit alliance with Soeharto, argue Mahasin and Wahid, will give excuses to others to attack Islam in general.[61]

An illustration of ICMI's conception of itself as a political party or mass-based political organization is the sale of shares in *Yayasan Abdi Bangsa*, the non-profit foundation established to provide funding for the various ICMI activities and which is technically the publisher of *Republika*. *Republika* launched the share sale scheme through advertisements in the daily early in 1993. One of the stipulations for share purchase is that the buyer's religion be Islam. The purpose of the share sales, according to *Republika* editor Adi Sasono, is to create an organized mass base symbolically committed to Islam through ICMI. Adi Sasono envisages the sale of shares to three million people with share sales limited to one share per family. Adi Sasono sees this as a group of people who then have a more committed core interest in change, based on Islam.[62] These symbolically committed Muslims will then form the basis of support for a process of democratization and de-militarization that Sasono says he envisions. Although senior ICMI and *Republika* editorial board member Soetjipto Wirosardjono does not agree with the "Muslim only" requirement for share purchase (because it feeds perceptions that ICMI is an "exclusive" organization), he explains that such requirements are the result of persistent feelings of "insecurity" among Muslims who have felt politically "traumatized" in the New Order. One of the purposes of ICMI he argues, is to moderate such feelings.[63]

Soetjipto Wirosardjono strongly disagrees with a plan to create a mass base for ICMI. Soetjipto says that he and Nurcholish Madjid reject the thinking of those activists who employ Islamic symbols for political purposes (including democratization and de-militarization), especially when they do not understand the meaning of the religious symbols they manipulate.[64] Soetjipto disagrees with the use of Islam for explicitly political purposes as outlined by Adi Sasono's share purchase plan and Sri Bintang Pamungkas' desire to create an Islamic political party. Yet, he also argues that this difference of opinion illustrates the necessity of ICMI: "to integrate the extremes into the discourse" and lessen Islamic "feelings of insecurity" that lead to the manipulation of Islam for political purposes. However, even young Islamic intellectuals such as Din Syamsuddin argue that "the most solid basis of politics is religion whether we like it or not."[65]

The possibility of ICMI becoming a political party is tied to its members' definition of membership criteria. Habibie has stated that "anyone who considers themselves to be an intellectual may join,"[66] while Imaduddin sees membership criteria as simply being based on "literacy." On whether or not he conceives of ICMI as a political party, Imaduddin argues that while ICMI is "not a political organization, it does have political goals." In fact, Imaduddin argues in a manner similar to Abdurrahman Wahid, that precisely because formal political participation is impossible in the New Order because of successful regime de-politicization strategies, people act politically outside the formal structures.[67] It is clear that NU withdrew from politics in order to participate more effectively in politics. The distinction between their approaches is fundamental, however. Imaduddin sees Islam as the natural political basis of the vast majority of Indonesians while Wahid argues that any appeals to religion for explicitly political goals will "re-confessionalize" Indonesian society with disastrous results, including provoking a clampdown on Islam by the armed forces.

"De-militarization" and democratization

"De-militarization" is another political objective articulated by some members of ICMI, including Dawam Rahardjo, Director of the Institute for the Study of Religion and Philosophy, Sri Bintang Pamungkas, and Adi Sasono. In a March 1993 interview with the weekly *Detik*, Dawam Rahardjo emphatically stressed his opposition to the nomination of General Try Sutrisno (then Chief of Staff of ABRI) for Vice President.[68] In particular, Dawam emphasized that Soeharto himself would have trouble accepting General Sutrisno and did not like being "dictated" to by ABRI to accept Sutrisno. Instead, Dawam advocated Minister Habibie, the Head of ICMI, as the ideal vice-presidential candidate. Senior ABRI figures mention this interview with Dawam Rahardjo as "evidence" of the anti-ABRI character of ICMI. Additionally, Habibie is generally not well-liked by ABRI and for his nomination to be advocated so strongly by Dawam was particularly galling to ABRI. Again, it is important to stress perception and appearance. Dawam is a well-known Islamic scholar and for him to speak out as a leading ICMI member against ABRI's candidate for Vice President firmly depicts ICMI as anti-ABRI in many officers' minds.

Adi Sasono argues that the "key issues" for ICMI are democratization and an eventual reduction in the military's political role. The problem with ABRI, he notes, is that it is worried about any challenge to its position. He suggests that the only power that may be able to successfully challenge ABRI is the movement led by Islamic intellectuals. Why? Because, Sasono reasons, only the Islamic intellectuals will be able to appeal to the masses for support. The key element of such an appeal for democratization will be based on religion, argued Sasono. He explains that this is only realistic because appeals based on religion will make it easier to organize people for democratization and de-militarization.[69] Sasono argues that ABRI knows a more democratic society would mean a reduction in the military's political role, and as a result, the armed forces seek to depict ICMI as "extreme" and desirous of an Islamic state. Sasono says that he in no way seeks the establishment of an Islamic state but that religion is simply the most effective means of mass organization for political change. He adds that Abdurrahman Wahid's depiction of ICMI as a "sectarian, exclusionary" organization whose goal is an Islamic state simply plays into ABRI hands and damages the chances of eventual democratization. Adi Sasono strongly rejects the suggestion that ICMI's political behavior encourages sectarianism and thereby heightens religious intolerance. He says that some of his relatives are non-Muslim and therefore he could never conceive of politics which would negatively impact his family in any way. But it is a fact, he reiterates, that aside from ABRI the only force that could be harnessed for significant social change such as democratization is Islam, as it is the religion of the Indonesian majority.[70]

Adi Sasono, Bintang Pamungkas, Din Syamsuddin, Dawam Rahardjo, and Soetjipto Wirosardjono all articulate support for a more democratic political system. With the exception of Adi Sasono, democratization is not, however, advocated as a central purpose of ICMI. Imaduddin argues, for example, that although he "believes in democracy, if the masses are still ignorant, backward and poor, I don't want democracy." Imaduddin agrees with Adi Sasono's contention that religion must be used to organize the people, but not for the purpose of democratization. Moreover, Imaduddin argues that "because Islam is for democracy, not against democracy," the question of democratic goals for ICMI is irrelevant.[71]

It appears that democratization is more an offshoot than a general objective for ICMI members. It may even be considered by some in ICMI as a tactical political strategy. One ICMI insider suggested that Muslims in ICMI believe that a more open, democratic political system would mean that Muslim interests would be better represented. A number of ICMI figures acknowledge that in a genuine democratic system they believe Muslims would simply "win." This, suggests Amir Santoso, is why some non-Muslims oppose democratization as they know Islamic parties would dominate.[72] Secular nationalists, Wahid, and non-Muslims do concede that because of their anxiety over Islam "winning at the ballot box" they seek Islamic willingness for specific minority-rights guarantees in any future political setting. ICMI members including Imaduddin and Adi Sasono argue that Islam is a "democratic" faith, and because of this guarantees for minorities are unnecessary. Adi Sasono adds that because Islam accepts Pancasila and because minority rights are "inherent in Pancasila" there is no need for special protection of minorities.[73]

"Proportionalizaton" and "*Kristenisasi*"

Calls for the redistribution of political "goods" (education, seats in Cabinet and in the MPR/DPR, and access to capital, for example) also form one of the broad categories of what some ICMI members want. Many in ICMI seek "proportionalization," or the distribution of appointments to the senior bureaucracy or in the DPR/MPR in proportion to the religious make-up of the population at large. That is, nearly 90 percent of seats in Parliament and Cabinet positions should be held by Muslims. Proportional representation of personnel is probably the clearest single objective of ICMI. There is also a strong strain of xenophobia, particularly against ethnic Chinese, in calls for "proportional" access to bank credit and business opportunities. There is a perception among some Muslim activists that the heavy domination of the Indonesian economy by Chinese-Indonesians automatically means that "indigenous" Muslim (non-Chinese) Indonesians have less access to the fruits of development.[74] Amien Rais argues that "racial minorities" have disproportionately benefited from development. Unfortunately, legitimate economic concerns often become linked to anti-Chinese perceptions in general. Aswab Mahasin laments that the periodic resurgence of anti-Chinese prejudices in the Muslim community constitutes the "chronic illness of Indonesian politics."[75] Even though PPP member Sri Bintang Pamungkas argues that Muslims must expand their share of national wealth, he rejects apportioning "blame" to the non-Muslims.[76]

For Amien Rais, a prominent member of ICMI and the Chairman of *Muhammadiyah*, a key problem in Indonesian society is "*Kristenisasi*" (or "Christianization") which must be reversed with proportionalization. Amien Rais argues that Christian propagation has accelerated in Indonesia since the 1970s and that Muslims are "victimized" by this process. He points to the large number of non-Muslim cabinet officials and ABRI officers during the New Order.[77] Several other ICMI-affiliated intellectuals, including young and generally thoughtful scholars also view the role of non-Muslims in government as partially responsible for the political handicaps placed by the New Order on Islamic political activity.[78]

Perhaps indicative of new-found confidence that ICMI provides protection for a more assertive Islamic perspective, Imaduddin, in an April 1993 interview, strongly attacked Benny Moerdani. At one time Moerdani was one of the most powerful members of the Soeharto government. He is a retired General and former Minister of Defense and Security (and a Catholic). Moerdani was dropped from Soeharto's Cabinet announced in March 1993. Imaduddin bitterly criticized Moerdani as responsible for both his own imprisonment in the 1970s and the trauma of Islam in Indonesia in general.[79] Amien Rais specifically blamed Ali Moertopo, Moerdani's mentor, for "bringing in too many Catholics." However, few other ICMI intellectuals (with the notable exception of Sri Bintang Pamungkas) will apportion responsibility for "Christianization" to Soeharto himself. Rather, Rais says, "although Soeharto rules like a king, he is not a king and is not responsible for everything."[80] Because ICMI is wholly dependent upon Soeharto and Habibie for protection, it perhaps is not at all surprising that today Rais or Imaduddin would be reluctant to say that Soeharto has always been responsible for appointments to his Cabinet. Christians in government have always served at the pleasure of Soeharto. Some members of ICMI say they can now cooperate with Soeharto in ICMI because they have "forgiven" him for favoritism of Christians in earlier years.[81]

There is also a sense among some ICMI supporters that the organization allows them to "seek revenge" on those they perceive as responsible for Islamic "trauma" in earlier years. CSIS, the think-tank established by Ali Moertopo who was the architect of the de-politicization strategies, is particularly singled out. Frequently, ICMI figures will say that ICMI's presence (and implicit political activism) is justified because "Catholics had CSIS."[82] Similarly, *Republika* is mentioned as the Islamic response to *Kompas* which is owned by Catholic Indonesians. In response to these comparisons, ABRI's Chief of General Staff, Lieutenant General H.B. Mantiri (a Christian) asked, "Why must they [ICMI members] always differentiate between Indonesians on the basis of religion?"[83]

Certainly, not all ICMI members call for strict proportionalization along the lines advocated by Amien Rais. For example, former bureaucrat Soetjipto Wirosardjono sees that Muslims will require "special attention" from the government in order to "catch up," especially in the field of education. Conversely, Abdurrahman Wahid argues that no citizen should be given preferential treatment. Wahid says that if the power structure truly represented the people and was humane and democratic "all" Indonesians would be better off.[84] Soetjipto argues that if all citizens are treated equally, like Wahid suggests, then it would take a very long time for Muslim education to improve. Meanwhile, non-Muslims will continue to better their educational standing and the educational gaps between Muslim and non-Muslim will remain. Soetjipto's worries are well illustrated by the construction of a luxury private school that reportedly will cater primarily to Christian children of Chinese-Indonesian business people. The school, in an elite suburb of Jakarta, has become a contentious issue and a vivid exhibition of the social gap. Interestingly, however, Soeharto's wife officially opened the school.[85] Soetjipto Wirosardjono concludes that this is evidence that Muslims do require "special attention," and that the "open competition" implied in Wahid's arguments cannot be allowed.[86]

The Cabinet announced by Soeharto in March 1993 is broadly representative of the religious affiliations of the population as whole and therefore it appears to respond to some Muslim concerns about the previous overrepresentation of non-Muslims. Out of over forty Cabinet posts, three are held by Christians, and one by a Hindu. Notably, however, Soeharto did not elevate any of the ICMI activists to the Cabinet or appoint them as members of the MPR in 1992. While the Cabinet does contain numerous Habibie allies who are ICMI members (such as Minister of Education, Wardiman, and Minister of Transportation, Haryanto Dhanutirto), it does not contain any of the ICMI activists – those persons who are much more interested in an Islamizing agenda.

Economic objectives

There is a sense among some ICMI members that the organization is dedicated to seeking a shift in the current strategies of *pembangunan*, [economic development] in both an ethnic and nationalist sense. Sri Bintang Pamungkas and Amien Rais in particular argue that the vast majority of poor Muslims have not benefited from the government's development strategies. Amien Rais promotes economic nationalism in which he allows that a form of Malaysia's New Economic Policy would be appropriate for Indonesia.[87] Rais argues that "racial minorities" have most benefited from *pembangunan* and that access to credit must be given to the "*pribumi*" [non-Chinese Indonesians]. Another ICMI member argued that Muslims should have proportional access to credit, bank loans, and other financial services.[88] Bintang Pamungkas implies that Muslim activists seek fundamental change in economic development strategies which, he says, do not address questions of mass poverty.[89] Other ICMI activists also state that the purpose of ICMI is to help the poor, "backward" Muslim majority develop economically.[90]

The activists' intentions for ICMI to promote a more equitable form of economic development that will benefit poor Muslim masses is sharply at odds with Habibie's own economic thinking. Even though Habibie states that ICMI battles Muslim poverty, he envisions a capital-intensive, technological leap forward for Indonesia and not the labor-intensive industrial development that would most help the poor masses. He is a tireless promoter of high-technology solutions for Indonesia and has been the primary supporter of Indonesia's domestic aircraft industry and nuclear power development. During his long tenure as powerful Minister of Technology, he has also emphasized human resource development and urged an overhaul of Indonesia's educational system to more adequately prepare students for a high-tech, industrialized era. However, Adam Schwarz points out the contradictions between Habibie's economic vision and the views of others in ICMI:

> Habibienomics is an elitist vision. Training a corps of engineers and skilled technicians will bring immediate benefits to a layer of well-educated Indonesians, but it will have little direct bearing on low income Indonesians, a much larger community. Quite possibly, the latter group will be disadvantaged by Habibie's plans because there will be less money available to spend on programs targeted at the poor. In fact, there is compelling evidence to suggest that Habibie's approach will exacerbate the wealth gap which is so heatedly criticized by Habibie's ICMI supporters.[91]

Clearly then, vastly different approaches to economic development are held by some prominent ICMI activists on one hand, and Habibie on the other. So what then is going on – how can ICMI as an organization be for the betterment of the uneducated poor Muslim masses while ICMI's patron and protector – Habibie – is committed to an "elitist" vision of economic development which may, according to Schwarz, actually harm the poor? Sri Bintang Pamungkas, a senior ICMI and PPP member, explained that this contradiction illustrates the weakness of ICMI. Bintang criticized ICMI intellectuals who privately disagree with Habibie's economic approach, but publicly ignore this difference in order to use Habibie to gain political power.[92] That is, Habibie's powerful political position and closeness to Soeharto provide the opportunity for the ICMI activists to have their voices heard on other issues.

ICMI POLITICAL STRATEGIES

The political strategy used by members of ICMI, especially the activist wing discussed extensively in the preceding section, is heavily reliant on the goodwill and protection of President Soeharto and the Minister of Technology and ICMI Chairman, B.J. Habibie. There is one frequent criticism of ICMI posed by both Abdurrahman Wahid and from inside ICMI, Sri Bintang Pamungkas, which has put ICMI on the defensive. Wahid and Bintang argue that ICMI is allowing itself and the Muslim activists and scholars associated with it to be used by Soeharto to broaden the legitimacy of his rule in the wake of increasing divergence of interests between ABRI and the President.[93] Wahid argues that such a strategy by part of the Islamic movement will only serve to target ICMI for eventual retribution by some elite contenders for power and influence. On the point of allowing themselves to be coopted and used by Soeharto, there is wide and frank acknowledgement among ICMI activists that this is indeed the case.

The central argument of ICMI activists, particularly Imaduddin, Amien Rais, and Adi Sasono is that, in Imaduddin's words, "in the name of ICMI you can say anything. They have to respect me now – behind me is Habibie and behind him is Soeharto."[94] Being used to support Soeharto is simply the price they are willing to pay for what some in ICMI see as the dramatic change in politics in recent years. For example, Bintang Pamungkas argues that he has never been able to speak out so frankly on controversial issues of national politics in his life. According to Bintang, the creation of ICMI and the *rapprochement* between Islam and Soeharto have legitimized his commentary. For example, he said that several years ago he would have been unable to give the *Detik* interview (March 1993) in which he said then Chief of Staff of ABRI, General Try Sutrisno, was inappropriate and unacceptable as Vice President.[95]

Bintang Pamungkas acknowledges that when Abdurrahman Wahid speaks of ICMI as a tool of the government, he is correct. However, Bintang argues, the "real ICMI" (the activist wing, not Habibie and his bureaucratic allies such as Wardiman) see this as an "opportunity" and is fully "conscious that it is being used" by Soeharto. Bintang argues that he realizes the purpose of Soeharto's sponsorship of ICMI was to garner support for his re-election in the MPR in March 1993. Yet Bintang says he was not surprised that there were no "real ICMI" (activists) in the new Cabinet. This is because the function of ICMI for Soeharto – at least until the next election in 1997 – is over. However, for ICMI activists such as Bintang and Nasir Tamara, their main victory is the institutionalization of ICMI and its organs, especially *Republika*. In fact, Bintang and Adi Sasono argue that it is good for ICMI that their activists were not elevated to the Cabinet. Why? Because they now are in an ideal position. ICMI is able to struggle for its goals – broadly defined as the establishment of an Islamic society (not an Islamic state) from a position neither in nor out of government. That is, if ICMI activists were to be brought fully into government they would be completely coopted. Yet by remaining under government, especially under Habibie's protection in ICMI, they are free to organize without becoming totally bureaucratized.[96] However, as noted above, in 1994 Bintang distanced himself from this strategy and now criticizes ICMI for being too close to the government.

Amir Santoso's analysis supports the above explanation by ICMI activists. Santoso argues that ICMI is very realistic and that its members know full well that Soeharto is using them, but they figure they should take such an opportunity and "get what they can for Islam" as long as Soeharto needs them.[97] Yet Aswab Mahasin argues that it is precisely this ICMI strategy that influenced his desire to become a "non-active" member. He rejects the "tacit alliance that Muslims in ICMI forged with the government." Contrary to the arguments of Imaduddin, Nasir Tamara, Amien Rais, and Adi Sasono, Mahasin contends that being coopted by the government is not an effective way to promote change because it too closely aligns Islam in general with a specific political side.[98]

Imaduddin contends that the beauty of ICMI is that it allows him and others to legitimately spread their message of Islamic society and to call for improvement in the life of the Muslim masses. Imaduddin says that in return for his abandonment of opposition to Soeharto and by allowing ICMI to seemingly support the government, he and other ICMI activists have the opportunity to spread the "ICMI message" across the country. The ICMI message involves many of the purposes and objectives discussed in the preceding section including: "proportionalization" in politics and economics, the possible creation of a committed Muslim mass base that could form the basis of a new Muslim political party, calls for de-militarization (and for some, democratization), and efforts to create a society in which law and government policy are imbued with Islamic values.

Imaduddin observes that because of official sponsorship of ICMI from Habibie and Soeharto, ICMI can build its mass base: "that's why Habibie continues to visit the *pesantran* [usually rural, traditionalist Islamic boarding schools]. His visits open the door for me, Amien Rais and others to spread the ICMI message to the masses." Imaduddin says that he could never do this before ICMI.[99] Whereas *Nahdlatul Ulama's* response to the New Order's "de-politicization" of society was to withdraw from participation in its repressive political system, other Muslims particularly those now in ICMI, argue that they achieve their goals within the

New Order structure even if this grants additional legitimacy to Soeharto.

"Forgiveness" for Soeharto

The ICMI strategy also involves a willingness to praise Soeharto and ignore his role in past government proscription of Islamic politics.[100] Adi Sasono applauds Soeharto's commitment to the *umat*: "Soeharto has done more for Islam than *Masyumi* ever did or even wanted to do." In matters of supporting Islamic politics, "Soeharto is more Muslim than Abdurrahman Wahid."[101]

In order to explain why they have abandoned criticism of Soeharto since joining ICMI, activists usually take one of two positions. Some simply assert, like Adi Sasono above, that Soeharto has changed, become a good Muslim, has done many things for the Muslim community, and is therefore deserving of support. More common, however, is an argument that says while in previous years Soeharto appeared to endorse actions that were damaging to the Islamic community and to Muslim politics, it is not actually Soeharto who is at fault. Rather, "blame" for the bad things that happened to Muslims (i.e., emasculation of political parties, the forced acceptance of *asas tunggal*, and the Tanjung Priok riots) is instead apportioned solely to "non-Muslim" members of the regime. As noted above, both young intellectuals associated with ICMI and senior ICMI leaders say they have "forgiven" Soeharto now that they understand it was the "Christians and Catholics" who were to blame. Indeed, they assert, Soeharto is to be praised for finally realizing the damage these non-Muslim advisors caused and then dismissing them. Those most frequently singled out for blame include the late Ali Moertopo (himself a Muslim, a fact dismissed by activists), Benny Moerdani, and senior economic advisors such as former Minister of Finance, Sumarlin, and former Coordinating Economics Minister, Radius Prawiro. However, Bintang Pamungkas says Muslims only hurt themselves by naively saying they can "forgive" Soeharto, because this approach too closely associates Islam with Soeharto's political liabilities. Says Bintang, "ICMI kills itself by being so close to Habibie and Soeharto."[102]

Adi Sasono explains that he does not seek a revival of "Islamic politics" in the old, confrontational, Islam versus non-Islam sense. Rather, Sasono, like many ICMI figures, supports Nurcholish

Madjid's conception of "cultural realism." That is, because the majority of Indonesians profess Islam as their faith, and because the proportion of Muslims in the MPR is higher than before, Islamic politics *is* Indonesian politics.[103] This is clearly a desire to articulate a vision of Indonesian society in which Islamic politics are not distinct from other kinds of politics.

The strategy to make use of Soeharto's perceived need for Islam was publicly explained in an interview Amien Rais gave in *Detik* in March 1993.[104] In this interview, Rais acknowledged that ICMI supports the status quo (including the re-election of President Soeharto). He explained that he and other members of the Islamic movement in Yogyakarta had previously outlined a number of different scenarios concerning the "succession issue."[105] In 1993 Rais revealed that they opted for a strategy he referred to as "*figur tetap, policy berubah*" [The person (or figure) remains, but policy changes]. In other words, he said ICMI opted to see President Soeharto remain as the nation's leader in a context in which government policy may change (same person, different policy). Rais argues that ICMI chose this as the most "realistic" option and labeled its support for a "same person, different policy" option as a "matter of strategic tactics." Rais argues that this approach is entirely "cultural" and not at all a "political" approach. He acknowledges that although there are some in ICMI who see the organization as a "stepping stone" to political power, this is not his objective. None the less, it is clear that the strategy calling for support of Soeharto and maintenance of the status quo (with the hope for changes in economic policy that Rais indicates should involve removing the dominance of a "racial minority's" grip on the national economy) is a deeply political approach with ideological implications.[106] Din Syamsuddin concurs with Rais by noting that "the grand strategy of Muslims has changed from struggle from without to struggle from within."[107] An ICMI insider acknowledges, however, that in 1994 the "same person, different policy" strategy had been revised by some ICMI activists to now call for a "different person, different policy." He said this change was due to recognition that Soeharto was using ICMI and preventing ICMI activists from obtaining high-level bureaucratic positions. It was also suggested that the "different person" in mind instead of Soeharto is the head of ICMI, B.J. Habibie.[108] Amien Rais has already suggested that the time has come to begin discussing the criteria for the next President in 1998.[109]

In agreement with the initial strategy outlined by Amien Rais, ICMI founder Imaduddin said that the ICMI interest is "to maintain the current power structure for at least the next five years so that ICMI can grow and become independent and strong. Then later we will not be dependent upon Habibie and Soeharto." There is also a distinct awareness that such a strategy is inherently weak. Imaduddin says that if something were to happen to Soeharto and Habibie before 1998 ICMI would be endangered.[110] Interestingly, virtually all ABRI officers interviewed concurred with this evaluation (see following chapter). A member of the military's parliamentary faction, Major General (retired) Sembiring Meliala, has publicly stated that Habibie's current position rests solely on support from Soeharto.[111]

In a political environment in which many groups are jockeying for position in the run-up to a long-anticipated "post-Soeharto era," ICMI has clearly opted for throwing the weight of "Islam" behind President Soeharto and Habibie. The changes hoped for with this approach, regardless of whether ICMI members choose to label it "political" or "cultural," may have profound political and ideological implications. Wahid and ABRI officers directly assert that ICMI's use of Islam for political objectives threatens the non-Islamic nationalist compromise enshrined in the Pancasila. Within the bureaucracy ICMI's politicking has also generated opposition. The Minister for Transmigration, Siswono Yudohusodo, criticized ICMI in 1994 for engaging in "sectarian" behavior and polarizing society. There was even speculation that Soeharto encouraged Siswono's attack on ICMI to weaken Habibie and balance contending forces within the bureaucracy.[112] Muslim thinkers such as Djohan Effendi and Aswab Mahasin, argue that the politicization of Islam through ICMI will unnecessarily revive anti-Muslim fears in non-Muslim communities. Religious minorities look with great alarm at Rais' apparent support of a Malaysian-style NEP for Indonesia in order to redistribute the economic goods in society away from "racial minorities" (code for the Chinese) towards non-Chinese Muslim Indonesians.[113]

The political strategy of ICMI is basically an issue for the activist wing of the organization. As noted in the preceding section, the bureaucrats who are also members of ICMI already have their loyalties tied to the regime, especially to Habibie and President Soeharto. The ICMI activist group perceives that members of

ICMI who were appointed to the Cabinet, such as Wardiman, the new Minister of Education and Culture, are not "real ICMI." Senior government officials including former Minister of Religion, Munawir Sjadzali, and former Interior Minister, Rudini, clearly see that there should be no explicit, independent ICMI political agenda.[114] Yet for the ICMI activists, the outlines of the strategy are fairly clear: overt reliance on Soeharto and Habibie to legitimize their participation in national discourse; hopes of encouraging Islamization ("proportionalization") of government from within and through ICMI influence; using ICMI to get their message to the masses; and using ICMI to effect a possible return to mass-based Islamic politics. To do all this some ICMI members are fully prepared to maintain the status quo for the time being so that ICMI can become entrenched and grow into an independent political organization.

ICMI and Pancasila

ICMI strategy also involves tacit agreement on several things not to say and do. First and foremost, Pancasila is never mentioned in a negative context. Opposition to Pancasila is seen by ICMI figures as a losing strategy. Similarly, Muslim politicians are extremely conscious to avoid saying they want an Islamic state. However, Sri Bintang Pamungkas observes that some Muslim apprehension regarding Pancasila has not completely gone away; it has simply gone underground.[115] Although Imaduddin sees Pancasila as essentially an Islamic conception, and thereby acceptable, he rejects it as the unifying ideology of Indonesia which, he contends, can only be Islam.[116]

As indicated in the preceding section on ICMI strategy, there does appear to have been a decision to abandon opposition to Pancasila. Amien Rais states that "the scariest thing is to be accused of being an enemy of Pancasila."[117] Others, including Nurcholish Madjid, argue that especially after the President enunciated Pancasila as an "open ideology" it has been easier for Muslims to see that Pancasila is not juxtaposed against their faith. Amir Santoso points out that the President's evaluation of Pancasila as an open ideology has given legitimacy to the interpretation of Pancasila in a non-threatening way for Islam. Using Soeharto's open ideology terminology, Islam is able to give Pancasila its own meaning.[118] One political scientist observes that some Muslims may have used Pancasila as a "loophole" to legitimize the role of Islam in the state and to advance Islamic interests in general. Pancasila, he argues, has become a "vehicle that can be used by groups other than Soeharto." Moreover, "Pancasila has become the safest way" for the Islamic movement to press for its interests.[119]

Although Islamic intellectuals are generally indifferent towards Pancasila, some ICMI members have used Pancasila to criticize the New Order political structure and government development policies. Sri Bintang Pamungkas argues that the undemocratic functioning of the MPR (of which he is an elected member representing the PPP) is not sanctioned by either the Pancasila or the Constitution of 1945. Bintang criticizes the lack of voting in the MPR (which is officially said to be incompatible with *musyawarah* and *mufakat*) as something which is not warranted by Pancasila. Pancasila, he argues, does not justify the unrepresentative form of governance the regime calls "Pancasila democracy." Bintang uses the same language employed by the New Order in 1966 when Sukarno was criticized for allowing the contravention of Pancasila and the Constitution. Bintang urges Indonesia to "return to the rails of Pancasila and the Constitution of 1945." According to Bintang, the nation has already left the intended meaning and path of Pancasila and is in need of correction.[120] Bintang also argues that the true implementation of Pancasila would require three developments: the democratic functioning of the MPR, the retreat of ABRI from politics (de-militarization), and a presidential term limit. Unlike Bintang, few ICMI members explicitly appropriate Pancasila to negatively appraise the regime in a forum in which they identify themselves as speaking from an ICMI perspective. Similarly, Bintang argues that ABRI must reduce its role in politics to be in accordance with the Pancasila and the Constitution.[121]

Another prominent intellectual associated with ICMI who uses Pancasila to negatively appraise development strategies is Professor Mubyarto, economist at Gajah Mada University and an appointed member of the MPR. Mubyarto criticizes national development (*pembangunan*) as "not Pancasila-ist" because of gross inequalities in regional levels of development. He argues that the concentration of industrialization and development in Java sacrifices the rest of the nation, especially the poorest areas in Eastern Indonesia. This form of development, Mubyarto argues, violates both Pancasila's principle of social justice (*Keadilan Sosial*) and national unity by heightening differences between the regions. The result of uneven regional development, he concludes, will be a degradation in levels of national unity which would damage Pancasila as a unifying national ideology. Similarly, growing inequality between rich and poor, the so-called "social gap," would be destabilizing and thus threaten the harmony and tolerance implicit in Pancasila.[122] In a similar vein, Bintang Pamungkas has argued that efforts to sustain equitable national development are hampered because of deviations from Pancasila and the Constitution.[123]

For the moderate members of ICMI, especially the former bureaucrat Soetjipto Wirosardjono, Pancasila is positively seen as having vague adhesive value in Indonesia's pluralist society. Soetjipto argues that Pancasila will always be the "anchor" of legitimacy for any government.[124] Although Pancasila is generally not problematized by most Muslims (either out of sincere conviction of its appropriateness for Indonesia or simply out of political expediency), there is diversity within ICMI regarding the meaning of Pancasila. While Soetjipto contends that Pancasila has legitimizing and unifying value in Indonesia, Imaduddin rejects Pancasila as a unifying nationalist ideology. Imaduddin argues that the only possible unifying element in Indonesia is Islam, not Pancasila or any other form of a nationalist ideology.[125] Amien Rais also agrees that "Islam is the glue that helps bond the nation together."[126] In striking contrast, Buchori Masruri, head of NU's Central Java branch, argues that Pancasila, not Islam, is the essential political formula necessary for Indonesian national unity.[127]

Democracy and ICMI

It is useful to focus attention on ICMI strategies as they relate to democratization and the armed forces. It seems clear that democratization is not the primary goal of many in ICMI. The main objective, in varying degrees, is to encourage the development of an Islamic society. Mohtar Mas'oed, political scientist at Gajah Mada University, argues that the core objective of the ICMI activists is to "empower the state in order to Islamize society and enact Islamic-value based laws and regulations." Mas'oed further argues that Abdurrahman Wahid and NU, on the other hand, "seek to empower the people" and in so doing both Muslims and non-Muslim Indonesians will be empowered.[128]

A good example of ICMI thinking on democracy relates to an oft-mooted plan to revise the electoral system. Several leading ICMI figures frequently mention their desire for a single representative electoral district system to replace the current proportional system of representation. In such a system a simple majority of voters would determine the winner in each district. A number of ICMI intellectuals suggest that this type of voting in an electoral democracy would ensure that "Islamic" candidates would win because Islam is the nominal faith of most Indonesians.[129] This rationale sharply contradicts the history of Islamic politics in Indonesia in which Muslim voting patterns have been far from monolithic in support of Islamic parties.

The government's closure of three of Indonesia's leading news weeklies in June 1994 illustrates the problematic position ICMI activists are in regarding a principal tenet of democracy: freedom of the press.[130] *Tempo*, Indonesia's pre-eminent weekly magazine, *Editor*, and a popular tabloid newspaper, *Detik*, had their publishing licenses revoked. *Tempo* was singled out by the government for "destabilizing" society. All three publications had reported widely on the central role of Minister Habibie in the government's purchase of thirty-nine ex-East German naval warships. The purchase was initially promoted by Habibie as good deal for Indonesia to be able to upgrade its Navy with modern vessels at rock-bottom prices. However, it was reported that the cost ballooned into a nearly $1 billion deal after all additional expenses were calculated (including refitting, munitions, and port improvements to handle the new vessels). Habibie was sharply criticized for the alleged cost overruns. Moreover, the publications reported on widespread disagreement within the government over the wisdom of the ships purchase. It was reported that the armed forces opposed the acquisition while the Minister of Finance, Mari'e Muhammad, questioned the escalating costs and refused to allocate Habibie's requested $1 billion.[131]

It was widely assumed in Indonesia that the publications were banned because they questioned Habibie and thereby indirectly questioned Soeharto's role in the decision. It was also generally assumed by most members of the press in Jakarta, and by democratization advocates, that Habibie was directly involved in the decision to ban the publications. However, the reaction among many ICMI activists, especially those close to Habibie, such as Nasir Tamara, insisted that Habibie was not responsible.[132] Others in ICMI argued that the publications, particularly *Tempo*, were themselves to blame. Leading ICMI figures argued that *Tempo* conspired with non-Muslims and the military to destroy Habibie's reputation over the ship purchase.[133] The issue was portrayed not in terms of press and other democratic freedoms, but one of Muslims versus non-Muslims. That the government's banning of the publications was the strongest attack on democracy in years was not a serious concern for many in ICMI. The ICMI daily *Republika* did not strongly condemn the bannings and stand up for the principle of press freedoms. However, *Kompas* did not strongly editorialize against the banning either. The *Kompas* position is perhaps due to the paper's reluctance to be perceived as in any way anti-Muslim (and this includes anti-Habibie/ICMI as well) because *Kompas* – as part of the Gramedia publishing group – had been singled out for blame by Muslims in the "*Monitor* Affair" in 1990.

The armed forces and ICMI

In their desire to "empower the state" and realize Islamization from above, ICMI activists seek a reduction in the political influence of ABRI. The *de facto* strategy that ICMI appears to stand for can be summarized in the following way: Islamization and/or democratization through de-militarization under the banner of Islam and the protection of Habibie. This strategy illustrates why there is much anxiety and tension between ABRI and ICMI. That is, such a combination of strategy and objectives raises all the ideological issues that most easily inflame the armed forces and contradict ABRI political thinking and ideology. Moreover, the personal and political relationship between Habibie and many in ABRI is poor and this tends to exacerbate tension between ICMI and the military. Conflict of personal and institutional interests between Habibie and ABRI partially arose after management responsibilities of the Indonesian arms industries were transferred to the Ministry of Technology under Habibie (who has served in this portfolio for nearly two decades). Thus, there is a conflict grounded in the political economy of these two powerful government agencies. However, President Soeharto's 1994 reshuffle of the ABRI leadership, especially in the crucial social and political affairs command, has eliminated several officers critical of Habibie and elevated others said to be sympathetic to Habibie and ICMI. Whether these personnel changes will have an eventual impact on ABRI perceptions of ICMI is uncertain, particularly because most other ABRI officers are still overwhelmingly suspicious of Habibie and ICMI. The ABRI Chief of Staff, General Feisal Tanjung, and the former Chief of Social and Political Affairs, Major General Hartono (who was promoted to Army Chief of Staff in February 1995), are often mentioned by ICMI members as sympathetic to ICMI. The ICMI daily *Republika* even named General Feisal Tanjung as its 1993 "Man of the Year." However, both officers have publicly warned against politicking on the basis on religious affiliation and Hartono has also strongly criticized the outspokenness of particular intellectuals.[134]

Even though many senior ABRI officers harbor negative perceptions of ICMI,[135] several ICMI figures insist that their organization enjoys either a good or neutral relationship with the military. When Imaduddin was asked in a *Detik* interview (April 1993) about the "impression that the relationship between ICMI and ABRI was less than harmonious," Imaduddin retorted "who says that? That's *fitnah* [slander]." Imaduddin would only allow that those in ABRI who are associated with a Christian intellectuals' organization (PIKI) would not like ICMI.[136] Similarly, the University of Indonesia's Professor of Law, Ismail Sunny, bluntly stated "it's not true that there is conflict between ABRI and ICMI."[137]

A number of ICMI figures in the early 1990s also insisted that former Chief of Staff of ABRI and now Vice President, Try Sutrisno, is "for ICMI."[138] Some ICMI members have said this impression is based on Sutrisno's well-known Islamic religiosity and an interview he gave to *Republika* in January 1993. In that interview Sutrisno stated that Islam is not a threat to the nation.[139] Nasir Tamara argues that this interview is symbolically important for ICMI and the *umat* because it demonstrates the changing relationship between Islam and the armed forces. While this may be indicative of a more devout military leadership, it does not automatically translate into political support for ICMI. However, Soetjipto Wirosardjono argues that before ICMI was even established he helped to garner approval from senior military and intelligence figures, including Try Sutrisno.[140] None the less, ABRI officers usually identify Sutrisno as part of a majority of officers who are wary of ICMI and concerned about the use of religion for political purposes.[141]

ICMI and Abdurrahman Wahid

ICMI's voice on democratization is partially a response to Abdurrahman Wahid. Wahid portrays himself as a genuine democrat, navigating the most "narrow path" between military rule and Islamic fundamentalism (see Chapters 2 and 5). There is no doubt that Wahid attempts to heighten his own democratic and nationalist, especially Pancasila, credentials by contrasting what he says is the inclusive, Pancasila-ist, democratic nature of NU with the allegedly exclusive, anti-Pancasila, and cynically manipulative (of Islam) nature of ICMI. In response, there are a number of common ICMI arguments.

First, and most commonly heard, is that Wahid represents himself, and not *Nahdlatul Ulama*. In fact, many ICMI figures point out that NU members have joined ICMI. Indeed, both Yusuf Hasyim, Wahid's uncle and frequent critic within NU, and Ali Yafie, the former *Rois Am* [titular spiritual head of NU], joined ICMI. However, two senior NU followers argue that NU is philosophically inclined to reject national political behavior based solely on religion. Achmad Buchori Masruri, the Chairman of NU for Central Java and a key player in the Rapat Akbar, also says he is a member of ICMI. However, Buchori firmly rejects the extreme positions of ICMI activists and argues passionately that Islam is quite content within the Pancasila state and he attacks those Muslims who say they accept Pancasila "only for tactical reasons."[142] Similarly, staunch NU follower and former Secretary General of PPP, Matori Abdul Djalil, argues that for NU in general, while religion provides ethical values, "our political behavior must always be based on nationality, not religion."[143]

Many ICMI activists agree with Wahid that they are being used by Soeharto. The difference, however, is that ICMI leaders say that being used by Soeharto provides the opportunity to advance the cause of Islam and realize an Islamic society. Wahid responds that such a strategy "re-confessionalizes" Indonesian politics and "wrecks" all efforts to recast Islam in a moderate, sincerely Pancasilaist, tolerant, and, especially, democratic form. Moreover, Wahid argues that when ICMI members speak of democratization, they simply have in mind a system where "Islam wins" and minority rights are not protected. According to Wahid, this would be a betrayal of the essence of Pancasila.[144]

Muslim figures prominently associated with ICMI argue that Wahid is simply angry at being unable to "monopolize the Islamic discourse."[145] Soetjipto Wirosardjono, formerly very close to Wahid, argues that the main problem with Wahid's views on ICMI is that they are colored by his personal and family background. Wahid, he notes, must carry on the burden and expectations of his family, which means he should be the nation's pre-eminent Islamic leader. Soetjipto adds that although Wahid worries that ICMI heightens social tensions by giving voice to Muslims' "insecurities" ("Christianization," for example), what Wahid does not realize is that ICMI serves as a place where Muslim perceptions of insecurity can be ameliorated and moderated.[146] However, by 1994 Wahid's criticisms of ICMI (as sectarian and damaging to Indonesia's tolerance of religious diversity) had been taken up by other national figures. The most prominent voice outside ABRI and NU was the attack on ICMI by Minister of Transmigration, Siswono Yudohusodo. The weekly *Forum Keadilan* [Justice Forum] noted that the Minister had voiced the same critique of ICMI that Abdurrahman Wahid alone had been expressing for some time.[147]

ICMI AND ITS IMPLICATIONS FOR POLITICAL DISCOURSE

ICMI's so far brief appearance on the political scene has had profound implications for Indonesian political and ideological discourse. Perhaps the most revealing comment on the implications of ICMI for political discourse came from Imaduddin, the self-described guiding force and intellectual founder of ICMI: "It's the only way to be free in Indonesia today."[148] For Muslims who have been searching for a way to play a legitimate political role compatible with the New Order's strict proscription of "confessional" politics, ICMI represents the legitimacy they have been seeking. In the opinion of ICMI activists, the right to contribute to political discourse and speak out on political issues far outweighs the "price" of being coopted and used by President Soeharto to bolster his own legitimacy. Abdurrahman Wahid frequently attacks ICMI members as "naive politicians" because they allow themselves to be used by Soeharto. Yet ICMI activists are fully conscious that they have been used to bolster the political position of President Soeharto. For this they offer no apologies. They do, however, calculate that they can equally take advantage of Soeharto's perceived need for them to advance their own political interests, particularly to promote their conceptions of an Islamic society.

Several major achievements of ICMI can already be identified. First, as suggested above, ICMI has legitimized the participation of Muslim activists in national discourse more so than any other development in the New Order. Leading ICMI figures speak of their new ability to break the monopolization of political discourse, especially by representatives of the historic *aliran* in Indonesian Islam. Soetjipto Wirosardjono specifically argues that ICMI has legitimized Islam's participation in national discourse. This achievement must strongly be qualified. As shown in preceding chapters, Islam never left the discourse. Nurcholish Madjid, for example, by calling for Islamic rethinking and the complete abandonment of desire for an Islamic state in the early 1970s, and Abdurrahman Wahid's dramatic infusion of pluralism and democratic issues into discourse about Islam, politics, and the state, indicate that political Islam was never wholly de-legitimized.

ICMI has successfully institutionalized itself in a very prominent fashion. ICMI membership has grown rapidly with branches in all provinces and most districts of Indonesia. ICMI branches have also been established overseas to cater to Indonesian (especially student) communities in Europe, the United States, and the Middle East. *Republika* is the daily voice of ICMI. Its editorial staff are senior ICMI leaders and organizers who assert that their main competition is *Kompas*. The ICMI academic think-tank, CIDES (Center for Information and Development Studies), is viewed by CIDES directors as Muslim competition for CSIS. Finally, the reduction in the number of non-Muslims in the Cabinet is also seen as attainment of one of ICMI's objectives (even though so-called "real ICMI" – the activists – were not selected). This, according to Soetjipto, contributes to eliminating feelings of "insecurity" among Muslims who felt "trauma" and bitterness at being locked out of meaningful participation in the early New Order.[149] Therefore, he sees that proportional Muslim representation in Cabinet and in the MPR is a "good thing" as it does begin concretely to show that Muslims are not a threat and should participate fully in government.

Ordinary Muslims throughout Indonesia, especially Java, are also reportedly pleased with ICMI. In Java Habibie is seen as the *jago* [hero] of ordinary Muslim Indonesians. According to Mohtar Mas'oed and Din Syamsuddin, the establishment of ICMI, combined with the President's *haj*, is widely interpreted by ordinary people as evidence of Soeharto's *rapprochement* with Islam and indicative of his sincere Muslim religiosity.[150]

Dissension

What, then, has happened? If the creation of ICMI is indicative of a new, more accommodative era in state–Islam reactions, is it not a good thing that some Muslims no longer feel they stand outside the state? Are the many initiatives by Soeharto to accommodate Islam – such as the education and religious courts legislation, establishment of ICMI, and creation of an Islamic bank – a genuinely healthy development which contribute towards a resolution of an Islam versus Pancasila dichotomy in Indonesian ideological discourse? What, then, are the implications for politics of the development of institutions like ICMI, which Nurcholish Madjid suggests are the natural consequence of cultural and educational trends extant in Indonesian society? Why, then, is ICMI so controversial? What makes it so provocative both within the Islamic movement, towards ABRI, and among some senior members of the bureaucracy?

The answers to the preceding questions are suggested in several ways. For Abdurrahman Wahid it is the "process" more than anything else that disturbs him. He argues that Soeharto has given opportunity for the legitimate expression of intolerant, and ultimately anti-Pancasilaist, Islamic political views in order to satisfy his own short-term political objectives. This process, Wahid contends, is a contravention of Soeharto's own path: the path of "de-confessionalization" and the de-linking of faith from politics so that a repetition of history – violence and destructive politics based on *aliran* affiliations – are forever avoided. Wahid goes so far as to argue that ICMI activists' promotion of an "Islamic society" camouflages a revived desire for an Islamic state which would contravene the compromise expressed in Pancasila and established at the founding of the Republic.

ABRI, on the other hand, is infuriated at the prominent entry into political discourse of an ICMI-identified (by ABRI) strategy of democratization (or Islamization) through de-militarization under the banner of Islam and protected by Habibie. Nearly all ABRI ideological thinking is challenged by such a formula for political change.

Yet it is not just ABRI, Wahid, and NU that criticize ICMI. Government officials, including several Cabinet Ministers, have acknowledged that they think the process of legitimate government accommodation with Islam, illustrated by ICMI, may have gone "too far." One recently retired senior government official acknowledged that he supported ICMI publicly because he was "ordered to do so," even though he considered the government's role in the creation of ICMI to be manipulative of religion – something that the government should avoid.[151] The Minister of Transmigration, Siswono, has bluntly said that ICMI is a "sectarian" organization. Moreover, although done quietly, prominent Muslim intellectuals such as Aswab Mahasin, Nurcholish Madjid, and Emha Ainun Nadjib, also question whether the perception of Islamic exclusivism in ICMI may be counterproductive for Islam and wonder if the organization has been captured by those who see Islam as a stepping-stone to political power.

Arguments from ICMI activists that "Islamic values" should inform and influence government policy, programs, law, and regulations heighten tension in Indonesian society. For example, Indonesia's leading human rights lawyer and prominent democratic activist (who has also defended Islamic activists' political rights in court), Adnan Buyung Nasution, argues passionately that the only criterion on which to judge any Indonesian should be "citizenship," and not religion. Moreover, he argues that it would be extremely problematic to "Islamize" law and to evaluate whether it was informed by Islamic values or not. The tolerant compromise established by Pancasila, regardless of its cynical manipulation against legitimate Islamic and other political activity in the New Order, would then be under threat, Nasution argues.[152]

ICMI as part of the "Pancasila-ization" of Islam?

Is it possible that the concerns of many opponents of ICMI are misplaced? Perhaps President Soeharto has managed to simultaneously accommodate the legitimate symbolic aspirations of Muslims in a positive fashion while "capturing" otherwise critical Muslim politicians in an organization indebted to the New Order. Similarly, has Soeharto adeptly managed to eliminate the outstanding Muslim concerns about the overrepresentation of non-Muslims in his Cabinet and the MPR while avoiding replacing them with Muslim activists that may still harbor reservations about the Pancasila state Soeharto has built? Soeharto continuously reminds both ICMI and the nation in high-profile addresses that "ideological alternatives" to Pancasila must never be allowed to reappear in Indonesia and that religious tolerance is crucial to national unity.[153] The President also warned ICMI to guard against revival of "sectarianism and primordialism."[154]

A senior ABRI officer in the Defense Ministry argues that Soeharto will never be "used" by ICMI and that the President has always been aware of threats to Pancasila.[155] Much evidence since the new Cabinet was announced by President Soeharto in March 1993 suggests that Soeharto never intended to give anything of substance to Muslim activists who may have been seeking to "empower the state" in order to "Islamize from above." Although several Habibie allies and government bureaucrats who belong to ICMI became Cabinet Ministers, not one identifiable Muslim activist from ICMI was selected for the Cabinet, even though many analysts and scholars have argued that this was, in fact, the main short-term goal of ICMI – to place its personnel in government. Amidst much controversy in late 1992, it was said that more Muslims and fewer Christians were appointed by the President to the MPR. However, the Chairman of the PPP, Ismail Hasan Metareum, protests that the MPR is "still only" 80 percent Muslim.[156]

The ICMI strategy of using Soeharto to enter the bureaucracy and position Muslims for an eventual power struggle in a post-Soeharto era may not have been successful thus far. Soeharto did drop the three most prominent Christian ministers and replace some of them with Muslim bureaucrats.[157] Although much was made of the replacement of the so-called "technocrats" by the Habibie-supported economic nationalists referred to as "technologues," their appointments were offset by Soeharto's formal appointment of prominent former officials (who were responsible for the form of development that Amien Rais and Sri Bintang Pamungkas hope to change), such as Ali Wardhana, as Special Economic Advisor. After the announcement of the Cabinet in March 1993 there was a good deal of speculation whether the new ministers reflected the economic nationalism associated with Habibie. This caused concern whether Indonesia would be able to maintain its excellent relations with international lending agencies if Habibie's proteges were in charge of the economy. Soeharto's appointment of former members of his economic team as official advisors served both to reassure overseas partners and to remind others that Habibie was not given free rein within the new Cabinet. Moreover, as economist Hadi Soesastro points out, the new economic team has generally adhered to responsible macro-level economic development policies.[158]

Has Soeharto then "trapped" Muslim activists in ICMI, a government-backed organization completely dependent upon the continued goodwill and sponsorship of Soeharto and Habibie without giving them real political power in government? (Clearly, ICMI activists see their dependency on Soeharto as purely temporary.) Has Soeharto successfully moved to reaffirm his legitimacy, partially based on his heightened Islamic credentials, with the masses while avoiding any significant concessions to ambitious Islamic activists associated with ICMI who hoped for policy change and further moves towards the Islamization of society? Indeed, Soeharto has disarmed his critics on the Islamic right. As outlined by former Religious Affairs Minister Munawir Sjadzali above, Soeharto has done many things that benefit the *umat*. But has Soeharto allowed the Islamization of the government? No. Not in the sense that Muslims who advocate a formalization of links between Islam and the government have made any significant short-term political gains.

The most important point that can be made at this stage is that political discourse in contemporary Indonesia is heavily influenced by the ICMI phenomenon. The implications of that participation in the discourse are not merely confined to answering whether ICMI succeeded in using Soeharto to Islamize the state, or even whether Soeharto has disarmed his Muslim political critics once again while using them to bolster his own legitimacy. Instead, the debate examined so far in this study between Abdurrahman Wahid and NU and Muslim activists in ICMI, definitively shows that contention over the meaning of politics based on Pancasila is still an acute element in national political and ideological discourse. Most significantly, ICMI contributions to ideological discourse include discussion of the role of ABRI in politics, limited advocacy for democratization, and the establishment of an Islamic society. These last three issues will be shown to have the greatest impact on how other voices interact with ICMI and what the concrete political implications of that interaction might be.

Neither the roles of Abdurrahman Wahid and NU or ICMI in political discourse can be adequately assessed without consideration of the thinking and ideology of the most powerful single institution in Indonesian society. Therefore, the following chapter will examine the role of the Indonesian armed forces in contemporary political debate as it pertains to Pancasila.

Chapter 4

The Indonesian armed forces

> Indonesia's unity and diversity should not be taken for granted. That is why ABRI is so obsessed with national unity. The philosophy of ABRI and Indonesia is grounded by Pancasila and the UUD '45 [Constitution of 1945]. It is a family-like democracy which calls for ABRI's active participation in all aspects of national life.
>
> General Try Sutrisno[1]

> For ABRI, the very existence of Indonesia is the essence of Pancasila. It is the highest formulation of the existence of the nation. And without Pancasila Indonesia will disintegrate, it's that simple.
>
> Vice Admiral Sunardi[2]

ABRI is the only national institution with both security and political functions. This is derived from its origins as a genuine "people's army" born in revolution and followed by the development of the "Middle Way" doctrine in the 1950s and *dwifungsi* in the 1960s. Moreover, ABRI perceives itself as the primary defender of the Pancasila state: a non-communist, non-theological, unitary state. ABRI's role as the defender of Pancasila is stipulated in the *Sapta Marga*, the virtually sacral soldier's oath.

As an institution ABRI is deeply imbued with a comprehensive ideological notion of itself and of the nation. As described in Chapter 1, this ideological vision is in part negatively defined. That is, Indonesia as a Pancasila state is often defined by ABRI's perceptions of threats to the state, which are synonymous with perceived threats to Pancasila. These threats are communism, an Islamic state, and "liberalism." General Nasution's key role in support of Sukarno's dissolution of the Konstituante in 1959 and the unilateral decree reinstating the Constitution of 1945 was a clear demonstration of military disapproval of parliamentary democracy.[3] Since that time the belief that liberal democracy is inappropriate for Indonesia has been a central tenet of ABRI ideology. This is reflected in ABRI's dominant role in conceptualizing the de-politicization strategies of the New Order. Future ABRI leaders are exhaustively instructed in ideological thinking. One of the largest component blocks of instruction time at the elite army senior staff college (SESKOAD) is study of Pancasila.[4] Most senior ABRI leaders speak frequently of threats to Pancasila and reassert its necessity for maintenance of Indonesian national integration and development.

Interviews with seventeen senior ABRI leaders (and consideration of the written views and other interviews of numerous additional officers) have demonstrated that Pancasila is a core referent for the military in contemporary political discourse.[5] Indonesian generals, air marshals, and admirals, with varying degrees of intensity and sophistication, perceive Pancasila as central to any explanation of ABRI's social-political functions and how those functions are linked to national unity and development. Moreover, officers often use Pancasila as a referent for discussion of any fundamental political issue. There is no doubt that ABRI contains multiple interests and personnel who have competing political or personal agendas. None the less, as William Liddle has aptly noted, ABRI is characterized by "a high degree of internal solidarity and loyalty."[6]

The purpose of this chapter is to focus on how and why ABRI participates in contemporary discourse. There are three broad areas of consideration. First, the ideological imperative for ABRI to maintain its role as a legitimate political actor is examined. One of the ways ABRI emphasizes its legitimate political role is to stress a concept known as "integralism." Integralism is a largely military supported ideological argument with roots in the Independence Investigating Committee debates of 1945 (briefly outlined in Chapter 1). Senior officers often define Pancasila "as an integralistic ideology."

Second, ABRI's participation in political discourse is linked to perceptions of specific institutional and ideological threats. ABRI uses Pancasila to define the boundaries of permissible political behavior in Indonesia. Because ABRI has historically considered political Islam a "threat" to itself and the nation, consideration is given to ABRI interaction with NU and Abdurrahman Wahid, as well as with ICMI. Additionally, ABRI has historically perceived liberal democracy as inimical to Pancasila.

Third, this chapter will examine why ABRI's Pancasila discourse is changing in the post-*asas tunggal* era. This is relevant because, as suggested in Chapter 1, it is difficult to identify tangible threats to national stability from communism and Islamic fundamentalism. Therefore, it is necessary to examine the way ABRI uses Pancasila to justify its role as defender of national stability in the current reduced-threat environment. ABRI has been forced to refine its ideological justifications in response to the changing perceptions of threats to the Soeharto regime.

Although this chapter assumes a fairly high degree of institutional solidarity within ABRI, it will also consider perspectives of individual ABRI officers which differ from official ABRI positions. For example, some officers have recently called for increased "openness" and democracy. This chapter will attempt to reconcile unrelenting ABRI warnings about liberalism as a threat to Pancasila on the one hand, with these officers' rhetorical support for democracy on the other.

Pancasila is also appropriated by ABRI officers to negatively appraise regime policies, programs (or the consequences of those policies), and even President Soeharto himself. ABRI's changing relationship with Soeharto will also highlight divergent interpretations and political uses of Pancasila.

ABRI'S "PERMANENCE" IN INDONESIAN NATIONAL LIFE

There is a firmly held ABRI conviction that its political and security role in national life is permanent. ABRI does not consider its stewardship of the nation as temporary or justified by unusual or particular circumstances. There can never be a "return to the barracks," as Indonesian officers contend that ABRI was never a barracks-bound institution.[7] Officers emphatically reject suggestions that there should be an end to the military's socio-political dual function.[8] Similarly, senior officers argue passionately that it is completely irrelevant to differentiate between the armed forces and civilians. That is, ABRI does not recognize a distinction between military and civilian domains of national life. Former

ABRI Commander General, Try Sutrisno, provides an example of this assertion:

> We are all one family, aren't we? Both ABRI and civilians have the same rights and responsibilities to advance the people. Together we all develop the Indonesian person. No one may feel that just one group holds all responsibility.[9]

An understanding of how ABRI perceives its political role is directly tied to the military's interpretation of Pancasila as an "integralistic" ideology. Senior officers argue that because Indonesian culture is "integralistic," a permanent socio-political role for the armed forces is justified. The former Deputy Commander of SESKOAD and a leading military ideologist, retired Brigadier General Abdul Kadir Besar, argues that it is simply "wrong" to base ABRI's political function on *dwifungsi*, or even the *Sapta Marga*.[10] These are man-made doctrines whereas ABRI's socio-political role derives from the conceptualization of Pancasila as an "integralistic" ideology.[11] Therefore, a brief review of ABRI's concept of "integralism" is necessary to understand its role in ABRI's definition of Pancasila in the 1990s.

Integralism

Integralism conceives of the state and society as an organic totality in which the primary emphasis is not on individual rights but social obligations. Arguments for a *negara integralistik* [integralistic state] originated in the constitutional and independence preparatory debates of 1945. The main proponent of integralism was a Dutch-trained Javanese constitutional scholar, Professor Soepomo. Soepomo argued that Indonesian political culture, especially Javanese village governance was based on family principles.[12] Soepomo contended that these principles were not suited to Western conceptions of parliamentary democracy with checks and balances and guarantees of individual human rights. Soepomo's arguments, however, did not prevail in the independence preparatory debates. Instead, the delegates opted for the establishment of Indonesia as a constitutional democracy, albeit with a very strong presidency.[13]

Even though Soepomo's arguments were not accepted by Indonesia's founders, his ideas have remained part of Indonesian political thinking. Soepomo argued that all individuals in the state were inseparable from each other and that the state was like a family where all components played crucial roles.[14] These ideas have been revived in official discourse since the late 1980s, especially in ABRI thinking. Previous studies of the military and politics in Indonesia have not revealed ABRI interest in integralism although it is frequently raised today by ABRI officers as the ideological foundation of both Pancasila and *dwifungsi*.

Brigadier General (retired) Abdul Kadir Besar's conception of Pancasila as an integralistic ideology provides an understanding of how Pancasila is interpreted and how threats to Pancasila are conceived by senior officers. Besar argues that all ideologies have philosophical roots and that "Pancasila is the modern ideological expression of integralist truths." That is, the five principles of Pancasila are an inseparable, coherent expression of indigenous Indonesian political culture, the essence of which is *kebersamaan* [togetherness]. "Togetherness" is best expressed in the Indonesian context, Besar insists, as the principle of *kekeluargaan* [familyness]. Besar explains that a family principle of governance means that Pancasila describes an inseparable set of relationships: between all people, between people and the state, between the rulers and the ruled, between God and mankind, and between "this world and the universe." The combination of these relationships, Besar concludes, is the integralistic state of which Pancasila is the modern ideological expression. According to Besar, all these concepts are part of the ideological curriculum of the senior military staff colleges, including SESKOAD. He says it is not surprising that today his "students" (current ABRI and political leaders, including Vice President Try Sutrisno) refer to integralism when discussing Pancasila and the role of ABRI in national life.[15]

Abdul Kadir Besar suggests several contemporary political implications of integralistic thinking. Besar argues that the first principle (belief in God) expresses a relationship between mankind and God and could never imply endorsement of a particular God or faith. Therefore, according to Besar, political developments which suggest that one group, or religion, especially Islam, should control the government or society constitutes a contravention of integralism and Pancasila. He argues that integralism requires the "majority" groups to be "especially sensitive" towards religious and ethnic minorities because the weak and the small are automatically the objects of state –

"family" – protection and care. That is, Pancasila as an integralistic ideology is deeply paternalistic and the government has the duty to protect all parts of the national family equally. The emphasis is on government duty towards individuals and groups rather than on individual rights. Checks on government power are unnecessary because this would hinder government ability to fulfill its protective duties towards all.[16]

Indeed, there are numerous examples of how ABRI officers conceive of Pancasila in an integralistic sense when explaining particular ABRI actions and behavior. For example, Lieutenant General Harsudiyono Hartas and Air Vice Marshal Teddy Rusdy argue that it is always ABRI that protects minorities.[17] Former Minister of Defense Benny Moerdani notes that "ABRI is always most powerful in dousing SARA [disturbances based on ethnicity, religion, race, and class] problems."[18] Both Hartas and Rusdy explicitly account for ABRI's behavior in terms of fulfilling ABRI's commitment to Pancasila as an integralistic ideology. Major General Hendropriyono, installed as Commander of the key Greater Jakarta Military Command in April 1993 (and replaced in November 1994), notes that one of his first challenges as Jakarta Commander was to overcome "SARA issues, such as the stoning of churches" in the city.[19]

ABRI takes great pride in its role as the defender of Pancasila as stipulated in the *Sapta Marga* [Soldiers' Oath].[20] However, Kadir Besar argues that ABRI's right to defend and interpret Pancasila is not justified by the *Sapta Marga*, the Constitution, or even the *dwifungsi* doctrine itself. Rather, he says it is the "culture of *kekeluargaan* [family-ness]" upon which ABRI participates in society. The other concepts are "man-made" whereas integralistic ideals such as the family state principles are rooted in Indonesian culture. Therefore, ABRI participation in national life simply "is." ABRI comes from the milieu of Indonesian society where all parts play an essential role in the system. Besar concludes that Pancasila as an integralistic ideology is the cultural and philosophical grounding of ABRI. Therefore, ABRI does not need special permission to participate in national politics.[21]

Although few senior officers speak as philosophically as Kadir Besar, it is clear that some elements of integralistic thinking, especially underlying the interrelatedness of ABRI and national unity, are recognizable in ABRI contributions to the Pancasila discourse. Lieutenant General Harsudiyono Hartas, for example, directly links ABRI thinking on Pancasila with integralism. Hartas argues that Pancasila "stipulates the unity of all things in the state," especially "God and the internal spirituality of all beings." Pancasila thus conceived, is "a relationship between mankind and the universe and it is uniquely Indonesian."[22] These are not the views of retired brigadiers alone; until May 1993 Hartas held one of the most powerful political positions in the Indonesian Armed Forces. Moreover, ABRI reference to integralism is not merely something invoked in private interviews. It is also explicit in public discourse. An example of how debate over integralism has recently been revived occurred at the Second National Awakening Seminar sponsored by Lemhanas (the National Defense Institute). There Hartas and civil rights attorney Adnan Buyung Nasution debated the appropriateness of integralism for Indonesia today. In this debate, Hartas said that Nasution's arguments for a separation of military and civilian functions constituted contravention of Indonesia as an integralistic state.[23]

Air Vice Marshal Teddy Rusdy and Vice Admiral Sunardi (Rusdy was a senior political advisor to former ABRI Commander General Try Sutrisno and Sunardi senior advisor to Ministers of Defense Benny Moerdani and Edy Sudrajat) both argue that Indonesia based on Pancasila is a state which functions as an organic whole and that none of its component parts – people, organizations, ideology, or territory – could ever be considered separate from the unitary Indonesian state. Most importantly, they argue that it is the supreme duty of ABRI to maintain this unity. For ABRI, Indonesia without Pancasila is virtually inconceivable. Unlike many other Indonesians, ABRI officers do not conceive of Pancasila as merely a political compromise between nationalists and religious groups. They see it as the essence of national unity. Benny Moerdani argues that above all Pancasila is a "way of life" and Admiral Sunardi contends that "without Pancasila Indonesia would disintegrate."[24]

In an era of increased challenges to military domination of politics, ABRI relies in part on its integralistic interpretation of Pancasila to justify its political role. This approach is difficult to challenge, because intangible but accepted cultural principles are cited to legitimize ABRI's political function. ABRI's integralistic approach is stronger than doctrines such as *dwifungsi* and *Sapta Marga* which can be challenged and possibly changed. Gajah Mada University political scientist Mohtar Mas'oed argues that for ABRI "integralism sanctions the indivisibility of the polity and because of this ABRI needs integralism more than other doctrines."[25] ABRI's political role is permanent and debate should not even be about ending *dwifungsi*, said Teddy Rusdy. It should be emphasized, however, that senior officers, and even Soeharto himself, do not discount the possibility that the military role could be altered, scaled back, or reduced in significant ways. Soeharto, Moerdani, Sutrisno, and others suggest that while they will not consider ending the dual function, they will consider a reduction in the numbers of officers staffing civilian positions in the bureaucracy. Moreover, President Soeharto and Try Sutrisno have said that the number of ABRI seats in the DPR can easily be reduced according to the wishes of the people. But the fundamental right of ABRI to retain a central political role cannot change.[26]

A final note is necessary on why ABRI uses integralism to justify its role as defender of Pancasila and national unity. In the early years of the New Order, ABRI's political legitimacy was more widely recognized than today. Indeed, there was a national consensus that deviations from Pancasila which occurred under Sukarno had to be corrected in ideological, economic, and political spheres. This consensus gave crucial support, especially from intellectuals and Muslims, to the New Order and to ABRI. Student activists and proponents of democratization generally supported the central role of the armed forces in politics at that time. Marsillam Simanjuntak, a leading member of Forum Democracy, human rights activist, and constitutional scholar, recalled that in the mid-1960s student activists and democrats saw the military as a potential agent of democratization and modernization. Therefore, at the urging of their mentors, such as Soedjatmoko, a prominent leader of the PSI (Indonesian Socialist Party) and later respected elder statesman and United Nations official, students and democrats supported the military.[27] However, today many of Indonesia's Muslim and non-Muslim intellectuals as well as proponents of democratization no longer view ABRI as their "agent." Instead, for many intellectuals and democrats the military is viewed as an obstacle to democratization (see Chapter 5).[28] Similarly, as suggested in the chapters on Abdurrahman Wahid and ICMI, there are increasing calls for "de-militarization" from the Islamic movement. In this environment of growing challenges to the military's political role, ABRI has sought to further legitimize its permanence in national life through reference to

Pancasila. This may be because ABRI recognizes that the national consensus evident in the 1960s no longer applies. David Bourchier suggests that this is the case:

> Integralism is essentially an ideological device deployed by Indonesia's rulers in an attempt to preserve and extend their grip on society in the face of demands by new social forces for greater political rights and effective limits on executive authority.[29]

THREATS TO PANCASILA

ABRI officers define various threats to Pancasila. These include any perceived challenges to its dual function role or any threats to national stability and unity as well as more specific threats. For example, the then Defense Minister, Moerdani, vowed to "crush any attempts to replace the Pancasila state ideology with religious or ethnic ideologies."[30] Former Chief of Staff (and Minister of Defense since March 1993) General Edy Sudrajat and Lieutenant General Hartas have both identified proponents of liberal democracy and human rights as threats to Pancasila and national unity. Hartas has also warned against the re-emergence of threats from the "extreme right," the usual official term for Islamic fundamentalism.[31] Furthermore, in a reference to Islamic threats to the state, Hartas warned of a rising tide of religious intolerance.[32]

Lieutenant General Harsudiyono Hartas explains how a number of different kinds of people could constitute a "source of danger to Pancasila." These include intellectuals (especially if the intellectuals are associated with mass movements where they can incite the people); business people and conglomerates if they only care for the accumulation of wealth and not for the good of all the people; individual members of ABRI (such as in 1965 when the PKI influenced some officers); certain bureaucrats "if they go outside" the accepted conception of Indonesia as a unitary, integralistic state; leaders of mass social organizations (especially religious leaders); religious figures if they put their own narrow religious interests ahead of national interests; and political parties if they simply promote "narrow party interests" and not the interests of the whole nation.[33] Thus, the potential threats to Pancasila are vast. In a similar vein, Air Vice Marshal Teddy Rusdy suggests viewing Indonesia's history as a pendulum swinging between left (communism) and right (religion). If any activity goes "outside the bounds" of the pendulum's normal arc, then it becomes anti-Pancasila. How then do we know what is "in" and what is "out" of bounds? Rusdy concedes that this is indeed very difficult to judge. However, the boundaries on the left are very clear he said, and marked by the communist-inspired September 30, 1965 movement. Rusdy says that on the right, two incidents have gone out of bounds: the *Darul Islam* of the 1950s and early 1960s and Islamic extremism in the 1970s. Rusdy adds that today ICMI is on the right-hand side of the pendulum's arc.[34]

The stability imperative

ABRI leaders speak of the need to maintain national social and political stability. "Stability" is identified as essential for economic growth and development. The political chaos of the 1950s is seen as having prevented economic development. Even though ABRI identifies a wide range of people and their activities as potentially anti-Pancasila, officers distinguish between threats to Pancasila that may be associated with a mass-based movement (which are by ABRI definition almost always de-stabilizing) and other less worrisome issues. For example, Rusdy argues that he considers threats to Pancasila from most proponents of liberalism and communism to be mild. He argues that such threats are 'in the realm of the intellectuals' and are no longer mass-based. On the other hand, he says that religion is so broad and all-encompassing that it is potentially a much greater threat to the Pancasila state.[35] The prioritization of "stability" over any increased openness in political life is known in Indonesia as the "security approach" to politics.

Overarching emphasis on the "security approach" is, however, under debate within ABRI circles. The extent to which there is disagreement is illustrated in a public debate between Try Sutrisno and the then Minister of the Interior, Rudini (a retired general). Rudini argued that the New Order's heavy emphasis on stability above all else should be abandoned. Rudini contended that increased public political awareness of global and national changes could not be accommodated by a sole emphasis on security and stability. Not all expressions of political behavior should be interpreted as potential threats to stability and Pancasila, Rudini argued. In response, ABRI Commander Try Sutrisno opined that even open debate about the appropriateness of the "security approach" was destabilizing. Moreover, Sutrisno argued that only those who have thoroughly studied Pancasila and other ABRI doctrines could thoughtfully participate in such public discourse.[36] In other words, threats to Pancasila disturb national stability, and these threats include discussion which should be avoided. However, some ABRI figures such as police Brigadier General Roekmini, a former member of the ABRI faction in the DPR and current member of the National Human Rights Commission, and former Speaker of the parliament, retired Lieutenant General Kharis Suhud, also argue that too much emphasis on stability alone quashes legitimate participation in the political system.[37]

Islam and ABRI threat perceptions in the 1990s

One of ABRI's most frequently mentioned potential "threats" to Pancasila is ICMI. This view directly contradicts the insistence of ICMI members that there is no problem in the ICMI–ABRI relationship. ABRI uneasiness with ICMI is linked to institutional and personal rivalries and dislikes. While ABRI does not blatantly accuse ICMI of being anti-Pancasila in public forums, numerous individual officers strongly suggest that ICMI's activities and its members' statements contravene Pancasila. Furthermore, it must be recognized that ABRI in many ways is more sophisticated and nuanced than in previous years regarding the question of Islam and the state. Part of this has to do with general sociological trends of greater religiosity among public officials and increasing government use of Islamic nomenclature.[38] Retired army Brigadier General Sudibyo argues that ABRI is much more tolerant and understanding of Islam than in the pre-*asas tunggal* era. He notes that there is no longer any automatic tendency in the armed forces to look for Islamic fundamentalism as the source behind security disturbances.[39] Vice President Try Sutrisno forcefully insisted in a 1993 interview while he was still Commander of ABRI that depiction of Islam as a threat is "clearly wrong."[40] Nevertheless, there does exist a great deal of concern within senior ABRI ranks about ICMI.

Abdurrahman Wahid also agrees that since the Tanjung Priok incident the armed forces have begun to carefully appraise the role of Islam in Indonesian society and no longer automatically view Islam as a state threat. Wahid partially credits the joint efforts of the then ABRI Commander Benny Moerdani (a Catholic), himself, and the *ulama* [religious scholars in NU] to gain greater mutual understanding in the 1980s. Moerdani was taken around the country to visit *pesantran* [traditional Islamic schools] by Wahid in order to make contact with the *umat*.[41] Furthermore, Moerdani and other prominent government officials addressed the 1989 NU Congress.[42] Moerdani's successor as Chief of Staff, Try Sutrisno, is widely praised as a devout Muslim. Indeed, one ICMI member approvingly described Sutrisno as the "first *santri* [devout Muslim] head of the armed forces."[43]

Indonesian scholars and officials have noted that the apparent decrease in ABRI and government mistrust of Islam in the past decade is a welcome and healthy development.[44] As the scholar Magnis Suseno observed, it was never a good thing for Islam to stand outside the state and the government.[45] Similarly, some ABRI officers have recognized this as a major change from previous years. However, recognition that ABRI is responding to broad sociological trends and developments does not necessarily mean that there is fundamental change in ABRI's basic conception of the Pancasila state. For example, many ABRI officers imply that ICMI activists are naive to assume that Try Sutrisno's devoutness would in any way make him sympathetic to ICMI as a political organization.[46]

ABRI and Abdurrahman Wahid

This study has already argued that two of the most prominent voices in contemporary ideological discourse are Abdurrahman Wahid (and NU) and the Islamic activists associated with ICMI. Both Wahid and ICMI have linked part of their participation in the discourse to references to ABRI. Wahid emphasizes his good relationship with ABRI and implicitly suggests that he shares with ABRI the broad goal of ensuring that politics remain "de-confessionalized" and that Islam should not again become the basis of political allegiance. Moreover, Wahid asserts that despite his goal of seeking greater democratization, ABRI still "accepts me as a nationalist because I am for a de-confessionalized state." Wahid, as noted in Chapter 2, seeks to navigate a political course between military domination of the state on one hand and Islamic politics on the other.[47] Some voices in ICMI, however, argue for de-militarization and the establishment of an Islamic society. ICMI members also insist that their relationship with ABRI is not unduly strained. Wahid, however, maintains that ABRI is worried about ICMI and that in a post-Soeharto era ICMI may be among ABRI's first targets.[48] What then does ABRI have to say? Given its own commitment to Pancasila, does ABRI appreciate Wahid's prominent reiteration of support for Pancasila in the discourse, especially as exemplified by the Rapat Akbar? Consideration will first be given to an examination of ABRI's relationship with Wahid, after which ABRI views of ICMI will be analyzed.

Abdurrahman Wahid is perhaps the only leader of a mass-based non-governmental organization that remains generally independent of the regime. A crucial element in Wahid's politics and his role in Pancasila discourse is his relationship with ABRI. Wahid specifically juxtaposes his position in NU with ICMI and argues that ABRI perceives ICMI as "a dangerous thing." Moreover, Wahid has said that ABRI leaders have told him "for all your sins of democracy you are better than them [ICMI] because you are still going for a nationalist state." Wahid acknowledges a close relationship with Benny Moerdani and notes that when Moerdani served as Commander of the armed forces, and later as Defense Minister, he met frequently with him, as often as once a month. But Wahid insists it is not only Moerdani but also others in ABRI, including "mid-level colonels, and brigadiers" who express appreciation for his nationalist credentials.[49] Wahid has been attacked over his close relationship with the Catholic Moerdani by other Muslims. However, Wahid strongly defends his relationship with Moerdani, insisting that such good relationships are helpful to protect the interests of the *umat* and to lessen ABRI suspicions of Muslim organizations.[50]

Wahid's relationship with ABRI may be changing, however. After a round of retirements and command reshuffles by President Soeharto in 1994 and 1995, Wahid has been left with few personal contacts in the upper reaches of the armed forces. Aswab Mahasin observes that Wahid has yet to develop effective relationships with some of the new ABRI commanders.[51] The extent to which Wahid's personal relationships with ABRI leaders has shifted is illustrated by Lieutenant General Hartono, former ABRI Social and Political Affairs Chief and army Chief of Staff since February 1995. Hartono, widely assumed to be a close ally of Habibie and sympathetic to ICMI, appeared to actively campaign against Wahid and even suggested he should be replaced as head of NU at the organization's December 1994 Congress. Wahid, however, argues that what matters most is not simply his own personal relationship with the generals, but the good rapport between ABRI and NU at the provincial, district and village levels. Wahid notes that he always urges the NU *kiai* to "cooperate with ABRI and the government as a partner in development." Furthermore, Wahid argues that NU and ABRI share a similar nationalist outlook that rejects Islamic exclusivism and that this shared perspective will persist regardless of personnel.[52]

However, at the elite political level, with the exception of Benny Moerdani (now retired from all government posts) many active-duty senior ABRI leaders do *not* express strong appreciation for Wahid's role as leader of the democratization movement. Almost all the officers interviewed for this study argue that even though ABRI recognizes Wahid as the legitimate representative of Indonesian Islam and the main leader of the *umat* (and not ICMI), he is not perceived by ABRI to play a constructive role as a leader of the democracy movement. Retired General Soemitro was the only ABRI figure who would go on record with strong praise for Wahid's creation of Forum Democracy in 1991. Soemitro also laments that the government has failed to understand Wahid and appreciate his expression of support for Pancasila at the Rapat Akbar.[53] Soemitro's praise of Wahid must be qualified in that he is not necessarily representative of ABRI. Although Soemitro is former Commander of the powerful KOPKAMTIB (armed forces' Command to Restore Security and Order), since the late 1970s he has become a frequent critic of the Soeharto regime and has openly called for Soeharto to step down. However, one active duty senior army general remarks that even though he is wary of Wahid's advocacy of democracy, he still sees that Wahid is "sincere and genuine, the real leader of the *umat*, and has advanced, broad-minded liberal beliefs that are politically ahead of his time."[54]

It is not only Wahid's advocacy of democratization which limits his appeal to ABRI. Former Ambassador to the United States, (retired) Lieutenant General Hasnan Habib, argues that although many in government respect Wahid personally and as a Muslim leader, he is viewed warily by many officials for a combination of reasons. Habib contends that Wahid's great personal charisma, political savvy, intelligence, and his huge popular base in NU positions him as the sole non-governmental figure with the ability to organize a mass-based political movement.[55] Indeed, Wahid sought to demonstrate this with the March 1992 Rapat Akbar. Wahid himself has acknowledged that since the withdrawal of NU from formal participation in politics he perceives NU's mass base as a crucial element in his political strategy to work towards a non-Islamic, genuinely democratic and politically de-militarized future. In June 1992 Wahid argued that

> NU is in a very good position, as the anchor of politics in Indonesia – PPP, PDI, and Golkar all need us, *the armed forces need us*; nearly everybody needs us because of our mass base, which we utilize very prudently.[56]

Following his re-election as NU Chairman in December 1994, Wahid advanced the same basic argument – that NU plays a unique national political role because all forces contending for power – especially in the run-up to the 1997 general elections – covet support from NU's mass base.[57] Yet it is precisely Wahid's mobilizing potential that ultimately limits his influence and appeal among ABRI officers. ABRI ideology stresses that liberal democracy is a central historic threat (the political chaos of the 1950s) and culturally incompatible with Pancasila as an integralistic ideology. For ABRI, Wahid's democratic credentials combined with his leadership of NU and his personal qualities may partly cancel out his nationalist, anti-Islamic state bonafides.

There is, however, reason to argue that Wahid and ABRI significantly overlap in their views on Pancasila. First, while Wahid seeks a democratic state and has called for democracy consistently since he began his public career in the 1970s, his arguments against revival of Islamic politics are equally important. That is, Wahid wants both a non-Islamic state – expressed through the religious tolerance in Pancasila – and a democratic society. Yet he favors maintaining the "de-confessionalization" process as his first priority. In this regard, his position is similar to ABRI's self-defined role as defender of Pancasila and protector of religious minorities. Wahid compares the twin threats of Islamic state and militarism in the following way:

> With the imposition of a one-sided concept of state, like the Islamic society, you can imagine that people in NTT [*Nusa Tenggara Timor*, Eastern Indonesia, a largely Christian area], East Timor, Irian Jaya, and Maluku, and all those people in

> Toraja, in Kalimantan, and the Batak people, [will not accept an Islamic society] and so the breakdown of Indonesian society will take place *if we change Pancasila into a sectarian ideology*. But if military rule perpetuates we won't be disintegrated along territorial dimensions, but instead it will be more like the breakdown of the fabric of society and the consent of the ruled.[58]

Wahid appears to argue that the most damaging threat to Indonesia would come from the establishment of Indonesia as an Islamic society, whereas the military threat is more diffuse, leading instead to a diminution in regime legitimacy. However, like the armed forces and other nationalists, Wahid argues that Islamic exclusivism will damage the unity of the nation by driving away the non-Muslim portions of the country. He argues that NU possesses the unique authority and legitimacy to keep the country unified. This is because NU under Wahid opposes Islamic politics that may lead to an Islamic state. Moreover, Wahid argues that because ABRI accepts the notion of equality of all citizens regardless of their religion, ethnicity, or regional origins, it has unwittingly accepted the basis of a future democratic civil society.

There are two dimensions to the overlap in the Pancasila message of both Wahid and ABRI. First, both believe in the need to maintain the separation between religious affiliation and political mobilization and participation. This similarity exists even though Wahid sharply criticizes ABRI's attempt to appropriate sole interpretive rights of Pancasila as well as its role of defender of Pancasila. This, Wahid argues, reduces the ideology to a political tool for perpetuating ABRI domination of the political system. Observes Wahid, "By saying they are the defenders of Pancasila, they in essence castrate Pancasila."[59]

A second similarity between Wahid and ABRI is that they both argue that Pancasila is "necessary" for Indonesian unity. The shared political objectives between ABRI and Wahid are evident in Lieutenant General Hartas' contention that Indonesia is a "religious state" in which the most serious threats to Pancasila are challenges to the religious tolerance expressed in Pancasila. Hartas further notes that rejection of religious tolerance threatens the territorial integrity of the nation, a position similar to Wahid's concern about the emergence of separatist tendencies in non-Muslim regions of Indonesia if government becomes more "Islamic."[60] Benny Moerdani states that "ABRI will always be prepared to defend the conception of Indonesia as a non-sectarian country."[61] Wahid adds that he and NU, as exemplified in the Pancasila message of the Rapat Akbar, are also prepared to defend the conception of Indonesia as non-sectarian. The key issue then is to consider what ABRI identifies as threats to the conception of Indonesia as a religiously tolerant, non-sectarian state. However, ABRI's perception of itself as the pre-eminent defender of Pancasila's religious tolerance is severely undermined by some of its own actions which are profoundly intolerant of religious freedom and independence. For example, since 1992 military authorities in North Sumatra have intervened in a complex leadership dispute in the largest Protestant congregation in Indonesia (known as the Batak Church). Human Rights Watch/Asia reports that ABRI intervention in the church included arrest and torture of pastors and other church officials.[62] However, outside of North Sumatra, the military role in this issue remains generally unknown and has had little impact on perceptions of ABRI as a protector of religious minorities.

ICMI AND ABRI: CONTENTION IN THE DISCOURSE

Although ICMI is a relatively new organization, its presence has generated intense hostility from senior ABRI leaders. ICMI has also had a polarizing effect within ABRI. Senior officers deplore the emergence of "pro" and "anti" ICMI members of the armed forces. However, several senior commanders are identified as sympathetic towards ICMI or personally close to Habibie. These include Lieutenant General Hartono, former head of ABRI's Social and Political Affairs division and Army Chief of Staff since February 1995, and the ABRI Chief of Staff, General Feisal Tanjung. None the less, numerous Indonesian civilian observers as well as ABRI officers, concur that most ABRI officers are either hostile or suspicious towards ICMI. ABRI concerns about ICMI are focused on several levels. First, ABRI officers attack ICMI on ideological grounds by arguing that it surreptitiously supports an Islamic state and therefore contravenes Pancasila. Second, ABRI rejects ICMI because of deep personal animosity towards its Chairman, Minister of Technology B.J. Habibie. Third, ABRI perceives that Soeharto backed the establishment of ICMI in order punish ABRI and manipulate the *umat* to increase his own legitimacy. Fourth, ABRI is suspicious of ICMI because it has added legitimacy to some Muslim activists' calls for the "de-militarization" of Indonesian politics.

Contravention of ideology

ABRI reference to ICMI is usually expressed in the context of wider views on what officers say is meant by the Pancasila state and what are the limits of ABRI's tolerance. For example, Hartas explains that threats to Pancasila can only be understood if Indonesia is conceived of as a "*negara beragama*" [religious state] of which the fundamental moral tenet is religious tolerance. According to Hartas, because Indonesia is a religious state it demands religious tolerance, otherwise the state will split along territorial and sectarian lines. Therefore, the first and second tenets of Pancasila are inseparable: national unity and religious tolerance. Hartas and Vice Admiral Sunardi reason that any threats to religious tolerance are, *ipso facto*, threats to national unity.[63] There is a generalized concern that ICMI could be the potential manifestation of newly politicized Islam. Although in 1991 and 1992 few officers were as worried as Abdurrahman Wahid on this point, in 1993 and 1994 a sharp polarization has emerged between ABRI and ICMI.

Several senior officers suggest that ICMI is breaking specific laws. They pointed to the 1978 P-4 legislation which contains a listing of thirty-six separate "values and norms" that must be followed regarding Pancasila.[64] One of the stipulations is that in order to fulfill Pancasila's first principle (Belief in God), people must "mutually respect and cooperate with followers of different religions and beliefs." Lieutenant General Hartas suggests that if any ICMI members consider Islam to be in conflict with any of the thirty-six points then they would be in disagreement with the Constitution itself.[65] One high-ranking active duty officer argues that raising the issue of "*Kristenisasi*" by people now associated with ICMI is a specific contravention of Pancasila because such views differentiate on the basis of religion.[66] One officer even allows that a small, though perceptible degree of Muslim/non-Muslim tension inside the armed forces has emerged in the past several years and he attributes this to the influence of ICMI. Another officer argues that ICMI has changed the definition of "what is a good Muslim" and that some Muslim officers who are not supportive of ICMI are said to be "bad Muslims."[67]

A number of officers remark that while they initially regarded ICMI as merely "odd" when it was first formed in December 1990, they now find it "dangerous." They contend that the establishment of an "exclusivist" organization for Muslim intellectuals is unnecessary as almost everybody is Muslim anyway. Air Vice Marshal Teddy Rusdy and Vice Admiral Sunardi reject an ICMI argument that a Muslim intellectuals' organization is justified because of the long-standing presence of CSIS, led in part by prominent Catholic intellectuals. Rusdy argues that, first, it is natural for minorities to associate together in such organizations. Second, he points out that CSIS was created and sponsored by two Muslim generals, Ali Moertopo and Soedjono Humardhani.[68] Moreover, Sunardi and Hartas argue that ICMI may be involved in creating a mass base, something that is both anti-Pancasila and sharply differentiates it from CSIS.

There is a sense among some in ABRI that ICMI is not a "nationalist" organization. Several officers offered the example of ICNU (*Ikatan Cendekiawan Nusantara*, Intellectuals' Association of the Indonesian Archipelago) as an appropriate grouping of intellectuals who prioritized "national," not "group" interests. In fact, Lieutenant General Hartas argued that ICMI combines many elements hostile to ABRI ideological thinking: it is "individualistic" in that it serves simply to advance the particular political agendas of individual activists, it is exclusively "Islamic," and it is "extreme."[69] This is important because both individualism (a trait of the West and not compatible with the principles of "togetherness" and the "family-like, integralistic state")[70] and Islam were never acceptable to ABRI as the basis of the state. These elements make the mere existence of ICMI problematic for senior officers like Hartas. Additionally, ICMI members' promotion of democracy and de-militarization only increase ABRI dislike for the organization.

Several final points as to why the military views ICMI as a potential threat to Pancasila and ABRI's role in the Pancasila democracy are noteworthy. First, Hartas and others see ICMI as a nascent political party. Hartas argues that its structure is "party-like" with a nation-wide grassroots organization and overseas branches. He says that ordinary political parties are not allowed to organize at the sub-district level. Hartas reasoned that because ICMI is acting like a political party it is already going against the understanding of Pancasila by "prioritizing" the interests of Muslims alone.[71]

Habibie and political power struggles

Within ABRI there is a considerable uneasiness over people associated with ICMI. For ABRI, these people fall into two categories: Habibie-related bureaucrats and the so-called (by ABRI) "radicals" (the ICMI activists). The person most clearly associated with ICMI in military eyes is B.J. Habibie, the General Chairman of ICMI, Minister of Technology, confidant of Soeharto, and promoter of a high-technology approach to economic development. When ICMI was created in late 1990 the most common ABRI description of Habibie was that he was politically "naive." By 1994 senior officers said that Habibie was perceived as politically ambitious and, for some officers, "dangerous."[72] One well-known general flatly stated that "if Habibie becomes president, this country will be destroyed."[73] However, the armed forces often would not attack Habibie directly on ICMI (because of the closeness of Soeharto to the whole ICMI project) but over other issues. The military's hostility towards Habibie is heightened by ABRI's perception that Habibie is trying to harness the power of Islam, through his leadership of ICMI, behind his possible political ambitions.

Habibie has been attacked on several specific, non-ICMI matters. One concerned the crash of a Merpati Airlines, Indonesian-made twin-engine commuter plane in late 1992. The plane was a product of the Habibie-led national aircraft industry, IPTN. Within hours of the plane's crash in a remote area (and death of all passengers and crew) Habibie publicly ruled out mechanical or engine problems as the cause. Instead, he said the only possible reason for the accident was human error committed by the pilot, Captain Freda Panggebean. This incident is relevant because nearly six months after the crash in interviews with senior active duty officers about ICMI it was raised as an example of what ABRI dislikes most about Habibie. Officers contend that Habibie's automatic defense of the aircraft (and arms industry) drains resources away from the armed forces. In other words, Habibie was criticized on issues that had nothing to do with ICMI.

Yet, in military thinking, ICMI is instantly linked to Habibie, regardless of the specific issue at hand.

The most serious dispute between ABRI and Habibie involved the purchase of the thirty-nine ex-East German warships (see Chapter 3). It was widely assumed that the military encouraged the press to report on the huge inflation of the purchase price as a way to imply that Habibie poorly managed the acquisition. Both ICMI members and ABRI officers believe that the military encouraged the reporting to discredit Habibie. Some ICMI supporters interpreted attempts to question Habibie's role in the warship purchase as attempts to denigrate ICMI and Islam in general.[74] These examples indicate the deep levels of conflict between ABRI and Habibie on numerous issues which spill over into broader ICMI–ABRI, or even ABRI–Islam relations.

ABRI's Interpretation of Soeharto's relationship with ICMI

Although there may not be agreement with ICMI in general, there is a strong element of thinking in ABRI circles which interprets President Soeharto's sponsorship of ICMI as a sophisticated ploy to "control" Islamic radicals.[75] Few officers would agree "on-the-record" with non-military analyses which suggest that Soeharto created ICMI partially to offset potential diminution in ABRI support for the President.[76] Yet, one senior retired ABRI officer provided the following unattributable frank analysis of Soeharto's sponsorship of ICMI: "ICMI is pure political manipulation by Soeharto because Soeharto was unsure whether ABRI would support him for another term in 1993."[77] As evidence that Soeharto is using ICMI for his own political purposes and not to "Islamize" government in any real sense, several officers point to the fact that no ICMI "radicals" were appointed by the president to the MPR. Although he disagreed with Soeharto's manipulation of Muslims to enhance his political legitimacy, one senior officer conceded that once the non-radical ICMI members were in the MPR, they became "trapped" in an institution still strongly influenced by Soeharto.[78] Additionally, after the announcement of Soeharto's new Cabinet in March 1993, much relief was expressed by ABRI that no "real" ICMI members were appointed to the Cabinet. That is, although bureaucrats who are members of ICMI were appointed to various Cabinet positions, they were not the "radicals" that worry ABRI in a more ideological sense. Yet, at the same time, because Soeharto did reduce the number of non-Muslims in the Cabinet, he succeeded in neutralizing one major complaint of some ICMI followers – that the reduction of Christian cabinet ministers was a presidential response to ICMI activists' perceived fears of "*Kristenisasi*."

It appears that officers worry most about the process, not the specific results of Soeharto's manipulation of ICMI. That is, officers simply do not like the fact that some of the activists in ICMI feel they "can say anything" because they are "legitimized" by Soeharto and Habibie. One officer allowed that in the President's strategy to finally coopt all remaining significant Islamic activists through ICMI, Soeharto may have "given too much." However, if what Soeharto has actually "given" Muslims in recent years is examined, then it should not too be worrying to ABRI. The nature of the regime has not changed and Islamic political values do not seem to appreciably influence government policy and law more than before. The Islamization of society and government is more in the realm of nomenclature and style – something which non-Muslims often note is entirely appropriate in a Muslim-majority country.

ICMI as legitimizer of Muslim voices

In Chapter 3 the presence of former critics of the regime in ICMI was noted. Questions were raised concerning how and why individuals previously hostile to Soeharto and suspicious of Pancasila, particularly the *asas tunggal*, could change and opt for a new strategy to take advantage of what some Muslims perceived as Soeharto's need for them. ABRI too, raises such questions. While some officers acknowledge that Soeharto may be using ICMI to coopt Islamic activists in a constructive, or at least controllable way, they also worry about "who" is in ICMI. In addition to Habibie (whom ABRI dislikes for many reasons that have little to do with ICMI *per se*), ICMI individuals who concern senior officers include Dawam Rahardjo, Imaduddin, Adi Sasono, Sri Bintang Pamungkas, and Amien Rais.[79] These are all persons generally considered to be ICMI "activists." Officers mention "idealists" like Nurcholish Madjid as not really involved in ICMI.[80] Clearly, ABRI does not have much faith that people have truly "changed" and become "Pancasilaist." This view contrasts with senior civilian members of government. Former Minister of Religion, Munawir Sjadzali, argues that he is fully convinced that the cooperative behavior and acceptance of Pancasila by many Muslim "radicals" is precisely because of a sincere change in their beliefs.[81]

The former head of Socio-Political Affairs for ABRI, Lieutenant General Hartas, identifies the same evidence of the importance of ICMI as cited by Imaduddin and other ICMI leaders. Hartas says that Muslim activists in ICMI see that they are part of the discourse and "they now feel they can say anything."[82] Similarly, the former Minister of Defense, Benny Moerdani, in reference to the interviews given by Dawam Rahardjo, Sri Bintang Pamungkas, and Imaduddin in *Detik* in March and April 1993 (see previous chapter), also notes that ICMI members "feel they are entitled to say anything."[83] It appears that the mere presence of ICMI activists' voices in the discourse is disconcerting to ABRI, particularly when these voices call for demilitarization or attack ABRI leaders.

It is also the case that no one in ABRI feels that ICMI activists are successfully using Soeharto, even though some ICMI members specifically state this is what they are doing. For example, former Governor of the elite National Defense Institute (Lemhanas), Major General (retired) Soebiyakto, insists that "the President has never been manipulated by anyone."[84] Additionally, there is unanimity among the senior officers interviewed that it is naive for ICMI activists to identify ICMI-sympathetic officers. They concede that a few individual officers may, for their own reasons, appear receptive or at least neutral towards ICMI. However, the notion that Try Sutrisno is a "*santri*" general and would therefore be sympathetic to the political goals of ICMI activists, is widely ridiculed. One senior officer argues that religiosity should not be confused with support for an Islamic political agenda.[85] (Indeed, it was Try Sutrisno as Commander of the armed forces who launched a fierce attack on allegedly Islamic-inspired rebels in the southern Sumatra province of Lampung in 1989.[86]) A basic fact of Indonesian Islam is that a majority of Indonesians, including Muslim military officers, have not historically channelled their political aspirations through Islam.

DEMOCRATIZATION THREATS TO ABRI'S PANCASILA

ABRI is deeply concerned about efforts to promote a more liberal democratic structure in Indonesia, particularly one which may restrict or diminish its political role as stipulated in the *dwifungsi* doctrine and in integralistic thinking. This is clearly one of the reasons why Abdurrahman Wahid is viewed warily in ABRI circles. Even though he and NU are perceived by ABRI as representative of the *umat* (while ICMI is not), his long-standing advocacy of democratization in Indonesia is not appreciated. While Hartas describes ICMI as "individualistic, Islamic and extreme," he could just as easily describe advocates of increased democratization as "individualistic, secular, and extreme."

There is also a persistent view in the armed forces – and from Soeharto as well – that people advocating democracy are not sincere. For example, former ABRI Chief of Staff and current Minister of Defense Edy Sudrajat has depicted advocates of democratization and human rights as threats to Pancasila. Sudrajat warns against "opportunists masquerading under the banner of human rights or the democratization movement who are ready to exploit any societal discord."[87] Some senior commanders specifically name human rights and democracy advocates, including Buyung Nasution and labor leader Mochtar Pakpahan as "traitors."[88] Similarly, in February 1993 Hartas warned that threats of national disintegration were heightened by people who "use the excuse of struggling for the environment, freedom, democracy, or human rights." Hartas argued that such "Western-influenced ideas" were incompatible when applied to analysis of the Indonesian Constitution. Instead, these ideas were destabilizing and disintegrative. Hartas illustrated his point with reference to a debate in Indonesian academic and government circles about whether the national police force should be formally separated from the rest of the armed services branches. Hartas noted that such proposals were indicative of "individualistic Western thinking" which does not understand the essential "unity and oneness of the people and the army, including the police."[89] This is also a striking example of how integralistic thinking is injected into the national discourse. Threats to ABRI's conception of Pancasila as an "integralistic ideology" in this example are not only Islamic "exclusivism," but also "Western ideas" including democracy and human rights.

Even more explicitly, the then commander of the greater Jakarta military district, Hendropriyono, has referred to both the Petition of Fifty and Abdurrahman Wahid's Forum Democracy as a "sickness."[90] Hendropriyono asks rhetorically regarding the Petition of Fifty and Forum Democracy "at what point [will they] cause widespread social unrest? If generalized social unrest is created [by Forum activities] we must slow it down. That cannot be tolerated." When he was asked what are the limits of [official] tolerance, Hendropriyono replied

> if the Petition of Fifty or Forum Democracy just want to criticize the behavior of individual bureaucrats, that is acceptable. However, if [they criticize] national policies and programs that have already been agreed upon by the government and whose goals are clear, then for the sake of national stability, unity, and integrity of the people, it [the policies] cannot be disturbed or undermined. And if the masses are incited, that cannot be tolerated.[91]

The limits of tolerance then, appear to be when speech or discourse may "incite" people to action. In the formulation by the Jakarta Commander, any participation in public discourse which may have the intention or consequence of causing "action," constitutes a threat to Pancasila.[92] Yet it was also Hendropriyono who cited one of his first duties as Jakarta Commander to protect Christian churches from acts of violence and religious intolerance. The precariousness of the "narrow path" outlined by Abdurrahman Wahid is aptly illustrated by this example of ABRI enforcement of religious tolerance while simultaneously rejecting democratization. ABRI is determined to quell what it depicts as threats to Pancasila from either liberalism or religion. Yet if Wahid, Muslim leaders, and other nationalists seek a democratic state which retains the tolerant essence of Pancasila, the challenge presented by ABRI is formidable. That is, ABRI's role in preventing SARA-based conflict and protecting minorities is appreciated by many, including Wahid and other democrats. This dilemma for secular nationalist democratizers (to retain ABRI's strong support for religious tolerance and opposition to an Islamic state while seeking to reduce ABRI's resistance to greater democratization) will be considered in the following chapter.

A fundamental difference in definition and interpretation of democracy between ABRI and others concerns the meaning of elections. The issue of voting is often problematic for both ABRI and the government. Voting, especially in parliament, is often seen by ABRI and the government as contrary to the ideals of *musyawarah* and *mufakat* [consultation and consensus] by which minorities are not humiliated by being outvoted. However, the notion of consultation and consensus as valued practices is also praised by others, including Kwik Kian Gie of the PDI and Abdurrahman Wahid. They both argue that voting should be the "last resort" to resolve differences and that it is a genuine public good to reach consensus and thereby avoid what Sukarno referred to as a democracy of "50 percent plus one."[93] According to this view, divisiveness highlighted by voting may create harmful tensions in Indonesia's heterogeneous polity. Yet, in terms of national elections, there is general recognition that voting is acceptable and should be secret. None the less, there is a sharp difference between General Try Sutrisno's description of the purpose of elections and the position adopted by Forum Democracy. Prior to the 1992 national elections, Sutrisno argued that "the election is not held to elect people who will formulate a new state principle." Elections are not to usher in change; they are to confirm the status quo. At the same time the Chairman of Forum Democracy, Abdurrahman Wahid, argued that the 1992 general elections constituted an opportunity for people to produce change.[94] Given the New Order's (and ABRI's) firmness on maintaining strict limits on permissible political behavior, it is not surprising that some members of ICMI argue that the only means of effective countervailing weight against the powerful armed forces is to politicize the masses through religion, as ICMI's Adi Sasono suggests.

Could it be that ABRI has helped destroy the political "middle" leading to unintended consequences? The successful de-politicization of politics has eliminated precisely the non-religiously based nationalist organizations that Hartas praises. For many Indonesians, Muslim or non-Muslim, there are few avenues open for effective political agitation and mobilization. NU remains a semi-independent organization that consciously opted out of the formal political structure to free itself from regime restrictions. Taking another approach entirely, though perhaps borne out of the same frustration with the "success" of de-politicization, some parts of the Islamic community chose to be coopted and used by Soeharto to create ICMI, an organization that may eventually become, in the views of some activists, an independent political organization. The notion that elections – contested by Indonesia's three legal parties, Golkar, PPP, and PDI – are not meant to produce change, encourages efforts to move outside the formal structure of New Order politics.

ABRI AND CHANGES IN PANCASILA DISCOURSE

There is a significant strain of ABRI thinking which has not yet been considered. This concerns ABRI members who cautiously advocate greater openness and democracy. Some also suggest that because ABRI is operating in a no-threat ideological environment since the adoption of the *asas tunggal*, its role in the New Order may need to change. Finally, this concluding section will analyze ways in which ABRI is using Pancasila to negatively appraise President Soeharto or regime policies.

Absence of threats?

Some ABRI thinking holds that there are actually very few manifest threats to Pancasila in the post-*asas tunggal* era. In Chapter 1, it was suggested that President Soeharto and ABRI have operated in what could be considered a "no-threat ideological environment" since 1985. Some ABRI figures argue precisely this point. For example, Hasnan Habib acknowledges that there are no longer any conspicuous threats to Pancasila. A "threat" to Pancasila, Habib argues, is constituted by anyone who has a plan or agenda to oppose Pancasila. According to Habib, this is no longer the case in Indonesia.[95]

The former Commander of KOPKAMTIB (Command to Restore Security and Order), retired General Soemitro, also argues strongly that although there once were serious threats to Pancasila, with the complete destruction of the PKI, this is no longer the case. Instead, Soemitro points out that the only contemporary threats to Pancasila are those "mistakes made by the government."[96] Although retired senior officers like Soemitro feel less constrained to speak openly than younger, active duty officers, there is an emergence of shared thinking that actual threats to Pancasila are not communism or Islamic fundamentalism but contravention by the government itself.

Retired Lieutenant General Habib and retired Brigadier General Sudibyo both argue that in the post-*asas tunggal* era Islam should no longer be "*dimusuhi*" [made an enemy]. In the era before *asas tunggal* the government often sought Islamic extremism behind any security disturbances. This is no longer the case, Sudibyo and Habib argue. Furthermore, Sudibyo explains that Islam is no longer singled out because ABRI is more sophisticated and more nuanced in the way it perceives threats. Former ABRI Commander Try Sutrisno says that perceptions of Islam as a threat are "clearly wrong."[97] Moreover, both Hasnan Habib and Sudibyo say that Soeharto's Islamic religiosity has had an effect in changing regime, including ABRI, attitudes towards Islam.[98] Major General (retired) Soebiyakto, former Governor of Lemhanas, also agrees that the major change in recent years is that "fundamentalism" is no longer a problem.[99] On the other hand, Soemitro has said that while the major change since the 1980s is that "everyone accepts Pancasila," it is partly because if they do not, they must face ABRI which defends the Pancasila based on *Sapta Marga*. Therefore, Soemitro notes, because one cannot oppose ABRI people have reappraised their positions on Pancasila.[100]

ABRI advocates of "openness"

Much more significant than selected comments by retired generals on the diminution of traditional threats to Pancasila are the actions and public commentary by other ABRI figures. The most striking development in this regard is the emergence in 1989 and 1990 of a group of members from the ABRI faction in the DPR who became vocal proponents of "*keterbukaan*" [openness]. Why, at the same time senior ABRI commanders such as Try Sutrisno, Edy Sudrajat, and Harsudiyono Hartas continue to issue strong and frequent reminders of persistent threats to Pancasila, including threats from "liberalism" and Western-style democracy, do other ABRI officers speak openly of the need for greater democratization? "Openness" was also strongly advocated by several Golkar members of the DPR.

The "openness" debate was partly spurred on by retired General Soemitro who, in 1989, called for democratic culture to be fostered, particularly in the DPR. Soemitro said that proper implementation of Pancasila and the Constitution means that the DPR/MPR should function as a representative institution, with the right to initiate legislation and with government being accountable to the peoples' representatives. Additionally, Soemitro called for more than one candidate for the Presidency and Vice Presidency and a more independent political party system.[101] Many of these points were taken up by ABRI faction members in the DPR. Most prominently associated with them were the Speaker of the House, retired Lieutenant General Kharis Suhud, Police Brigadier General (at the time a Colonel) Roekmini, Major General Saiful Sulun, and Major General Samsuddin.[102]

President Soeharto's description of Pancasila as an "open ideology" has been appropriated by some officers to legitimate their advocacy of "openness" in the DPR. It was noted in the preceding chapter how some Muslim intellectuals argued that Soeharto's reference to Pancasila as an open ideology provided a "loophole" to advance Islamic political interests. In his August 1990 Independence Day Address President Soeharto reiterated his interpretation of Pancasila as an "open ideology." Two ABRI DPR faction members have used Soeharto's remarks and Pancasila language to legitimize their own participation in the DPR's "openness" debates. For example, Major General Samsuddin argued that "what is clear, as the President said on August 16, is that we must cultivate differences of opinion. If we can't do that it means we don't understand Pancasila."[103] Even more explicitly, Brigadier General Roekmini said that she and her colleagues in the DPR did not initiate the "openness" idea, but rather it was Soeharto himself. Roekmini referred approvingly to an address by Soeharto in which he described Pancasila as an open ideology.[104]

Harold Crouch argues that ABRI-promoted "openness" has been used by military leaders as "a weapon to undermine Soeharto."[105] It appears that because prominent supporters of "openness" and increased democratization in the ABRI faction in the DPR were not reappointed, that arguments in favor of less democratic advocacy (regardless of the nature of ABRI disagreements with Soeharto) have prevailed. Yet, what is clear is that the discourse is more porous than ever, that even for a disciplined, relatively unified institution such as ABRI, the Pancasila message is not always uniform. This is because threats and dangers to a "de-confessionalized" Pancasila state are no longer obvious. This does not mean that ABRI is by any means less supportive of the basic structure of the state built by the New Order. While calling for democratization and openness, retired General Soemitro still firmly attributes national prosperity and stability to the implementation of the de-politicization strategies which de-linked political party activity from "primordial" (religious, racial, ethnic) affiliations.[106] It is the very success of the "Pancasila-ization" of politics that allows a widening of the discourse, even within ABRI circles.

The military's view of the government's June 1994 closure of *Tempo*, *Editor*, and *Detik* illustrates the limits of military support for openness. For example, the armed forces reportedly encouraged the reporting of internal government opposition to Habibie's role in the purchase of ex-East German warships.[107] Some officers, including National Human Rights Commission member, retired Brigadier General Roekmini, lamented the closures as a setback to gradual movement towards democratization in Indonesia. Roekmini stresses that ABRI was anxious to show that the armed forces opposed the press bannings and were, instead, "on the side of the people."[108] Despite these views, regular army troops, along with the police, physically attacked protestors who were demonstrating against the bannings in Jakarta on June 27 and August 4. Lieutenant General Mantiri, the Chief of General Staff, argued that it was ABRI's duty to prevent destabilizing public demonstrations regardless of their purpose. Moreover, Mantiri argued that although the government should be introspective and correct its own shortcomings, others must not be allowed to oppose the government.[109] Therefore, regardless of ABRI's satisfaction at seeing Habibie blamed for the press bannings, military perceptions of the destabilizing potential of mass demonstrations convinced ABRI to crack down on public expressions of opposition to the press closures.

Appropriation of Pancasila

There are indications that some in ABRI are using Pancasila to negatively appraise the regime, or Soeharto himself. For example, Hartas and Abdul Kadir Besar both imply that the regime is to be faulted for not being integralistic enough. Others, including Hartas, stress the need for ABRI to correct deviations in Pancasila. For example, Hartas notes that his superiors must be willing to be corrected – that is their duty, based on the political culture inherent in integralism.[110]

Retired General Soemitro also suggests that there is a problem with the use of Pancasila in the New Order today. He argues that it should be interpreted by all parties and groups. Soemitro praises Abdurrahman Wahid's Forum Democracy as a "medium for all members, representatives, political groupings, even [individuals] from the government to discuss the interpretation of Pancasila." Soemitro adds that "as it [the interpretation of Pancasila] is now it is dominated by the government, . . . whoever is in power. It's not sound."[111] Cautious suggestions for corrections to the implementation of Pancasila often involve discussion of the wide "social gap" (income disparities) in Indonesia today. For example, former Governor of the National Defense Institute (Lemhanas), Soebiyakto, identified capitalism as an ideological threat.[112] Speaking on the social gap, former Defense Minister Benny Moerdani has argued that huge differences between rich and poor constitute a contravention of Pancasila's humanitarianism.[113] Many officers also note that one of their greatest worries is that income inequality and differential levels of prosperity in different parts of the country will be exploited through appeals to religion. Officers seem aware that "Islamic security threats" in recent years are not so much caused initially by religion *per se*, but instead by inequitable social and economic conditions. For example, the allegedly Islamic-inspired security disturbances in Lampung and in Aceh are actually outgrowths of local perceptions of economic discrimination or social inequalities associated with uneven distribution of the benefits of development. In Lampung, land tenure was the base cause of the disputes while in Aceh, perceptions that the local people were not the primary beneficiaries of massive petro-chemical and gas projects, played a role in stimulating unrest. Roeslan Abdulgani (former head of the Presidential Pancasila Advisory Team) argues that the most dangerous threats to Pancasila – and to the nation – are gross inequalities in the development process which breed social discord and resentment and are then exploited by appeals to religion, race, ethnicity, and class.[114]

In addition to the "openness" debate as a change in the post-*asas tunggal* era, there has been a specific shift in ABRI political behavior, explicitly justified by the acceptance of Pancasila in recent years. Beginning with the general elections in 1987, ABRI sought to present itself as "above" party politics and not necessarily the automatic backer of Golkar, the government party.[115] In a revealing interview with *Tempo* magazine, Lieutenant General Hartas explained the relevance for ABRI of changes in society since *asas tunggal.* He was asked how it could be, given ABRI's consistent support for Golkar in national elections from 1971 to 1982, that beginning in 1987 ABRI would appear to somewhat distance itself from the government party.[116] Hartas responded that up to the mid-1980s the nation still had to deal with the ideological enemies of Pancasila. But now, Hartas argued, "everyone accepts Pancasila as their basis and all socio-political forces have fulfilled the conditions [of having Pancasila as their sole principle]." Although it is true that ABRI created Golkar, according to Hartas, ABRI should not limit itself to endorsing just one political party. ABRI's task, Hartas said, is to protect all socio-political organizations because all of them are Pancasila-ist. Hartas added that threats to Pancasila now arise from specific individuals in society and not necessarily whole political organizations (although this view contrasts with ABRI views of ICMI).[117] Similarly, the then Assistant Chief of Staff for ABRI's social and political affairs, Major General Suryadi Surdirja, acknowledges that one of the major successes of political development in the New Order is the acceptance of Pancasila and *asas tunggal* by political organizations.[118] Thus, the discourse has changed – all accept Pancasila – and this has the political implication of allowing ABRI to argue that it treats all political parties equally and avoids sole sponsorship of Golkar. It must be acknowledged that ABRI's stance in this regard is intimately connected to its tense relationship with Soeharto. In the 1980s Soeharto demonstrated his ability to firmly control Golkar, especially in singlehandedly naming its leadership in 1987. Even though in mid-1993 Minister of Defense, General Edy Sudrajat, stated that Golkar "must be led by a member of the ABRI family," Soeharto succeeded in having his civilian Minister of Information, Harmoko, become the new Chairman of Golkar in October 1993. Moreover, Soeharto designated much power in the Golkar proceedings to Minister Habibie. Officers often cited their "loss" of the Golkar chairmanship as further evidence of the poor relationship between Soeharto and the armed forces.

ABRI's contemporary Pancasila discourse can be summarized by recognizing what is new in its participation in debate concerning Pancasila and what remains the same in the post-*asas tunggal* period. First, integralistic thinking has become a more frequent referent for ABRI leaders. Pancasila is often interpreted as an integralistic ideology in which the military's socio-political functions are legitimized not merely on the basis of *Sapta Marga*, *dwifungsi*, or even the Constitution, but on the deeply embedded political culture of Indonesia. Second, ICMI's appearance on the national political stage is cause for deep concern among many in ABRI. ICMI is identified as potentially incompatible with the religious tolerance of the "de-confessionalized" and de-politicized Pancasila democracy. Although there is appreciation of the improved relationship between Islam and the government and recognition of Soeharto's strategy to coopt remaining Muslim intellectuals and politicians in a government-controlled and thereby "safe" organization, there is concern that the process of cooptation has "gone too far." The presence of Habibie as the General Chairman of ICMI, as well as the prominent activities of other well-known Islamic intellectuals and activists in ICMI, clearly infuriates many ABRI officers and has polarized discourse. Could it then be considered something of a strategic mistake for ICMI activists to rely so heavily on Habibie?[119] This question will be reconsidered in the Conclusion. Certainly, there is agreement between Wahid, ABRI, and even ICMI activists that their heavy reliance on Habibie for protection is a high-risk strategy.

While ICMI members are ready to blame ABRI, especially retired non-Muslim generals such as Benny Moerdani, for Muslims' political frustrations in the New Order, ABRI officers often identify Habibie (especially in his capacity as head of ICMI) as the cause of ABRI's political frustrations and worries over the country's political direction. An ABRI perception of ICMI as supportive of a strategy of democratization (or, Islamization) through de-militarization under the protection of Habibie and Soeharto weakens ICMI's ability to successfully institutionalize itself. This is both because of widespread ABRI opposition to this strategy and because it further problematizes the Soeharto–ABRI relationship. Moreover, ABRI officers perceive that Soeharto's sponsorship of ICMI has been done to "punish" ABRI.[120]

Although NU is viewed as the most legitimate mass-Islamic organization, Abdurrahman Wahid's leadership of Forum Democracy also troubles ABRI. Entrenched ABRI suspicions of liberalism and liberal democracy tend to neutralize the nationalist credentials that Wahid believes keep him in good standing with ABRI. There is, however, significant overlap in the desire from both Wahid and ABRI to maintain the process of ensuring that politics in Indonesia does not return to religiously based political mobilization.[121] Finally, the military's relationship with Soeharto is reflected in ABRI Pancasila discourse, notably the appropriation of Soeharto's "open ideology" terminology by ABRI DPR faction members and the wariness of officers over Soeharto's manipulation of Islam through ICMI for his own personal political needs.

A number of elements of ABRI's Pancasila discourse remain unchanged, however. These include ABRI's institutional obsession with enforcing avoidance of SARA issues (with notable exceptions, however, such as the military manipulation of the North Sumatra Batak Church). This fixation interlocks with the anxieties of Abdurrahman Wahid, secular nationalists, and religious minorities. Additionally, ABRI's commitment to the maintenance of Indonesia as a unified state is intimately linked to Pancasila and its own *dwifungsi*. Finally, there is the persistence of perceptions of an ideological threat from Islam despite a more tolerant view of Islam in general. Other Indonesians, however, notably Muslim intellectuals (including both Wahid and many in ICMI), worry that ABRI has not completely abandoned its previously exaggerated suspicions of Islam. Some members of the civilian elite worry that ABRI may again seek to depict an "Islamic threat" in order to continue justification of ABRI's role as the defender of Pancasila and the state from threats on the "extreme right."

Chapter 5 will take into account a diverse range of "secular nationalist" voices in the Pancasila discourse. It will consider proponents of democratization and religious minorities, as well as a number of voices in the bureaucracy. Many issues discussed in the present chapter on ABRI will be revisited, particularly concerning the debate between advocates of democracy and ABRI.

Chapter 5

Secular nationalists

> Every nation has its limits; we have a limited openness, and the limits are not communism and not an Islamic state. And Pancasila is the Indonesian expression of those limits.
>
> Y.B. Mangunwijaya[1]

> I want to build a civil society. But you cannot unify the country based on religion. It must be based on sameness of citizenship, regardless of religion.
>
> Adnan Buyung Nasution[2]

The Indonesians considered here as "secular nationalists" share a number of broad ideas about politics. Most advocate greater democratization and seek to preserve a religiously tolerant Pancasila as the basis of the state. At the most general level secular nationalists consider religion and other "primordial" affiliations an inappropriate means for channelling political aspirations. Secular nationalists contend that all Indonesian citizens should be treated equally by the government. Abdurrahman Wahid argues that "the idea of secularism is the impartiality of the state *vis-à-vis* its citizens."[3] The rule of law should apply equally to all Indonesians, regardless of religion or ethnicity. Secular nationalists argue that religious tolerance and equality of citizenship are tightly linked to the preservation of Indonesian national unity.

Democratization and political openness also concern some secular nationalists. Secular nationalists not only reject religious politics, they also oppose an undemocratic role for ABRI in government. While secular nationalists may appreciate ABRI's secular view of politics, they reject its integralistic interpretation of Pancasila which legitimizes a permanent political military role. They also disagree with ABRI's use of Pancasila to justify denial of certain human rights in the name of "national stability" and security.

Secular nationalists come from a broad range of backgrounds. They include civilians, Muslim intellectuals, democracy advocates, and human rights activists, as well as leading figures from Indonesia's religious and ethnic minorities who seek a secular national political system. Members of the political parties, particularly from PDI and Golkar, as well as a number of government bureaucrats, also enunciate a secular nationalist viewpoint.

This chapter will highlight a key problem for secular nationalists. Many perceive their political agenda in terms similar to those expressed by Abdurrahman Wahid's "narrow path." Secular nationalists seek greater democratization and reduced military political dominance, while avoiding Islamization of government. Yet the way to navigate this narrow path constitutes an acute dilemma. Some secular nationalists argue that despite ABRI's authoritarianism and paternalistic political behavior, it still stands as the only effective guarantor of national unity and religious and ethnic rights.

Pancasila is also appropriated by secular nationalists to legitimize political positions and criticize government policies. Among several examples of Pancasila "appropriation" to be analyzed, the use of Pancasila by the Catholic Bishop of East Timor, Carlos Belo, is of particular interest. The significance of Belo's participation in political discourse is his ability to appropriate official ideology to sharply criticize government policy.

Many secular nationalists are associated with Forum Democracy, under the leadership of Abdurrahman Wahid. Forum Democracy has played a leading role in contemporary discourse, at times acting to counter ICMI. The Forum also provokes ABRI's concern that it advocates democratic ideas incompatible with the government's conception of "Pancasila democracy."[4]

FORUM DEMOCRACY

Forum Demokrasi was established in March 1991 by a group of about forty-five prominent intellectuals.[5] The organization is not incorporated as a formal association, but simply as a "discussion" or "working group" under the chairmanship of Abdurrahman Wahid. Although many well-known and respected intellectuals from various religious, academic, and political backgrounds are associated with the Forum, Wahid tends to have a dominant voice, much as he does with NU. The daily *Pelita* has argued that it is precisely because of Wahid's leading role in Forum Democracy that it is controversial. *Pelita* aptly observes that the appearance of the Forum is a significant political development precisely because Abdurrahman Wahid is its leading voice: "Wahid is a political figure that must be accounted for."[6] Marsillam Simanjuntak, a leading democracy activist, has said that it was a conscious decision of the Forum to choose Wahid as chairman in order to draw as much attention as possible to the association and to lend it credibility.[7] An examination of the reasons for the establishment of Democracy Forum will illustrate the political and ideological implications of the group's secular nationalist perspective.

Purposes and objectives of Forum Democracy

In a press conference called to announce the creation of Forum Democracy, Wahid cited the rise of "sectarianism" in Indonesia as the primary concern of the group. Democracy could not develop in Indonesia in a climate of increasing religious and ethnic hostility. Such tension, Wahid argues, is having a divisive impact on the nation. There are multiple and interconnected purposes of Forum Democracy, according to Wahid and its supporters. First, its establishment was provoked by a perception of dangerous examples of religious and ethnic intolerance. The most troubling case for those associated with the Forum was the "*Monitor* Affair" in October 1990 (see Chapter 3). The *Monitor* case, argued Wahid, demonstrates that some groups in society are willing to manipulate religious issues in order to prioritize their own needs – a development that he says is damaging to democratization efforts.[8]

The establishment of ICMI in December 1990 also prompted the formation of Forum Democracy. Wahid has repeatedly indicated that he believes ICMI is a prime example of political exploitation of religion which prioritizes "exclusive," narrow Muslim group interests over national concerns. According to Wahid, by promoting the interests of Islam, ICMI promotes an undemocratic vision of Indonesia. In a published interview, Wahid argued that ICMI will "alienate non-Muslims" and nominal Muslims, and thereby

> aggravate the already strong divisions and misunderstandings in our society between different religious, ethnic and cultural groups, especially if Islam is seen to be trying to manipulate the government just for its own benefit.[9]

However, when asked publicly if it is his intention for the Forum to offset or directly challenge ICMI, Wahid demurred. For example, in an interview with the daily *Suara Karya*, Wahid was asked if the Forum was intended as a "challenger" to ICMI. Wahid responded, "No, there is no connection with ICMI at all." Wahid then noted that his concerns for democracy and worries about sectarianism are long-standing and existed prior to ICMI's creation. Wahid also explained his "shock" at the undemocratic and sectarian attitudes expressed by Muslim intellectuals "as individuals, not as ICMI members" who supported the banning of *Monitor*.[10] Yet it is precisely these "individual intellectuals" who joined ICMI two months after the "*Monitor* Affair."

Wahid says that because of rising sectarianism in Indonesia, a purpose of the Forum is to encourage a "return to the commitment to national unity." For Wahid, the Forum "constitutes a vehicle for pushing a national integrative process through the elimination of sectarian-oriented groups." Wahid also argues that the Forum exhibits a genuine Pancasila-ist and nationalist orientation. Wahid repeatedly emphasizes that Forum Democracy is supportive of Pancasila so there is no way he can be accused of promoting values incompatible with the state ideology or the Constitution.[11] In this respect, Wahid combines both his desire to encourage democratization with his goal of promoting a secular and religiously tolerant society.

Although not mentioned when he announced the creation of the Forum, Wahid has accused members of the Islamic movement, especially those associated with ICMI, of exaggerating the *Monitor* Affair in order to depict Islam as under siege from Christians. This approach, according to Wahid, allows Muslim activists to justify their attempts to establish an Islamic society. Moreover, Wahid argues that the behavior of leading members of the Islamic community regarding the banning of *Monitor* reflects attitudes incompatible with democracy and its attendant, inseparable freedoms, including the freedom of speech.[12]

Additionally, Wahid laments what he argues is government complicity in the rise of sectarianism and the manipulation of racial and religious issues for short-term political gain. Although he added,

> I am convinced that Indonesia's silent majority is pluralistic in attitude and tolerant of diversity. It's the rigidity of government policy which leads to repression [of opinion] and it is repression which causes sectarianism.[13]

Wahid and other secular nationalists and democracy advocates such as Buyung Nasution contend that because people find it difficult effectively to participate in the restrictive New Order political system, they often turn to religious and ethnic issues to mobilize politically.[14] One leading Muslim intellectual supportive of secular democratization argues that because some Muslims have not found effective avenues for political expression through the parties and existing structure, they use religious and racial issues for political purposes. They are simply "taking the only available road" for political expression in the New Order.[15] A well-known non-Muslim intellectual worries that the success of New Order "de-politicization" has "forced politics into the mosque and the church where there is still some autonomy from government."[16] Wahid fears that the Chinese Indonesians may become targets of Muslims' frustrations with the New Order's authoritarianism.[17]

Government reaction to Forum Democracy

Immediately after the appearance of Forum Democracy, government ministers and senior ABRI officers issued highly critical statements. Admiral (retired) Sudomo, Senior Coordinating Minister for Political and Security Affairs in 1991, questioned the need for the Forum. Sudomo said that Indonesia is already a "Pancasila democracy" and therefore has no need for Forum Democracy. Both Sudomo and the ABRI spokesman at the time, Brigadier General Nurhadi, were disturbed by the establishment of the Forum which implied genuine democracy had not yet been achieved in Indonesia. This is a consistent ABRI complaint against democracy advocates. For example, in July 1994 the deputy head of social and political affairs for ABRI stated that democratic critics of the government speak "as if there is not democracy at all in Indonesia."[18]

An editorial in *Pelita* illustrated the reasons for the government's concern. *Pelita* argued that although Indonesia had successfully created a "formal" democratic system, it did not function as a true democracy.[19] Nurhadi submits that a potential problem with the Forum is that it may contribute to the process of creating narrow groupings – a process that Wahid says the Forum acts against. Moreover, Nurhadi worries that Forum Democracy will try to change the views of the masses and therefore contravene the "floating mass" concept in which masses are to remain depoliticized.[20] As shown in Chapter 4, ABRI is suspicious of any political developments or personalities that may potentially influence ordinary people. One of the original participants in the Forum, Arief Budiman, a well-known scholar and government critic at Satya Wacana University in Central Java, responds that the group is not an activist political organization. Its purpose, according to Budiman, is to inculcate a democratic spirit and knowledge among the people.[21]

In response to ABRI and government suspicions, Wahid underscored several points. First, he argues that Forum Democracy is not a mass-based organization and that it will not become a political party. The Forum, he adds, will also not become a political "pressure group." One year after the founding of Forum Democracy, Wahid emphasized that it had only expressed "hopes and wishes [for democratization] and nothing more than that. There have been no demonstrations, no shouting."[22] Wahid promised that the Forum would never be anything more than a refuge for "contemplative and reflective thought," and unlike ICMI, it would not be activist and take up specific political issues. Forum Democracy, which has limited itself to a general concern for democracy, would also be different from the Petition of Fifty which has advocated particular political issues (often anti-Soeharto).[23]

The government reaction to the establishment of the Forum is illustrative of contemporary discourse in several ways. First, it indicates an almost instantaneous suspicion that new organizations will disturb national stability and incite the masses. As shown in Chapter 4 on the armed forces, military obsession with maintenance of stability *qua* stability is foremost in ABRI thinking. Moreover, ABRI officials are particularly wary of Wahid because he combines extraordinary charisma, intelligence, and connection to a popular mass following in NU which remains outside the complete influence of the New Order. Wahid was careful to emphasize in his dialogue with government and military authorities following the announcement of the Forum's establishment that his role as head of the Forum was completely divorced from his role as head of NU. Therefore, he argued, there is no mass-base connection to society at large.[24]

The challenge posed by Forum Democracy

Although the initial concern of the Forum was that rising sectarianism, religious intolerance, and manipulation of religion for political ends created major obstacles for democratization in Indonesia, other issues were also frequently mentioned. Moreover, the Forum came under increasingly conspicuous surveillance and suspicion by authorities and security forces. In 1992 the Forum's meetings were banned or broken up by police, and official warnings were given to the Forum and Abdurrahman Wahid in the months prior to the general elections in June 1992. The legal basis for the "banning" of Forum meetings was always explained by police authorities as a lack of proper permits needed for large gatherings.[25]

There were two major reasons for heightened official concern in 1992 over the Forum's activities, especially regarding its leadership by Wahid. First, prior to all general elections in the New Order there has always been increased government desire to maintain security and stability. After all, as Try Sutrisno has explained, the general elections are not meant to produce change.[26] Yet the Forum and Wahid personally advocated precisely that – change. For the New Order, political change is automatically associated with chaos and instability.

Of particular concern to the Forum is the issue of presidential succession. For some participants in Forum Democracy, the issue of presidential succession is central to consideration of the prospects for democratization in Indonesia. For example, Marsillam Simanjuntak asks "is democratization possible without dealing first with succession as a problem?"[27] In February 1992 the Forum issued a statement which laid out the issues with which it was most concerned. Two points in the six-point statement are noteworthy. In addition to reiterating its commitment to democracy, the Forum noted its concern that people in "dominant positions resorted to violence to resolve problems." The Forum also stated that it "views the succession issue as an important matter which is inextricably linked to the democratization process." The Forum added that it was prepared to give "special attention" to the problem of succession as one of its "short-term programs."[28]

Second, whereas ICMI, according to Amien Rais, clearly opted for a strategy that sought the continuance of President Soeharto in office (so that he and Habibie would be able to continue their protection and sponsorship of ICMI), Forum Democracy implied that it wanted change.[29] The Forum never called for President Soeharto not to seek another five-year term. However, as shown in Chapter 2 regarding *Nahdlatul Ulama*, the failure to endorse Soeharto, or mere silence on the issue of his continuance in office, was construed by the President's supporters as evidence of disloyalty.

Shortly after the Forum's February Statement, senior officials and Lieutenant General Harsudiyono Hartas openly questioned the group's intentions. Hartas submitted that Forum Democracy was in contravention of Pancasila. Hartas argued that the statements issued by the Forum "confused the public" and often contradicted fundamental tenets of the 1945 Constitution and Pancasila. Hartas stressed that there would be no prohibition of the Forum as long as its actions did not cause unrest and instability. Hartas argued that supporters of the Forum acted as if "they were still affiliated with the previous era and this can be seen from their statements on justice, human rights, and democracy." Such language refers to the government's contention that the period of liberal democracy in the 1950s was incompatible with Pancasila and Indonesian political culture. Hartas urged the Forum not to cause "agitation." Moreover, Hartas warned that Forum Democracy should avoid any effort to seek fundamental change. He also noted that the Forum could only exist "if its activities are within the proper boundaries, and their intention is not to change the existing system."[30] The language Hartas used to delegitimize the Forum is remarkably similar to the way Air Vice Marshal Teddy Rusdy described ICMI as possibly "out of bounds of Pancasila."[31] Similarly, the Jakarta ABRI commander, Hendropriyono, also cautioned Forum Democracy not to challenge existing government policies or programs.[32]

Wahid directly responded to Hartas' suggestion that the Forum contradicts Pancasila and the Constitution. Wahid challenged Hartas to show him which article of the Constitution or which principle of Pancasila had been contravened. "Show me which ones [principles that are contradicted by the Forum]. I ask for proof," demanded Wahid of Hartas.[33] Hartas' warnings to the Forum and Wahid came shortly after two Forum meetings were banned by police, one in February and the other in April 1992. The April 20 meeting was intended by the Forum as a *Halal bi Halal* [traditional gathering to mark the end of the Islamic fasting month]. In addition to most Forum supporters, other prominent national figures were present at the gathering including the Chairman of the PDI at that time, Soerjadi, and retired General Soemitro. No official reasons were ever given for the banning other than the Forum's failure to possess proper permits for such gatherings. The banning elicited strong criticism from members of the DPR, including leading Golkar and PPP figures. Oka Mahendra of Golkar asked, "How can the police stop a traditional Islamic gathering on the basis of security reasons?"[34] Barely a week later Wahid was prevented from addressing a meeting of the PPP in Surabaya and the Coordinating Minister for Political and Security Affairs, Sudomo, reported that President Soeharto asked him to "monitor" Democracy Forum.[35]

It was difficult for authorities to portray Wahid's and the Forum's activities as "out of bounds" and contrary to Pancasila. Not only did Wahid challenge such accusations, he asserted that the Forum is, in fact, most "Pancasila-ist" and that democracy is an Indonesian concept. Attempts to restrict its interpretation in a non-liberal fashion are not justified by any provisions of the Constitution or Pancasila.[36] *Kompas* editorialized that Wahid and Forum Democracy were indeed based on Pancasila and the Constitution.[37] Citing the government's contention that Pancasila should be considered an "open ideology," the *Kompas* editorial saw it as entirely appropriate that non-governmental groups such as the Forum sought to promote democratization. Just as it was extremely difficult for the government to prohibit NU's Rapat Akbar in March 1992 because its purpose was to express loyalty to Pancasila and the Constitution, so too was it possible for Wahid, *Kompas*, General Soemitro, and others to support the Forum's activities as genuinely "Pancasila-ist."

Wahid and Forum Democracy are accused of advocating "liberal" ideas, such as the need for electoral choice through fair and effective elections. Wahid argues that such accusations ignore the original intent and meaning of Pancasila. It was, and remains, a "political compromise between democrats, supporters of a theocratic state, and nationalists." Pancasila, according to Wahid, allows all Indonesians to "come along together in a nationalist, unified state." It is not Pancasila *per se* that guarantees democracy. Pancasila stipulates a tolerant society upon which a democratic polity can exist. Wahid argues that it is the body of the Constitution which is the democratic document, and which stipulates that voting is permissible and allows for a measure of free speech and human rights.[38] Wahid argues that when Pancasila is used by the authorities to justify an undemocratic system or to attack Forum Democracy, then it is the regime "that is cheating on Pancasila."[39]

There was also intense pressure from the government on Wahid to quit Forum Democracy. Wahid relates that he was told by one of Soeharto's allies that his democratizing activities put him in opposition to Soeharto and that this constituted reneging on a commitment he made not to develop conflict with the President. Wahid argues that he was told he could reduce the friction either by endorsing Soeharto for another term or by leaving the Forum. Wahid said that he would do neither and instead threatened to quit NU. In fact, Wahid argues that if forced to make a choice between the democratization movement and the Islamic movement, "my choice is clear, I will leave the Islamic movement."[40]

Within weeks after the formation of Forum Democracy debate opened between ICMI and Wahid over his role as head of the Forum. The ICMI–Forum exchange illustrates fundamentally different perspectives on the relationship between government and Islam. For example, Adi Sasono, who sits on the editorial board of the daily *Republika* and is a leading ICMI member, replied to Wahid's argument that the rise of sectarianism demanded better inculcation of democratic values. Wahid argued that sectarian problems, such as the *Monitor* case, differentiate between Indonesians on the basis of religion and damage the prospects for democracy. On the contrary, Sasono argued, sectarianism does not constitute a major national issue in relation to democratization. Sasono, in an interview with *Pelita*, argued that because Indonesian citizens are also members of the global *umat*, it was natural and proper for the government to serve the religious interests of its citizens. The real obstacles to democratization, contended Sasono, were economic and educational inequalities, particularly the concentration of economic power in certain groups.[41]

NU, Forum Democracy and Wahid's secular democratic vision

Before we move to consideration of several examples of how Pancasila and official ideology have been appropriated by secular nationalists, it is necessary to note that there is a distinction between the way Wahid uses Pancasila as leader of NU compared to the way he uses it as leader the nation's democratization movement. The NU strategy envisioned by Wahid is primarily one of "de-confessionalization" – to prevent the re-occurrence of disintegrative politics based on religion. It is also to ensure that Indonesian Islam is divorced from petty political maneuvering that may damage the interests of the *umat*. Such maneuvering could create suspicions that Muslims are not fully committed to Pancasila and the state. The use of Pancasila in the Rapat Akbar illustrates this approach and attempts to establish NU as a Pancasila-ist organization *par excellence*.

The Forum strategy, on the other hand, places much more emphasis on promoting democracy but with a strong concern for a religiously tolerant society as a condition for democracy. In Wahid's mind the relationship between a tolerant "Indonesianized" Islam and a healthy democratic polity is inseparable. However, for political purposes, he cannot emphasize that he uses his mass base in NU as a force for democratic change, particularly when such change is automatically viewed by the authorities as a threat to the existing Pancasila democracy.

In his capacity as leader of Forum Democracy and as a politically secular nationalist, Wahid goes far beyond his NU message that Pancasila is a necessary precondition for both a democratic society and the healthy position of all religions in Indonesia. Wahid argues that the politically secular basis of society is established with adherence to Pancasila:

> If you reject primordialism and accept Pancasila, you must also eventually accept political liberalism. Because primordialism means inequality, that only people from certain origins will be equal. This mitigates against secular nationalism, including the philosophy of ABRI."[42]

Wahid adds, however, that even though the logic of liberalism – treating citizens equally before law – is contained in Pancasila, adherence to the ideology's tolerance is not enough for democracy. "If you want to achieve political democracy you need more than Pancasila," according to Wahid. Wahid elaborates that democratic secular nationalists seek three basic conditions that will allow the development of genuine democracy in Indonesia. First, there must be a separation of the state and civil domains. Wahid argues this has not happened in the New Order, which has subscribed to an ABRI-derived integralistic vision of the organic totality of the state. Second, there must be a separation between civil society and government. According to Wahid, this separation entails the autonomy of civil society and will necessitate basic freedoms of expression, association, and movement. Finally, Wahid argues that a separation of powers *within* government is essential for creating a true democracy. There must be an internal government system of checks and balances. Wahid argues that New Order politics are characterized by a military-derived "integralistic secularism." That is, the New Order is politically secular, but in an undemocratic way that fails to distinguish between either state or civil domains. Democratic secularism, however, requires separation of governmental powers and a clear distinction between state and civil society. However, for Wahid and other secular nationalists, there is at least a shared agreement with ABRI that Indonesia should be a secular society. Wahid contends that secularism is the first step towards a democratic society and that it could be established independent of – or at least prior to – genuine political democracy.[43]

OTHER DEMOCRATIZERS

Three additional examples of the secular nationalist perspective are provided by Adnan Buyung Nasution, T. Mulya Lubis, and Marsillam Simanjuntak.[44] Nasution is perhaps the most famous Indonesian human rights lawyer. He is the founder of one of the first non-governmental organizations dedicated to human rights and democracy, the *Lembaga Bantuan Hukum Indonesia* [Indonesian Legal Aid Institute], known as LBH. Nasution is also a co-founder of the American journal *Human Rights Quarterly*. T. Mulya Lubis, a prominent lawyer and democracy advocate, followed him as director of LBH and now heads a human rights foundation in Jakarta. Marsillam Simanjuntak, a medical doctor, was a student activist in 1966 and now devotes his energies to democracy and legal issues. All three stress that the rule of law in Indonesia should apply equally to all citizens.

Nasution's published doctoral dissertation, *The Aspiration for Constitutional Government in Indonesia*, exemplifies part of the secular nationalist perspective. In particular, Nasution argues that liberal democracy did not fail in the 1950s because it was incompatible with Indonesian political culture, but because it was made to fail by the arbitrary dissolution of the Konstituante by General A.H. Nasution and Sukarno. What matters most for Buyung Nasution, Mulya Lubis, and Marsillam is the rule of law. Issues should not be evaluated according to their compatibility with Pancasila, but on the basis of their constitutionality. All three support increased democratization and Forum Democracy.

Buyung Nasution, Marsillam and Mulya Lubis also express anxiety about ICMI. Nasution argues that "you cannot unify the country based on religion."[45] Nasution's argument on the role of religion in Indonesia is the opposite of ICMI founder Imaduddin's argument that only Islam can be the integrative basis of Indonesia.[46] To ensure national unity and democratic politics, the only applicable criterion should be "sameness of citizenship," argues Nasution. Yet Nasution's advocacy of the rule of law, despite his rejection of Islamic politics, has earned him the enmity of the armed forces. In early 1993 when Lieutenant General Hartas spoke of a "virus" of Western-educated liberals using the cover of democracy, human rights, and the environment to advocate change, Hartas was in part referring to Nasution.[47] Similarly, another high-ranking general has referred to Buyung Nasution as a "traitor" to Pancasila for his advocacy of human rights and democracy.[48] Moreover, despite Wahid's contention that ABRI's secular nationalism provides some common ground between civilian democrats and the military, senior officers none the less remain deeply hostile to democratizing ideas advocated by Wahid, Nasution, and others.

Even though Nasution and ABRI are at odds over democracy and human rights, Nasution nevertheless argues that ABRI governance is at least somewhat "more rational" than would be the case in an Islamic state. Although both are undesirable, a fundamentalist religious state would be a greater obstacle to democracy than a military-dominated state in Nasution's and

Wahid's view.[49] However, for secular nationalist democrats like Buyung Nasution, the armed forces often present a far more immediate concern than Islamic politicking. For example, in July 1994 police entered the LBH headquarters in Jakarta and arrested forty-one students who were holding a peaceful demonstration, including a hunger strike to protest at the government's banning of *Tempo*, *Editor*, and *Detik*.[50]

Despite the immediate setbacks to democratization directly experienced by LBH, Nasution argues that ICMI also weakens the democratic process. According to Nasution, by using the "symbols of religion" to establish Islamic solidarity, ICMI succeeds in unwittingly weakening the prospects for democratization. Why? Because, Nasution argues, non-Muslims as well as politically secular Muslims may choose to support ABRI if they perceive that ICMI – or any other group – appeals to religion as their organizing base. Mulya Lubis too, argues that ICMI "revives a narrow vision of society" and as such is damaging the prospects for democracy.[51] However, Nasution strongly warns that supporters of secular democratization should not exaggerate threats from "primordialism":

> We must have faith in the rationality of the Indonesian people. All those enemies – the enemies of primordialism and SARA, should not serve to scare us into legitimizing authoritarian rule in Indonesia. Yet I'm afraid that some moderates and democrats, will be *too* afraid to move actively towards changing the authoritarian system, to make the leap to a democratic future.[52]

Nasution cautions that appreciation for the religious tolerance implicit in Pancasila should not frighten Indonesians away from working towards genuine democracy.

POLITICAL PARTY AND "MINORITY" COMPONENTS OF THE SECULAR NATIONALIST VOICE

There are also non-Forum Democracy contributions to the secular nationalist voice which are scattered among different institutions and emanate from a religiously and politically diverse group of intellectuals. Some secular nationalist voices are part of the government's formal political structure, particularly from Golkar and PDI, while others stem from ethnic and religious minorities.

Minority ethnic and religious voices

Chinese Indonesians have appreciated the political secularism and stability of the New Order. The state, especially ABRI, has generally guarded against anti-Chinese violence and provided an environment in which many Indonesians of Chinese descent have flourished economically. Adam Schwarz observes that despite the New Order's prohibitions on Chinese cultural and political expression,

> there is no denying that the Chinese have benefited from the changes Soeharto has wrought. The gradual depoliticization of Indonesia reduced the Chinese community's political vulnerability while Soeharto's attention to economic development created an economic climate in which the business skills of the Chinese could be put to good use.[53]

However, there are indications that in recent years anti-Chinese sentiment has increased in Indonesia. In particular, there is an undercurrent of anti-Chinese feeling in the current Islamic revival in Indonesia.[54] Additionally, the May 1994 labor riots in Medan, North Sumatra were partly motivated by an anti-Chinese element. Some local Chinese business people in Medan reported they felt relieved when ABRI troops restored security in the city.[55]

One of the ways that resentment of Indonesian Chinese is voiced is through the frequent expression of concern regarding economic disparities that have become increasingly conspicuous during the past decade of rapid economic development.[56] Some Islamic activists identify the Chinese-Indonesian-owned business conglomerates as particularly harmful to Islamic interests. One Indonesian Buddhist leader argued that it is dangerous to constantly link ethnic Chinese to economic inequalities. Lieus Sungkharisma, the head of *Gemabudhi* (Indonesian Buddhist Young Generation), contends that efforts to blame wealthy Indonesian Chinese for the "social gap" may cause instability and violence. If such unrest is provoked, he says, the victims will not be rich Indonesian Chinese – a minority of the overall ethnic Chinese population – but the ordinary middle-class and poor Indonesian Chinese. Sungkharisma argues that Pancasila stipulates that all Indonesians, including the ethnic Chinese, must live together in peace.[57]

President Soeharto may also have contributed to feelings of anxiety on the part of some ethnic Chinese. In 1991, in what was interpreted as part of Soeharto's efforts to court Islamic political support, the President summoned Indonesian Chinese owners of the major conglomerates to his ranch in Bogor, south of Jakarta. There the President lectured the business tycoons on the need to divest some of the shares of their conglomerates to indigenous (non-ethnic Chinese) businesses. The occasion was filmed and shown on the national television network. An official impression was given that only ethnic Chinese are responsible for the economic gap in society. Non-Chinese business leaders, many of whom are also extraordinarily wealthy, were conspicuously absent from the audience. This has fueled public perception that the Chinese are responsible for the nation's economic disparities. One observer wrote that "in one fell swoop Soeharto had undone a great deal of New Order effort to sweep ethnic divisions under the carpet."[58] This in turn plays into the hands of those who see "*Kristenisasi*" and Islam versus non-Islam in zero-sum terms.[59] This also puts ethnic Chinese in an awkward position. They are grateful to the New Order for the peace and stability it has brought them. Yet they are uncomfortable at being manipulated so conspicuously. Such manipulation appears to be an effort to respond to questions of who are the primary beneficiaries of development.[60]

Other studies have shown that Indonesian Chinese have often demonstrated their support for the New Order's vision of the "Pancasila state" in a very explicit fashion. For example, leaders of the *Tridharma* school of Indonesian Buddhism specifically cite Pancasila as the state ideology which protects and legitimizes their beliefs. Since the violence of 1965–1966 and accompanying anti-Chinese perceptions from the government which linked the PKI coup attempt to communist China, Chinese religions in Indonesia have sought to portray their cultural practices as fully "Pancasila-ist." For example, *Tridharma* religious texts identify their faith as a "Pancasila belief," complete with a monotheistic god. Indonesian Chinese *Tridharma* religion shows how some Chinese have appropriated Pancasila to present themselves as committed to a nationalist vision.[61]

Other religious minorities also rely on Pancasila and are concerned with how to maintain secular politics in Indonesia. For example, in comments on the relationship of the Catholic Church to the state, Yusuf Wanandi says the dilemma for Catholics has been "how to maintain themselves as a part of Indonesian society where they are a minority, and at the same time struggle for democracy and social justice."[62] Consideration of several prominent intellectuals will show how their participation in Pancasila discourse is both part of a broader secular nationalist voice, and how it overlaps with other views. Professor Franz Magnis Suseno, the Jesuit scholar of philosophy and ethics in Jakarta, Pastor Eka Darmaputera, a Protestant scholar of Pancasila, Y.B. Mangunwijaya, the activist priest in Yogyakarta, and Carlos Belo, the Bishop of East Timor, all illustrate Christian clerical views of Pancasila which exemplify secular nationalist viewpoints. All argue that Pancasila is an integral part of the Indonesian state. Additionally, several people demonstrate ways in which Pancasila is appropriated to defend their views or to implicitly question the Pancasila credentials of regime policies. Magnis Suseno and Mangunwijaya have also been participants in Forum Democracy while Belo strongly supports it.

Magnis Suseno argues that there is a need for Pancasila values in Indonesian society. He argues that it is extremely important to distinguish between the "function" and "intention" of Pancasila. While the government may use Pancasila as an ideological tool against perceived opponents (the "function" of the ideology), and while this may worry some people, this does not mean that the basic values of Pancasila lack relevance for society. The ultimate core value of Pancasila is religious, ethnic, and regional tolerance, according to Magnis Suseno. In fact, the Javanese cultural influence on Pancasila is a good thing, according to Magnis, who argues that the Javanese-derived belief that the state can be "religious" but not theocratic or linked to a particular faith is central to Indonesian national unity.[63] The Javanese see a mystical unity between people and God and the path towards this unity can be through any religion. Each person may choose their own religious path. Thus, Magnis Suseno argues that Pancasila is more than a political compromise negotiated before the founding of the Republic; it also expresses aspects of Javanese culture that promote a tolerant national society in which no one group forces its beliefs on the rest.[64]

There is a concern expressed by Magnis Suseno as well as other secular nationalists, including Mochtar Lubis, Abdurrahman Wahid, and Goenawan Mohamad, that the tolerant essence, the "intention" of Pancasila, will be lost if people focus simply on the ways in which Pancasila may be used as a political tool against Islam or against democracy.[65] Mangunwijaya argues that even though the state itself does not live up to the ideals of the ideology, this does not reduce the necessity of Pancasila. Mangunwijaya argues that "the state in its everyday praxis is no longer Pancasilaist, no longer based on the Constitution of 1945." Yet Mangunwijaya also argues that Pancasila expresses the "limits of the state" and therefore remains essential.[66]

A leading member of the Indonesian Protestant community has been a vocal participant in Pancasila discourse. Eka Darmaputera is a Protestant pastor in Jakarta and is author of a major study of Pancasila, *Pancasila and the Search for Identity and Modernity in Indonesian Society*. Darmaputera offers a comprehensive analysis of Pancasila in contemporary Indonesian national life in both this book and a paper he delivered to an Indonesian Democratic Party (PDI) seminar.[67]

Darmaputera raises a number of the key issues most often cited in the secular nationalist discourse. First, he assumes that Pancasila is necessary for Indonesia and that it is the illustration of how extraordinary cultural diversity can be peacefully accommodated within one nation. The compromise that Indonesia is religious, and not a secular state, is the key aspect of Pancasila. Darmaputera argues that Pancasila is the expression of a unifying nationalist identity. He acknowledges that in a formal and institutional sense, Pancasila is firmly implanted in Indonesia, particularly since the promulgation of *asas tunggal*.[68] Yet he questions whether in practice the nation is moving away from the intention of Pancasila. Darmaputera argues that despite "progressively brighter" inter-religious relations in Indonesia, there have also emerged in recent years disturbing signs of "primordial sentiments, especially religion."[69]

To account for the re-emergence of politics that threatens national integration, Darmaputera argues that a complex combination of political and economic factors are responsible, including a "revival of "primordial religious sentiment." This has occurred, in part, because of the emergence of an "alliance between political power and religion." He concludes that collaboration between political power and religion "endangers national unity." He also argues that his warning about the rise of religious primordialism "is not because I am a Christian, but because I am a nationalist and a Pancasilaist." He then identifies the promulgation of Islamic-oriented religious court and education laws (see Chapters 2 and 3) as evidence of government policy and regulation that is specifically directed at followers of a particular faith. He argues that law and government behavior should apply equally to all citizens (recall Nasution's "sameness of citizenship"). Because of these developments, Darmaputera worries that the nation no longer appears "inclusive and non-discriminatory." Therefore, he concludes, "this proves that it is indeed true that threats to Pancasila are real. And, as expressed by our Head of State, the biggest dangers come from within the country."[70]

APPROPRIATION OF PANCASILA

Just as Pancasila is appropriated by Abdurrahman Wahid, and ABRI, others use the ideology to legitimize their critiques. In a remarkably frank interview following the so-called "Dili Incident,"[71] the Catholic Bishop of East Timor, Carlos Belo, made frequent use of Pancasila and state ideology to support his arguments. Bishop Belo was asked how he thought groups that are not supportive of East Timor's integration with Indonesia should be treated. He replied by saying that if Pancasila, especially the second principle (just and civilized humanitarianism), is followed, then problems concerning opponents to integration can be resolved without military measures.[72] Based on the national motto *Bhinneka Tunggal Ika* [Unity in Diversity], Belo argued that the unique attributes of East Timor should be recognized by the central government so that the province can be given special status. Belo asserts that because Indonesia is a state which values diversity and heterogeneity, then East Timor's particular characteristics should be recognized as well. He noted that this would include granting East Timor a form of regional autonomy as one means of resolving the persistent obstacles to peaceful integration.[73]

Furthermore, Belo insisted that he must "speak out if the people experience oppression and treatment that is unfair and in contradiction with Pancasila." Belo argues that he speaks out not simply to "oppose" [the government] but to "correct things that are not Pancasilaist." Belo argued that it is precisely because East Timorese are aware of the ideals of Pancasila, the Constitution, and their rights as citizens of Indonesia, that they are restless and appear opposed to integration. Belo maintains that the Indonesian citizens of East Timor are not treated like ordinary citizens and this is the cause of dissatisfaction.[74] Belo also accused the central government of creating a "police state" in East Timor which is incompatible with Pancasila. Belo was asked about the activities and presence of intelligence agents in East Timorese society. His response is illustrative:

> [I have] the impression that this nation is a police state. All behavior, activities, speech, is watched and under surveillance . . . Because that happens I feel that I have experience living in a police state. *From the results of my study of Pancasila, I think this is not the Indonesia that was intended by the Pancasila.*

Belo added that he sees Pancasila democracy as something that should be more politically open and to that end he expressed his strong support for Forum Democracy.[75]

It is very difficult for authorities to allege that Belo's support for increased autonomy and democracy for East Timor is in any way subversive. He carefully and consistently invokes Pancasila in defense of his arguments. The success of Belo's approach may, however, be only in the realm of participation in the discourse itself. The mere fact that Belo appropriates Pancasila to legitimize his views does not mean that East Timor will be given more autonomy or have the intelligence and military presence reduced. Importantly, Belo does not question Timor's integration with Indonesia as this would ensure that his arguments were never heard. Yet to speak of Pancasila and the Constitution, and to speak of East Timorese as Indonesians whose rights as citizens are not respected, may be an effective approach for promoting East Timor interests and participating in national discourse.

Political parties: a Golkar voice?[76]

Golkar is one of the key institutional pillars of the New Order. Some original Golkar activists envisioned that the party would come to embody the dominant secular nationalist perspective, albeit supportive of the government. Today, however, Golkar does not effectively promote a single nationalist vision of Indonesia. According to former Golkar official Rachman Tolleng, now a leading figure in Forum Democracy, "Golkar was supposed to be the secular nationalist middle" that would have accommodated "moderate, nationalist, non-Islamic political orientations" which were left without an effective institutional base following the New Order's consolidation of the nationalist parties into the PDI.[77] Yusuf Wanandi, a student activist in the early 1960s and initial supporter of Golkar, argues that "we have failed completely in our efforts for it [Golkar] to become a nationalist party."[78]

The lack of a distinct secular nationalist Golkar voice is due to its inability to emerge as an effective independent political organization in the 1990s. There are no "Golkar" views on the great issues of the day because all the various New Order factions are also present within Golkar. That is, there are staunch ABRI supporters, Soeharto loyalists, and a group of civilian cadres recruited by Sudharmono in the mid-1980s. Typically, Indonesians describe Golkar as being composed of "streams" representing ABRI, the civilian bureaucracy, and Golkar. A telling illustration of the deep cleavages in Golkar is found in the list of names suggested by various government factions in April 1993 regarding possible nominations for the new party Chairman. Among others, both the Information Minister, Harmoko, a close Soeharto confidant and a civilian, and Lieutenant General Harsudiyono Hartas were put forward. Harmoko was the only civilian name mooted at this point while ABRI maintained that a retired officer must lead Golkar. Yet ABRI was unsuccessful in retaining the chairmanship of Golkar after President Soeharto made clear his preference for Harmoko, who became the new Chairman in October 1993.

Despite these cleavages, if several Golkar civilian leaders are considered alone, secular nationalist voices within Golkar are discernible. The views expressed by Sarwono Kusumaatmadja, former Golkar Secretary General and Marzuki Darusman, formerly a leading Golkar proponent of "openness" in the DPR, are most appropriately considered as exponents of a secular nationalist perspective. Sarwono has been retained in the new Cabinet, announced in March 1993. He is now the Minister for the Environment. Marzuki Darusman, a member of the National Human Rights Commission since 1993, was at the forefront of the ABRI-sponsored "openness" debates from 1989–1992. His failure to be placed high enough on the Golkar electoral roles to ensure his election or to be appointed by the President to the MPR in 1992 was widely interpreted as punishment for his advocacy of democratization and openness. In broad terms, the "progressive" Golkar functionaries promoted by former Chairman and Vice President Sudharmono, such as Sarwono and Marzuki, support democratization (albeit within the basic structure of the current political system) and reject political organization and mobilization on the basis of religion.

Sarwono stated in a late 1992 interview that he disagrees with "people who organize themselves [politically] along religious lines."[79] In the interview Sarwono made several important points regarding the political system similar to arguments made by Wahid, religious minorities, and the PDI (considered below). Importantly, Sarwono rejects the suggestion that district-based system of voting would be a welcome democratic change. He argues that in such a system the "small parties" would have no voice. A district system would be "extraordinarily bad" for Indonesia, Sarwono argues, and could create an "extremely authoritarian regime."[80] As noted in Chapter 3, advocates of a district-style political system (majority winner in an electoral district takes all) are primarily Muslim activists who contend that such a voting system and ensure that Islam dominates politics democratically. As shown above, other secular nationalists are also concerned that the "wrong kind of democratization" could result in Islamic political domination.

On ABRI, Sarwono indicates a position consistent with other secular nationalists. For example, when asked in an interview about the possibility of students playing a role in political change, Sarwono observes that in 1966 the students were effective only because they were allied with the armed forces and intellectuals.[81] That is, Sarwono implies that ABRI and civilian secular nationalists have found common political ground before and perhaps could do so again. Moreover, William Liddle argues that Sarwono's conception of Golkar's role in future democratization clearly leaves important room for ABRI participation.[82]

Marzuki Darusman is the epitome of a secular nationalist politician, although one who believes that it is possible to work for democratic change from within the system. Like the ABRI DPR faction members who advocated "openness" and the PDI members discussed below, Sarwono and Marzuki basically advocate the "better functioning" of the existing system. Marzuki supports an independent political party system, especially an independent Golkar, the right to initiate legislation in the DPR, and parliamentary supervisory ability over the functioning of government. Marzuki notes that nothing in Pancasila or the Constitution prohibits the democratic reforms he seeks.[83]

On the issues of sectarianism and the role of religion in politics, Marzuki argues that Abdurrahman Wahid is sincere in his concerns and is not exaggerating the issue. Marzuki, like Buyung Nasution, Aswab Mahasin, and Wahid, worries that if Indonesians perceive that the existing political system does not satisfy their aspirations, then SARA issues will become more easily exploitable.[84] Writing in *Editor* shortly before it was banned by the government in June 1994, he criticized the emergence of sectarian politics and regretted the exclusive nature of ICMI:

> In the context of ICMI, it's clear there is no place for those who are non-Muslim. But for those [organizations] which are nationalist oriented, there will always be a place for those from any religious or ethnic background.[85]

However Marzuki, like Buyung Nasution, Wahid, and Marsillam Simanjuntak, argues that the responsibility for the emergence of groups like ICMI is the political structure of the New Order. Marzuki argues that "they [people in ICMI] react against the political culture that does not value differences of opinion." The current system is imbued with weak political institutions, including the parties which do not present viable alternatives to "exclusive" political agitation.[86] Clearly, both Marzuki and Sarwono seek to develop a political system that will reduce the appeal of religious and ethnic issues in the political process, a key element of the secular nationalist discourse. Yet Golkar as a whole is deeply split into various factions, a result of contention between Soeharto and ABRI for influence and control of the party.

The Indonesian Democratic Party (PDI)[87]

Some leaders of the PDI argue that their interests as a minority party are partially realized by a political structure based on Pancasila and its implicit defense of minority rights. For them, the referent is not only the religious tolerance inherent in Pancasila, but the fourth principle which stipulates an Indonesian-style democracy based on *musyawarah* and *mufakat* [consultation and consensus]. Through such procedures, some PDI officials maintain that its voice is more readily heard than by a strict majority voting system. Moreover, through the person of Megawati Sukarnoputri (Sukarno's daughter) as the current head of the party, the PDI can link itself directly to the secular nationalist struggles of Indonesia's early independence years.

Soerjadi, Chairman of the PDI until 1993, observes that he does not believe that the DPR/MPR is functioning in accordance with the intentions of the Constitution. If Pancasila were truly followed, according to Soerjadi, PDI as part of the "family state" would be included in actual governing, and not just hold seats in a relatively powerless parliament. (This is similar to the argument advanced by Brigadier General Roekmini, formerly of the ABRI faction in the DPR and Sri Bintang Pamungkas of the PPP and ICMI.) Soerjadi argues that a formal "opposition" party is not wanted or desired in the parliament as that would ensure that minority parties would always lose. In November 1992 Nurcholish Madjid gave a lecture in which he argued that it was appropriate for the emergence of genuine "opposition" parties, and that the PPP and PDI should acknowledge that they are "opposition."[88] Then Secretary General of the PDI, Nico Daryanto, immediately rejected the idea because "Pancasila democracy does not recognize the idea of opposition parties" and this was also because Indonesia has a "family" system which stresses consultation and consensus.[89]

Therefore, Soerjadi sees that the Pancasila concepts of consultation and consensus in place of outright voting on all important issues is necessary to protect the interests of minority parties. At the same time, however, Soerjadi argues that this principle is not fully implemented in the DPR and in government. If consultative procedures were genuinely followed by the government, then PDI members would sit on the Cabinet (no members of PDI or PPP are Cabinet Ministers). Soerjadi also argues against establishing a district-based voting system. He sees that with such a system minorities would not have the voice they now have under the general system of proportional voting in national elections combined with *musyawarah* and *mufakat*.[90]

Kwik Kian Gie, one of Indonesia's leading economists and a senior PDI leader, argues that Pancasila's *musyawarah* and *mufakat* are crucial in Indonesian politics:

> the best aspects of the current political structure are its obsession to reach decisions by *musyawarah* [consensus], as

> expressed in the fourth principle of Pancasila. It is not a must, but everybody is obsessed and is embarrassed if we do not try it first. I personally regard this as very good.[91]

Kwik adds that the other positive aspect of the system is a strong presidency which, when combined with a consensus-building decision-making process, results in stable government. However, the biggest political problem is that the DPR is not allowed to function in accordance with its constitutionally given rights and responsibilities (to initiate legislation, to hold government accountable, and to have free and open debate), according to Kwik. Nevertheless, the culturally derived aversion to opposition and voting, Kwik argues, gives the small PDI a "larger voice" than it would otherwise have. Kwik adds, "minorities will lose in a pure voting system so PDI does not want this. By preserving *musyawarah* I force them to listen to us."[92] Soerjadi and Kwik clearly endorse Pancasila-derived consultation and consensus as necessary to protect the rights of small parties.

In December 1993 Megawati Sukarnoputri, a charismatic and widely popular figure, was elected as head of the party. Many of Sukarno's children – Megawati, Rachmawati, and Guruh – are all active in the PDI today. According to Kwik Kian Gie, the Sukarno children explain that the PDI is the natural choice for them as it was the nationalist vehicle of their late father.[93] The PDI, then, is the only formal political party that can link itself directly to the original nationalist parties. Previously the weakest of the three parties, under Megawati, the PDI has the potential to function as an independent secular political force. If so, Megawati will have to move the PDI beyond the chauvinistic nationalism of the earlier nationalist parties and become a genuine democratic force as well. Moreover, according to Abdurrahman Wahid, Megawati is one of the only Indonesians who can genuinely command the loyalty of a popular mass base within an established political party.[94]

THE SECULAR NATIONALIST DILEMMA

Secular nationalists include a diverse group of Indonesians who do not channel their political aspirations through Islam or Islamic institutions and organizations. This includes many non-Muslims as well as Muslims who opt for a non-religious outlet for their voice.

Secular nationalists tend to have a stronger commitment to liberal democracy than the other voices considered in this study, especially ICMI and ABRI. This chapter has shown that Abdurrahman Wahid considers himself both a secular nationalist democratizer and a Muslim leader. A component of the secular nationalist voice is also derived from religious and ethnic minorities, especially Protestants, Catholics, and Indonesian Chinese. For these people there is a particularly acute dilemma regarding their desire to strive for a more democratic society, and their tendency to perceive themselves as vulnerable to political Islam. These perceptions create ambivalence over potential democratization in a post-Soeharto era.

For nearly all contributors to the secular nationalist voice Pancasila is perceived as necessary for Indonesian unity and stability. Even for secular nationalists who express their concerns primarily in terms of the constitutionality of politics and law, their views on religious tolerance and the role of ABRI vividly illustrate their dilemma over reducing the military role in politics while retaining what some see as ABRI's protection of Pancasila.

An implication of this thinking is that potential democratizers who are associated with ICMI are deprived of possibly powerful alliances with secular nationalists. Simply the perception that ICMI "re-confessionalizes" Indonesian politics puts the non-military voices for democracy in opposition to ICMI activists. Moreover, potential democratizers in ICMI stress the importance of Soeharto's continuance in office while some secular nationalists, notably those associated with Forum Democracy, see presidential succession as a key precondition to democratization.

Those voices staunchly opposed to what they argue is the military-dominated, non-democratic nature of the New Order are, however, also in fundamental agreement with one of the basic strategies initially advocated by many early New Order supporters and implemented primarily by ABRI: the de-linking of religious, ethnic, and racial affiliations from organized political behavior. However, the "success" of that policy may have impacted more on secular nationalists than on Indonesians seeking to channel their political aspirations through Islam. This is because people who may have been most comfortable, for example, with the Indonesian Nationalist Party (which was fused into the PDI), have no natural independent organizational base. Whereas for Muslims, there are both long-standing organizations and, moreover, the faith itself. Perhaps most significantly, in the 1990s there is also ICMI. There are few channels open to secular nationalists to promote significant political change. The PDI (despite Megawati's personal popularity) and the PPP are weak parties while Golkar is a tool of the government and primarily responsible to Soeharto. This leaves Islam which is perhaps the only effective means for organizing politically. Unfortunately, many Indonesians see that this endangers the nationalist underpinnings which guarantee national unity.

Forum Democracy, although a small informal grouping of intellectuals, represents the kind of cross-cutting nationalist association that appeals on the basis of the idea of a unified democratic Indonesia rather than "primordial" affiliations. However, there are no indications that the Forum could serve as an effective agent for political change. It exists for discussion purposes only at an elite level. Only if Wahid were to use his NU power base might this occur. Yet a mobilization of NU for secular nationalist democratization is highly unlikely given the diversity of NU views and its formal position as a "non-political" socio-cultural organization.

Importantly, this chapter has shown that although Wahid has the most prominent voice, especially in his role as head of Forum Democracy, he does not dominate the secular nationalist perspective. A wide variety of intellectuals from various backgrounds express a vision of society not unlike Wahid's – a democratic society, but yet one in which the democratic process is so structured to protect the rights of minorities in a non-sectarian society. Most of these voices express profound concern regarding their perception of rising religious and ethnic intolerance.

The dilemma of the secular nationalists is really one regarding a question of limits. That is, it is not that secular nationalists are paranoid of Islamic political aspirations. Indeed, many prominent secular nationalists are also Muslim. Moreover, many people associated with the secular nationalist voice specifically acknowledge that the relationship between Islam and the government is more healthy today and that it is a good thing that political Islam is no longer unnecessarily identified as the cause of threats to national stability. However, there is concern which revolves around the question of at what stage the reasonable accommodation of the interests and values of the Muslim majority might reach a point at which the legitimate interests of Indonesia's multiple minorities – religious, ethnic, regional, or even political (such as PDI in the current political structure) – are restricted or circumscribed. Ambivalence related to this question underlines much of the secular nationalist participation in the discourse. And yet, as Abdurrahman Wahid argued, secular nationalists perceive they are treading a "narrow path" between the choice of an "Islamic society" on one hand or continued domination by ABRI or Soeharto on the other.

Chapter 6

Conclusion

The meaning of Pancasila discourse

> the search for a viable form of people's sovereignty as enunciated by the Constitution is still an ongoing process despite the acceptance by consensus of the Pancasila principle.
>
> Editorial, *Jakarta Post*[1]

> Old rivalries, based on ideological differences in the Old Order, resurface in the New Order.
>
> Abdurrahman Wahid[2]

REVIVAL OF IDEOLOGY

The broad purpose of this study has been to evaluate the meaning that discourse about Pancasila has for our understanding of Indonesian politics, particularly in the 1990s. Contrary to the tendency in many analyses of Indonesian politics to ignore Pancasila, this book demonstrates that Indonesia's political elite considers Pancasila to represent key ideas in contemporary politics. The study indicates that elite arguments over what kind of political system Indonesia should have are part of the Pancasila discourse. These arguments include questions regarding the relationship between Islam and government, the role of the armed forces, national unity, presidential succession, democratization, and even economic development.

This study has shown that Indonesia is a country which has "made more of ideology than others."[3] Indonesia, and more particularly its elite, is deeply concerned with ideology. For nearly thirty years the Indonesian New Order has perceived a need both to have a constitutionally enshrined ideological basis of the state (the *dasar negara*) and to proscribe other non-state ideologies for fear of their "primordial" links to society. Indonesia is based on an ideology of limits. Yet while the national ideology expresses what ideologies the state should *not* embrace, it also enunciates positive values necessary for nation-building.

Pancasila appeals constructively to Indonesian citizens to build a nation based on humane values such as ethnic, religious, and regional tolerance, and social justice. This is Pancasila at the level of "intention." Pancasila was intended to be the formulaic representation of the "idea" of the Indonesian state. This study has argued that contention over the meaning of Pancasila as the dominant state idea is an acute part of contemporary political discourse. Pancasila also performs the most basic function of any official ideology – it legitimizes authority. Additionally, in the 1990s, Pancasila is also appropriated by non-state actors to legitimize challenges to the government.

Elite perceptions of a "dangerous" revival of non-state ideologies are very real. Military officers, senior government bureaucrats, Abdurrahman Wahid, secular nationalists, democrats, and non-Muslim intellectuals perceive that old ideological disputes have re-emerged in recent years. One observer told the Indonesian Democratic Party (PDI) that he was afraid that once-settled questions concerning the basis of the state have been rekindled in the 1990s.[4] ABRI officers express concerns that ICMI legitimizes Islamic appeals to "primordial" loyalties. Almost equally as strong, ABRI perceives liberal democratic ideas to be incompatible with Pancasila.

The significance of elite concerns of a recent revival of ideas incompatible with Pancasila must be situated in the context of the origins of the New Order. The New Order contends that ideological debate, as witnessed from 1945 through both the Konstituante and Sukarno's Guided Democracy period to 1965, prevented effective national economic development and political stability, both essential for nation-building. Instead, national elites became mired in polemical debate over ideological issues. Moreover, the New Order saw that the ideological positions of the political elite were often tied to programmatic and policy imperatives that were intricately linked to "primordial" affiliations, or *aliran*, of mass Indonesian society. Proponents of an Islamic state (or simply of a more formalized link between government and Islam) appealed to the more *santri* (devoutly Islamic) elements in society. Communists, with appeals for land reform, economic redistribution, and calls to the agricultural and industrial proletariat attracted the less devout *abangan* poor. Secular nationalists appealed yet again to other Indonesians, including non-Muslims, who channelled their political aspirations through more cross-cutting secular organizations.

Not only did ideological appeals divide Indonesians along religious lines, they also distinguished on the basis of ethnicity and region. According to the New Order, the ultimate result of a nation deeply split in seemingly irreconcilable ways, and led by an elite who actively manipulated the masses for support, was violence and retribution meted out along "ideological" lines. In the minds of many New Order supporters, it was the perception of a causal link between "ideology" and chaotic, violent political behavior that contributed to a belief that society must be "de-ideologized." New Order supporters argued that the ideological orientations of elite politicians must never again be allowed to influence the masses. The New Order believed that history showed that when given the chance to organize politically, ordinary people were most easily attracted to mobilization based on "primordial loyalties." However, not all politically secular nationalists, Muslim intellectuals, and even dissident ABRI officers, expected the New Order to proceed so completely with the de-ideologization of society so that almost all independent political organizations became strictly controlled in ways that frustrated legitimate channelling of political aspirations.

By promoting Pancasila as the sole ideology (*asas tunggal*), officials of the New Order hoped to sever the connection between *aliran* and mass political behavior. To this end, the New Order sought to carry out the de-politicization of society, based largely on the thinking of key New Order strategist Ali Moertopo. The de-politicization strategy has been variously called "de-ideologization" or "Pancasila-ization." More recently Abdurrahman Wahid has referred to this process as "de-confessionalization," with the emphasis on ensuring that politics is not based on one's "confessed" religion. After the destruction of communism, government officials and ABRI officers perceived the most extreme manifestations of threats to the de-politicization process to be from proponents of a formalized link between Islam and the state. Liberal democracy, associated with the political and economic chaos of the 1950s, has been the other main ideological threat to the Pancasila state as perceived by the government of President Soeharto and the armed forces.

Political Islam is not the only "revived" ideology that has caused concern among members of the elite. Senior ABRI leaders in particular identify demands for human rights and democracy as incompatible with the New Order's Pancasila. For example, the Chief of General Staff, Lieutenant General H.B. Mantiri argues that "Western" concepts of democracy and human rights are "old" ideological issues whose inappropriateness for Indonesia was demonstrated by the "failure" of the parliamentary democracy period in the 1950s.[5]

When Indonesian elites express worry over the revival of "old ideological issues" it is not difficult to understand their fears when considered against the background of political thinking on the danger to the state of ideology linked to ethnic, religious, and regional affiliations. Moreover, consideration of the voices of Wahid, ABRI, and politically secular nationalists has shown that they consider President Soeharto to be partially responsible for encouraging, perhaps unwittingly, the ideological and political revival of Islam. Therefore, it is necessary to review whether President Soeharto has indeed been responsible for the "revival of ideology" in the 1990s.

SOEHARTO'S VOICE IN THE 1990s

Chapter 1 indicated that the voice of President Soeharto on Pancasila is notably different in the post-*asas tunggal* era. Speeches such as Soeharto's 1980 remarks which prompted vigorous dissent from the Petition of Fifty on the grounds that Soeharto had personally appropriated Pancasila for his own political needs have not been repeated. Instead, Soeharto speaks of Pancasila as an "open ideology" and is much less explicit today in identifying his perceptions of threats to Pancasila. There are very few examples of presidential discourse on Pancasila in which specific "enemies" of the government are identified as enemies of Pancasila. This contrasts with the interpretation of Soeharto's Pancasila speeches in 1980 as partially directed at NU for its opposition to the Pancasila education legislation in 1978.

One of the concerns of Muslims was that Pancasila was a "secular" ideology and was particularly informed by Soeharto's belief in Javanese philosophical antecedents to Islam. These concerns have disappeared in the post-*asas tunggal* era. No longer are worries voiced that Soeharto has an exclusively "Javanist" interpretation of Pancasila that is inappropriate for the Islamic-majority nation. There have been no widely reported remarks similar to his famous speech to the KPNI (Indonesian National Youth Committee) in which Soeharto said that Javanese culture is closely identified with Pancasila and helps to most clearly explain the ideology. No longer do Muslims see that President Soeharto gives Pancasila an anti-Islamic, Javanese cultural interpretation which would heighten Muslim concerns over Pancasila as an ideology of Javanese political culture. However, the President's "Javanese-ness" has not disappeared; on the contrary, it remains an integral part of his value system. There are several indications of this. First, in 1987 his daughter published a two-hundred page collection of Soeharto's Javanese philosophy. Second, in unscripted remarks at a Javanese language congress in July 1991, the President urged the nation's intellectuals to consider the applicability of the Javanese philosophy of life to further Indonesia's development.[6] Islamic activists would like to see Soeharto today as a "good" Muslim willing to use the power of his office to promote Indonesia as an Islamic society. Reality is more complex and may be less comforting to Islamic activists. President Soeharto is a Muslim Javanese deeply imbued with Javanese syncretic philosophy and therefore will always retain a deep suspicion of overtly Islamic politics. Former Minister of Religion, Munawir Sjadzali, argues that Soeharto has only allowed greater government attention to Islam because he perceives that most Muslims no longer question Pancasila.[7] What would happen, however, if President Soeharto's perceptions changed and he felt, as do senior ABRI commanders, that certain Islamic political behavior contravenes Pancasila? However, part of the ICMI activist strategy demands belief in Soeharto's Islamic sincerity in order to justify his coopting of Muslim activists within ICMI. Muslim intellectuals clearly endorse Soeharto's enunciation of Pancasila as an "open ideology." Yet Soeharto's conception of Pancasila's openness surely does not extend to allowing it to be appropriated or contravened by the emergence of political movements whose ultimate goal may be substantial political change or eventual challenges to the New Order itself. None the less, as indicated in Chapter 3, political activists in ICMI argue that Islamization of society is most strongly advanced by Soeharto's short-term continuance in office. No longer do Muslims raise concerns that Soeharto is "too Javanese" or that he uses Pancasila against Islam.

Does Soeharto's well-known *rapprochement* with political Islam in the post-*asas tunggal* period mean that the President and, through him the New Order government, is less supportive of Pancasila as the ideology of de-politicization and a religiously neutral state? Has Soeharto contravened the New Order's interpretation of Pancasila by encouraging Islamic politics? Chapters 4 and 5 indicate that there is a perception among ABRI and secular civilian nationalists that by encouraging Islamic politics in order to enhance Soeharto's legitimacy a worrisome process has been initiated which may eventually contravene Pancasila. That is, some ABRI officers, Wahid, and secular nationalists argue that the manipulation of Islam for political purposes, particularly *vis-à-vis* the armed forces, re-ignites fears that "primordial" affiliations will once again come into play in Indonesian politics. After vigorously proscribing the organizational ability of Islam as a force for political mobilization throughout the New Order, some fear that Soeharto has unwittingly encouraged just such a development through his sponsorship of ICMI.

Such fears may be exaggerated, however. Most evidence suggests that Soeharto is firmly committed to the essentials of Pancasila as a religious, though non-Islamic, state ideology tolerant of diversity. This is particularly clear from both the composition of the MPR announced in October 1992 and the new Cabinet, unveiled in March 1993. None of the Islamic activists that worried ABRI, Abdurrahman Wahid, and secular nationalists have been appointed to these bodies. It is the case that Muslim representation in both the Cabinet and the MPR does more closely resemble the proportion of Muslims in the general population. However, Muslim activists who may be supportive of formalized links between the state and Islam do not appear in the MPR or Cabinet. Therefore, Soeharto is able to neutralize demands for "proportionalization" expressed by Muslim activists without allowing those who advocate an Islamizing agenda into government.

The fear that Muslim activists would use ICMI as a "Trojan Horse" to surreptitiously enter government by appointment has not materialized. ICMI activists were deeply disappointed with Soeharto's 1993 Cabinet appointments. The degree of ICMI activists' awareness at having been manipulated by Soeharto is reflected in the commentary by ICMI members cited in Chapter 3. Indeed, ICMI members who were appointed to the Cabinet, such as Wardiman, the Minister of Education and a key Habibie lieutenant and leading ICMI administrator, are derided by activists as "not real ICMI."[8] Retired senior government officials also acknowledge that Soeharto did not allow Islamic "radicals" in the government and this helped to reduce their fears that Soeharto had "gone too far." However, ICMI's presence in the bureaucracy has provoked increased tension among civil servants. Some bureaucrats nervously recount in private conversations to the effect that if they do not join ICMI they are considered "bad Muslims" by fellow bureaucrats supportive of ICMI.

There was some additional evidence that Soeharto was seeking to balance the voices of Islam in ICMI by sending positive signals to NU and Abdurrahman Wahid. Perhaps the most interesting is Abdurrahman Wahid's report that he believes Soeharto was attempting to repair relations with him and NU. As evidence, Wahid said that the new Minister of Religion, Tarmizi Taher, has been instructed by the President to "take care of the *ulamas* [Islamic scholars, many of whom are followers of NU]." Moreover, Wahid says that the government has promised to consult with NU more fully on issues relating both to the *haj* and in transmigration matters.[9] On a personal level, Wahid notes that President Soeharto offered to pay all hospitalization costs incurred by his wife following a serious automobile accident. In a political culture where personal gestures are extremely important, Wahid interprets Soeharto's moves as indicative of a desire to placate NU, Wahid himself, and to repair some damage left from the obvious manipulation of ICMI throughout 1992.[10] Moreover, media reports suggest that Cabinet Minister Siswono's high-profile criticism of ICMI as a "sectarian and exclusive" organization in 1994 was made with Soeharto's blessing.[11] Yet government efforts to depose Wahid as head of NU in December 1994 suggest Wahid's earlier optimism on improvement in his relationship with Soeharto was misplaced.

In the post-*asas tunggal* period there is also plenty of evidence of an uncompromising government approach to all overt manifestations of Islamic fundamentalism and violence. Three examples vividly illustrate this. First, in February 1989 (noted in Chapter 4) a swift military operation was mounted in the South Sumatra province of Lampung against a group of people identified by the government as Islamic extremists. Then Commander of the armed forces, Try Sutrisno (who has been hailed as a friend of Islam because of his *santri* status by some in ICMI), bore ultimate responsibility for the operation as, of course, did President Soeharto. In July 1989 the government announced that twenty-five Muslim extremists would be tried on charges of seeking to create an Islamic state.[12] There were also military operations against Islamic supporters of the small "Free Aceh" movement in North Sumatra.[13] In 1992 a Muslim preacher was sentenced to an eight-year jail term for opposition to Pancasila.[14] The government and ABRI also responded quickly to scattered attacks on churches in East Java in November and December 1992.[15]

Although Soeharto does not speak directly of specific threats to Pancasila in the 1990s as he did in 1980 and prior to *asas tunggal*, he maintains a consistent public voice on Pancasila. Notably, in speeches before two ICMI congresses Soeharto urged Islamic intellectuals to "guard against the emergence of alternative systems to Pancasila" and to reiterate the position of Pancasila as the sole principle of national life.[16] Soeharto and his ministers continue to frequently stress the importance of religious tolerance.[17] In other words, although Soeharto no longer appears to use Pancasila to delegitimize political behavior of others or to explicitly proscribe Islamic politics, he continues to express the fundamental values of the New Order's conception of a tolerant, religious, though non-Islamic, state.[18] Soeharto has even warned against sectarianism using language almost identical to Abdurrahman Wahid's frequent warnings.[19] Soeharto has also urged religious groups to work together in the interests of national unity and has issued general warnings about any efforts to challenge Pancasila.[20] Thus, Soeharto's Pancasilaist position is still strongly enunciated. The failure of ICMI activists to be appointed to either the MPR or the Cabinet, and the consistency of Soeharto's statements on religious tolerance as the core issue of Pancasila, indicates the President has not abandoned his concept of a nationalist, non-Islamic state. However, it is possible that Soeharto may have unwittingly – in efforts to expand his personal political legitimacy – weakened the New Order's prohibition of religious politics.

In the final analysis, Soeharto seems to have been engaged in a long-term strategy similar to that advocated by the Dutch colonial advisor, Snouck Hurgronje, in the 1920s: the vigorous promotion of Islam as a spiritual and cultural force combined with strict prohibition on Islam as a political force. As Nurcholish Madjid suggests, Soeharto has managed to flexibly adapt to the social and cultural Islamization of Indonesian society. In numerous circumstances Soeharto has sought to depict himself in more Muslim settings when he is acting as "citizen Soeharto" and not in his "political" capacity as President of Indonesia. For example, in April 1993 President Soeharto was shown on television speaking to Javanese farmers in his capacity as head of the *Yayasan Amal Bakti Pancasila* (a private Soeharto family foundation to promote mosque construction and religious projects). Soeharto repeatedly stressed to the farmers that he was supportive of this foundation and of promotion of Islam "not as president" but "only as head of *Yayasan Amal Bakti*."[21] In August 1993 "citizen" Soeharto even became the chief patron of ICMI. Former Minister of Religion, Munawir Sjadzali, states that Soeharto had refused for years to undertake the pilgrimage to Mecca as "President" but that he would consider it as a private citizen or when he was "retired."[22] Clearly, Soeharto attempts to separate Islam as a private matter from his role as President. "Citizen" Soeharto, however, is also President Soeharto and therefore the political implications of the appearance of heightened piety and sponsorship of ICMI are extremely important. While fears that Soeharto has "gone too far" in his accommodation of Islam and contravened the tolerant compromise of Pancasila are not necessarily supported by all recent political developments, it is essential to recognize that some Indonesians consider the danger to be the initiation of a *process* of allowing the Islamization of politics.

Which of the voices considered in this study are most relevant to political outcomes in Indonesia? A great deal of consideration was given to Abdurrahman Wahid, other Islamic intellectuals, secular nationalists, including democratizers, non-Muslims, and members of Golkar. It remains true, however, that Indonesian politics are still dominated by two authoritarian institutions competing for power – the armed forces and the presidency. For example, the sheer power of ABRI and the presidency is well illustrated by the bannings of Indonesia's most popular and respected publications in 1994. Despite sweeping disagreement with this action (including some from within ABRI itself), the armed forces were easily able to prevent widespread dissent. The military clamped down for the sake of "stability," as well as because of their fundamental rejection of liberal democracy and its attendant freedoms. President Soeharto was able to react to a perceived personal challenge (the questioning of the warship purchase) with few, if any, damaging repercussions. Ideological evidence that the armed forces and the presidency remain dominant is also shown in that non-governmental voices have felt compelled to adopt the official ideology to legitimately participate in political debate.

While some secular nationalists believe that the armed forces provide protection against a possible Islamic state, others are careful not to overstate this concern for fear of justifying a continued military political role. Adnan Buyung Nasution warns that exaggeration of such a hypothetical choice only frightens people away from democracy. Politically secular nationalists and non-Muslims who worry about an "Islamic" political future must also recognize that ABRI is probably less concerned about minority religious rights than national stability. Indeed, ABRI's conception of Pancasila as an integralistic ideology prioritizes what officers perceive as "national" interests over individual rights. Military intervention in the Batak Church crisis in North Sumatra should give pause to those who perceive that ABRI always adheres to a position of religious neutrality.

ICMI reliance on Soeharto for sponsorship must be considered a strategy of weakness, at least in the short run. Muslim activists have realized in the post-*asas tunggal* era that opposition to Pancasila prevents an Islamic voice in national discourse. Some ICMI activists clearly acknowledge that their reliance on Soeharto and Habibie is a high-risk and rather weak strategy. Indeed, ABRI perception that people within ICMI advocate de-militarization through Islamization and/or democratization under the sponsorship of Habibie may indelibly mark ICMI as an "enemy" of the armed forces and therefore, as an enemy of Pancasila. Muslims who seek to promote a more formal link between the government and Islam are forced to rely upon the goodwill and accommodationist attitudes of President Soeharto because it is the only strategy available to those who have been unrelentingly denied the opportunity to express an Islamic political voice during the New Order. Therefore, participation in the discourse by many Indonesians is predicated on recognition that ABRI and President Soeharto continue to set the parameters of political debate. Those parameters, however, are increasingly blurred in the 1990s.

The political significance of apprehension

The Indonesian elite is gripped with a high degree of apprehension about Indonesia's political future. Based on the interviews in this study, several major reasons for this can be discerned. First, the elite is preoccupied with the issue of the succession of President Soeharto. Most political and ideological issues are in some way connected to succession politics. For example, ABRI seeks to deepen its legitimacy by enunciating the concept of "integralism" which defines Pancasila as a fully indigenous ideology in which the military is an indisputable part of politics. Such an intensification of ABRI efforts to further legitimize its role is necessary because of uncertainty regarding President Soeharto. Presidential and military interests are no longer automatically shared. Furthermore, because of an eventual political future without Soeharto and the 1945 generation of officers whose link to the revolutionary struggle granted them personal legitimacy, it is not surprising that ABRI seeks greater institutional and ideological justifications for its dual function.

The Indonesian Islamic elite is divided over how to deal with Soeharto and the issue of succession. ICMI strategy is dependent upon Soeharto's continuance in office until at least 1998, so that the President can maintain his sponsorship and protection of ICMI. ICMI activists plan that this period will allow the institutionalization of ICMI as a potentially powerful national Islamic political organization that will be well positioned to contest the political configuration of the post-Soeharto era.

Abdurrahman Wahid and like-minded Muslim intellectuals and politically secular nationalists have also been deeply involved in succession political planning. NU's Rapat Akbar in March 1992 was used by Wahid to make an important distinction between endorsing Soeharto's continuance in office and reiterating NU's loyalty to Pancasila and the Constitution. Furthermore, Wahid fears that if Muslim activists push for an Islamized polity in the post-Soeharto era this will generate a military backlash that will impede democratization efforts.

Additionally, Wahid argues that his re-election as Chairman of NU in 1994 ensures that NU will retain its key balancing position in Indonesian politics. NU, according to Wahid, will be in a unique position to influence the general elections in 1997 as well as to play a role in a possible presidential succession in 1998.

Moreover, Wahid adds that ABRI's appreciation for NU's "nationalist outlook" will help smooth the way towards a more democratic future.[23] However, as suggested in Chapter 4, the armed forces' deep-seated anti-liberal ideology makes it doubtful that ABRI would support democratic change under any circumstances, despite Wahid's optimism.

Many members of the elite fear the potential revival of "old ideological issues" and "primordial" politics. In particular, fear of future political and institutional links between Islam and government is so great that it may create tacit alliances between ABRI, secular nationalists, and Abdurrahman Wahid. Yet it is difficult to point to pervasive, nation-wide examples of "sectarianism" and Islamic activism that explicitly justify fear of an Islamic political future.

However, two major forces encourage such apprehensions. The first is awareness among the entire elite of international Islamic revival and political activism. There is an ever-present concern that international fundamentalist developments will reach Indonesia. These concerns were most alarmingly raised by Abdurrahman Wahid's widely publicized letter to President Soeharto in March 1992. In that letter Wahid said that if the government frustrated his efforts to develop a democratically-inclined *umat* tolerant of diversity then there would be potential for an "Algerian" situation. The analogy suggests that if the military clamps down on Islamic political activity it will weaken the forces of democratization and simultaneously radicalize the Islamic movement.

Leaving aside whether Wahid's scenario is unnecessarily alarming (keeping in mind the lack of pervasive fundamentalism in Indonesia), its mere enunciation in public discourse has an impact. Part of the intention of this study is to draw attention to the role of ideas, beliefs, and perceptions in political debate. As stated in the Preface, such perceptions do not necessarily have to be "accurate." Yet many secular nationalists and ABRI officers would often use the Algerian analogy of a nightmarish political future to argue that movement towards formalization of links between Islam and the state must be avoided at all costs. It is not that many members of the elite actually believe that Algeria is an accurate analogy, but it is used as a vivid rhetorical image in political debate.

The role of political perception is crucial in understanding the role of Islam and its relationship to Pancasila in Indonesia today. In the Indonesian context of a long-standing political culture (in pre-colonial, colonial and post-1945 independence eras) that highlights syncretism, social tolerance, and a flexible, inclusive Islam, simply the *perception* of a desire to Islamize government and politics is viewed with great alarm by Muslims and non-Muslims alike. Aswab Mahasin says that some Indonesian Muslims still need to recognize that "being a member of the Islamic community does not necessarily commit one to a Muslim political alliance or grouping."[24]

The second reason for apprehension over a revival of ideology is memories of communal violence that surged through Indonesian villages and towns from October 1965 to early 1966. Abdurrahman Wahid says that while no one mentions those killings today, "it is foremost in all our minds."[25] The targets of communal violence were allegedly communists. The instigators of many killings were often Islamic organizations – including NU's own youth wing, the Ansor – which justified the killings in terms of *jihad* [holy war]. The beneficiary of the elimination of the PKI at the time was the ABRI-backed New Order. But the example has not been lost on many Indonesians. While few recall those events openly, those who do including Wahid, speak with fear that such horror could be unleashed again *if* political programs and ambitions are tied to deeply held religious beliefs.

It is the perception not so much of concrete acts of "sectarianism" in contemporary politics, but of a process that conjures up links to mass society that is most troubling for some Indonesians. The government, especially ABRI, perceives that the masses can be politically mobilized not just by religion but by democracy and other issues. Politically secular nationalists also worry about links between emotional ideological issues and mass behavior. Most frequently mentioned are the "*Monitor* Affair" and the harsh reaction from within the Islamic community to a lecture given by Nurcholish Madjid in November 1992 advocating an inclusive, tolerant Islam. Nurcholish Madjid's remarks – and the reaction they provoked – are illustrative of both the paradoxes within the Islamic community and reasons why secular Indonesians fear the Islamization of Indonesian society.

In November 1992 Nurcholish Madjid gave a public lecture in which he argued that Islam was essentially "borderless." He said that Islam means "surrender to God" and this surrender should not be taken to mean surrender to any particular religion. So, Nurcholish argued, anyone who surrenders to God, including "people of the book" (Christians and Jews) may also be considered Muslim because Islam is a universal faith. According to the Jesuit scholar Franz Magnis Suseno, Nurcholish Madjid's lecture is a theological effort to show that "non-Muslims can be accepted in the grace of God."[26] While Nurcholish advocates an inclusive view of Islam, highly appropriate to Indonesia's pluralism and diversity, he has been fiercely attacked over this theological argument.[27] For example, the lecture prompted some radicals to accuse Nurcholish of "Zionism" and betrayal of Islam. The emotional and strident reaction within the Islamic community towards Nurcholish Madjid's lecture on the fundamental sameness of all religions illustrates wide theological and political cleavages both within ICMI and the wider Islamic community. Goenawan Mohamad suggests that the visceral attack on Nurcholish over this lecture was partially because some Muslims in Indonesia are intent on demonstrating the distinctiveness of Islam, thus legitimizing Islamic politics.[28] Nurcholish Madjid's argument, however, tends to theologically "blur" the boundaries between Islam and other religions in Indonesia. Such blurring of religious boundaries dilutes political appeals that Islam is deserving of special government attention.

A danger for the future of peaceful Indonesian politics lies in the possibility that fears and apprehensions extant in society may be consciously exaggerated and exploited. This process cuts every possible way. For example, it is not unlikely that officers could perceive that an exaggeration of an "Islamic threat" may advance ABRI's efforts to re-emphasize its role both as defender of Pancasila and guarantor of domestic stability. Indeed, many Indonesians express precisely this fear that ABRI will overstate a political danger from Islam and in so doing will hinder democratization efforts. Similarly, exaggerations of "Christianization" and purported Christian plots to suppress the Muslim majority are used to strengthen a case for greater government attention to Muslim interests. The rhetoric of so-called "Christian conspiracies" is typified by accusations from some activists that *Tempo* conspired with non-Muslims and the military to denigrate Habibie, and through him ICMI and Islam in general, through coverage of the ex-East German warship controversy.[29] In turn, however, Christian overreaction to the legitimate expression of

Islamic values in an overwhelmingly Muslim society feeds Islamic perceptions of anti-Muslim Christian scheming.[30] For example, attacks on churches in East Java in late 1992 were provoked by an inflammatory anti-Muslim tract written by an evangelical pastor.

An unintended consequence of the New Order's de-politicization of society may have been the elimination of a moderate secular channel for political expression. That is, as permissible means for expressing political aspirations were increasingly constrained within the structure of the New Order's "Pancasila democracy," there were virtually no outlets for secular democratic voices. Yet, for some Indonesians, Islamic organizations, although ostensibly non-political, provide a forum for political behavior. Both NU and ICMI illustrate the political activities of "non-political" bodies. A key difference, however, is that NU under Abdurrahman Wahid emphasizes a basically "secular" political approach while ICMI encourages a more exclusively Islamic view of politics. For politically secular democrats, there is a perception that they have no place to go in the New Order. They must navigate a "narrow path" between the twin authoritarianism of the armed forces and the presidency while trying to maintain a secular political approach. Chapter 5 indicated that some politicians intended Golkar to become the independent vehicle for expression of a secular nationalist perspective. Today, however, Golkar exists simply as the "directorate-general" for winning elections, according to former Golkar Secretary General Sarwono.[31]

INTERNATIONAL DIMENSIONS

Despite the fact that Indonesia has the largest Muslim population in the world, it is rarely considered in Western analyses about Islam, particularly in discussion of a so-called "Islamic threat." For example, in several articles on Islam and politics in popular American foreign affairs journals, there is not a single mention of Indonesia.[32] This is striking for three reasons. First, there are more Muslims in Indonesia than in any other country. Second, Indonesia suggests a successful example of a politically secular government managing to promote Islamic cultural and spiritual interests on the one hand while strictly proscribing the use of religion as a vehicle for political mobilization on the other hand.

The efforts of the New Order deserve examination in a comparative context with, for example, the governments of Egypt, Algeria, and Pakistan. Third, Islamic intellectual and cultural life is thriving in Indonesia. The thinking of Indonesian Muslim intellectuals on how to reconcile Islamic political imperatives with modern, industrializing societies in a democratic context requires attention. The Philippines' Ramon Magsaysay Foundation award to Abdurrahman Wahid for his leadership of *Nahdlatul Ulama* as a "force for religious tolerance, fair economic development, and democracy in Indonesia" depicts an Islam not widely understood or appreciated outside Asia. It is rare in Western discourse for Islam, Islamic organizations, or prominent Muslim personalities to be referred to as forces of tolerance and democracy. Yet the example of Indonesian Islam, in attempting to represent democratic aspirations within a nationalist context despite contradictions within the Indonesian Muslim community, provides needed balance to understanding the politics of Islam.

It is extremely interesting, however, to note the arguments of one observer who emphasizes ideological and political threats to the West from Islam. Although Judith Miller does not mention Indonesia, her analysis mirrors arguments swirling around contemporary Indonesian discourse on Pancasila, Islam, politics, minorities, and government. Miller's article echoes Abdurrahman Wahid's fears that some Muslims may manipulate democratic processes so that a duly elected Muslim "majority" government will then "extinguish democracy in the name of Allah." "Free elections" she argues, "seem more likely than any other route to produce militant Islamic regimes that are, in fact, inherently anti-democratic."[33] Clearly, Indonesian anxieties regarding political Islam's intentions are not unique to Indonesia. In this case, however, the writer would surely be less pessimistic if the democratizing efforts of neo-modernist Indonesian Islamic leaders like Abdurrahman Wahid were also considered.

Soeharto's *rapprochement* with Islam as well as minority concerns in Indonesia are paralleled in Ghassan Salame's argument that special consideration by governments of Islamic interests need not endanger minorities or produce a radical outcome. Again, speaking of Islam in general, but accurately reflecting, in part, both Nurcholish Madjid's and Abdurrahman Wahid's views, Salame argues

> whatever the outcome of Islamist attempts to dominate governments, the re-Islamization of societies is proceeding. That fact is becoming an obsessive worry of non-Muslim minorities and secular members of the intelligentsia, though not necessarily of the man on the street. Most governments seem unable to stop the movement, when they do not inadvertently accelerate it through indiscriminate punishments.[34]

Such a precise rendering of the dilemmas in Indonesia – from an analyst who fails to mention Indonesian Islam at all – should highlight the necessity of paying closer attention to how the Indonesian government has thus far managed the state–Islam relationship. Of particular concern should be the way in which the New Order seems to have pleased ordinary Indonesian Muslims with its sponsorship of Islam as a religious force while ensuring that Indonesia remains a Pancasila/nationalist state. The success of the New Order pursuit of such a strategy up to now even leads Wahid to become a more fervent proponent of "de-confessionalization" than Soeharto himself.

Again, while not referring to Indonesia, Salame none the less highlights a dilemma faced by Soeharto's, and perhaps even a successor's, government. He notes that secular governments in Islamic-majority countries, faced with the ongoing cultural "re-Islamization" of society, seek to accommodate some interests of the moderates and at the same time, "hit at the extremists." Yet, Salame argues, the distinction between the moderates and the extremists in Islamic movements tends to become blurred as they join forces for strategic purposes – the advancement of Islamic interests in general. When this blurring occurs, "governments face a catch-22 dilemma. If they lump Islamists together, they tend to help the most extremist; if they distinguish between them, they have to placate the moderates with new concessions."[35]

Is this what is going on today in Indonesia? Is the reason that ICMI so disturbs both Wahid and the democratic elements in the Indonesian Islamic movement, as well as non-Muslims, secular intellectuals, and ABRI officers, because the so-called "extremists" gather in ICMI, an ostensibly "moderate" and non-political organization? As Wahid argues, the perception that an organization exists to seek a more Islamic government may result in the military taking action against it. Yet, if this happens, it will polarize views and legitimize extremist positions. Or is Soetjipto

Wirosardjono correct in arguing that ICMI is actually helping to moderate the extremes and eliminate or reduce old feelings of Muslim bitterness towards the New Order?

Finally, consideration of the degree of international intellectual and political cross-fertilization of Islamic ideas is necessary. For example, if Abdurrahman Wahid, Nurcholish Madjid, and others succeed in more widely promoting ideas of a democratic, pluralist, nationalist Islam in which the political imperative to establish an Islamic state is irreparably severed from theology, then what impact will this have on other Muslims in the global *umat*? To what degree will the Indonesian variant of Islam become a "model" Islam? Abdurrahman Wahid argues that Indonesia is poised to be "the savior of the Islamic world." Wahid argues

> all that the West sees in Islam is radicalism and its incompatibility with modern, open, democratic politics. Indonesia, however, has the opportunity to show that politics based on confession – in Algeria or Iran – is not the only way. Not only can modernity and open politics exist in a Muslim-majority society, and here in Indonesia, but it can also be nurtured so that democracy can flourish well in Islam.[36]

Importantly, the case of the Indonesian *umat*'s struggle to come to terms with state ideology, exemplified by *Nahdlatul Ulama*'s embrace of Pancasila as a nationalist ideology, may represent a form of Islam fully compatible with secular national politics, democracy, liberalism, and non-confrontational relationships with the non-Muslim world.

Both for Indonesianists and comparativists in general, dismissal of Pancasila in Indonesia, or national ideologies elsewhere, as a gloss on "real" politics will ensure that crucial political issues and values remain unconsidered. Fundamental Indonesian political ideas and beliefs are expressed with reference to Pancasila. It is therefore a necessary avenue of analysis for a comprehensive understanding of Indonesia's national life.

The importance of national ideologies should not be underestimated. Suggestions that international ideological debate ended with the collapse of the Soviet bloc ignores important ideological and political developments in Indonesia and other countries. Indonesia illustrates ongoing contention over ideological differences. These differing perspectives are most explicitly given voice by Muslims, the armed forces, and politically secular nationalists and democrats.

Indonesian political discourse suggests that while authorities use Pancasila to restrict the permissible boundaries of political behavior, there is also unifying value in a national ideology whose appeal cross-cuts religious, ethnic, and regional affiliations. The broad Indonesian acceptance of the formulaic expression of national unity in Pancasila reminds us again of the appropriateness of Harry Benda's exhortation to seriously study the "significance of ideologies in the multifaceted process of 'nation-building.' "[37] The relevance Indonesians attach to Pancasila in contemporary discourse clearly illustrates the central value of national ideology in a culturally diverse society.

Notes

INTRODUCTION: THE IDEOLOGY OF TOLERANCE

1 Carol Gluck, *Japan's Modern Myths: Ideology in the Late Meiji Period* (Princeton: Princeton University Press, 1985), pp. 3 and 6.
2 David Apter contends that a primary function of ideology is to support and justify authority. See Apter, "Introduction," *Ideology and Discontent* (New York: Free Press of Glencoe, 1964), p. 18.
3 Pancasila, unlike other ideologies, does not contain a program of action and a prescription of how to reach a desired political or social future. Pancasila is basically a statement of humane values which are nearly impossible to refute at face value. It is not abstract but operational definitions of Pancasila that matter and it is Indonesian political actors who control the definitions.
4 Sukarno, *Pancasila: The Basis of the State of the Republic of Indonesia* (Jakarta: National Committee for the Commemoration of the Birth of Pancasila, 1964), pp. 13–38.
5 Mangunwijaya's comments were made in reference to the author's presentation of a paper, "Pancasila Discourse in Soeharto's Late New Order," Monash University Conference on Indonesian Democracy, December 17–21, 1992, Monash University, Australia.
6 On the appropriation of ideology, see for example, James C. Scott, *Weapons of the Weak: Everyday Forms of Peasant Resistance* (New Haven: Yale University Press, 1985), pp. 318–322, 340–347.
7 On the ideological education programs see, for example, Myra Diarsi, "The New Order State Hegemony: Analysis of Dominant Ideology in Primary School Textbooks," paper, seminar on ideology at Yayasan SPES, March 18, 1992; Aris Arif Mundayat, "The Rite of 'Tujuhbelasan' [17th of August — Proclamation of Independence Day]: Ideological Dissemination Under Soeharto's Regime," paper, Ideology in the New Order Workshop, Indonesian Democracy Conference, December 21, 1992; Michael Morfit, "Pancasila Orthodoxy" in Colin MacAndrews, ed., *Central Government and Local Development in Indonesia* (Singapore: Oxford University Press, 1986); and Geoffrey L. Gunn, "Ideology and the Concept of

Government in the Indonesian New Order," *Asian Survey* XIV, no. 8 (August 1979), pp. 751–769.

8 *Nahdlatul Ulama* (NU) is the largest mass-based Islamic organization in Indonesia with between 20 and 30 million members. Founded in 1926, it has often been defined as the "traditional" and "Javanese" stream of the Indonesian Islamic movement. Abdurrahman Wahid is the most powerful leader of a non-governmental organization in Indonesia both because of the huge mass base under his influence and because of the force of his renowned intellect and undisputed charisma.

9 ICMI, or *Ikatan Cendekiawan Muslim Indonesia* (Indonesian Muslim Intellectuals' Association) was formed in December 1990 with the strong support of President Soeharto. ICMI membership is comprised of a wide range of Islamic scholars, government bureaucrats, and former regime critics. ICMI is widely perceived, even by many of its members, as partially reflective of a desire by Soeharto to shore up his mass political base in light of a decline in support of the President from the armed forces. The head of ICMI is B.J. Habibie, Minister of Technology and a close ally of Soeharto. ICMI has grown rapidly since its inception — it now supports an academic think-tank (CIDES), and a daily newspaper (*Republika*). See Chapter 3 for a full treatment of ICMI.

10 ABRI is the acronym for *Angkatan Bersenjata Republik Indonesia* (Armed Forces of the Republic of Indonesia).

11 Interviews, Abdurrahman Wahid, September 17, 1994 and June 18 and 24, 1992; see also Adam Schwarz, "Islam and Democracy," *Far Eastern Economic Review* (*FEER* hereafter), March 19, 1992, p. 32.

12 Hartas, now retired, is a member of the Supreme Advisory Council. Interview, Lieutenant General Harsudiyono Hartas, April 28, 1993.

13 *Muhammadiyah*, founded in 1912, is the second largest Islamic organization in Indonesia. Unlike NU, *Muhammadiyah* is considered a "modernist" Islamic organization with a primarily urban-based membership. The terms "traditional" and "modernist" are, however, of limited utility in describing and understanding Indonesian Islam and its political role in the 1990s. See, for example, Greg Barton, "The Impact of Neo-Modernism on Indonesian Islamic Thought: The Emergence of a New Pluralism," in David Bourchier and John Legge, eds, *Democracy in Indonesia: 1950s and 1990s* (Clayton, Victoria: Centre of Southeast Asian Studies, Monash University, 1994), pp. 143–150.

14 Almost all the senior ABRI officers interviewed define Pancasila as an "integralistic ideology." Such a definition has political and ideological implications which are examined in Chapter 4.

1 ORIGINS OF DISCOURSE: POLITICS AND IDEOLOGY SINCE 1945

1 In Indonesian: *Badan Penyelidikan Usaha Persiapan Kemerdekaan Indonesia*; hereafter referred to in the text as the Investigating Committee.

2 "Secular" refers here to those politicians who did not mobilize politically on the basis of religion, particularly Islam.

3 Adnan Buyung Nasution, *The Aspiration for Constitutional Government in Indonesia: A Socio-Legal Study of the Indonesian Konstituante, 1956–1959* (Jakarta: Sinar Harapan, 1992), p. 59.

4 The concept of an "integralistic state" (or simply "integralism") conceives of the state and society as an organic totality in which the primary emphasis is not in terms of individual rights or limitations on the powers of government, but in terms of social obligations. Integralism is considered in following sections of this chapter, as well as in Chapter 4 on ABRI.

5 See the text of the original speech in Sukarno, *Pancasila: The Basis of the State of the Republic of Indonesia* (Jakarta: National Committee for the Commemoration of the Birth of Pancasila, 1964), p. 19.

6 In the Preamble to the Constitution of 1945 the ordering is slightly different with Belief in God as the first principle.

7 See Sukarno's speech, (1964); and Bernhard Dahm, *Sukarno and the Struggle for Indonesian Independence* (Ithaca: Cornell University Press, 1969), pp. 294–295. See also Adnan Buyung Nasution (1992), chapters 1 and 2.

8 Donald E. Weatherbee, *Ideology in Indonesia: Sukarno's Indonesian Revolution* (Yale University: Southeast Asia Monograph Series, no. 8, 1966), p. 26.

9 In Indonesian this is expressed as *kerakyatan yang dipimpin oleh hikmah kebijaksanaan dalam permusyawaratan/perwakilan*. This is generally translated as "peoples' democracy which is guided by wisdom in the unanimity arising from consultation and consensus through representation." See *The 1945 Constitution of the Republic of Indonesia* (Jakarta: Department of Information, 1972).

10 See Sukarno's "*Lahirnya* Pancasila" speech in Sukarno (1964), pp. 28–30; and Bernhard Dahm (1969), pp. 296–297. See also General Abdul Haris Nasution's description of *musyawarah* as an Islamic term in Nasution, *Pancasila Democracy Today and Tomorrow* (an account of the legislative achievements of the Provisional People's Consultative Assembly, MPRS, 1972), p. 5.

11 Ali Moertopo, one of New Order's early strategists and key politicians, explicitly argued this point in the late 1960s and early 1970s. See, for example, Moertopo's collected works in *The Acceleration and Modernization of 25 Years' Development* (Jakarta: Yayasan Proklamasai, CSIS, 1972). The central importance of Ali Moertopo's thinking on Pancasila and politics in the New Order is examined at greater length below.

12 Later Minister of Religion and the father of the current Chairman of NU, Abdurrahman Wahid.

13 Wahid Hasyim's remarks are cited in Harry J. Benda, *The Crescent and the Rising Sun: Indonesian Islam Under the Japanese Occupation* (The Hague: W. van Hoeve Ltd., 1958) p. 189.

14 Adnan Buyung Nasution, (1992), pp. 10–11, 63–64, 103–105 and Muhammad H. Yamin, *Naskah Persiapan Undang-Undang Dasar 1945* [Preparatory Documents of the Constitution of 1945], vol. I (Jakarta: Yayasan Prapanca, 1959), pp. 153–154, 264.

15 See Mohammed Hatta, *Memoir* (Jakarta: Tintamas, 1978), pp. 454–458; and Adnan Buyung Nasution, (1992), p. 64. See also the analysis of Hatta's – and Christian nationalists' – fears in B.J. Boland, *The Struggle of Islam in Modern Indonesia* (Slightly revised reprint) (The Hague: Martinus Nijhoff, 1971 and 1982), pp. 23–37.

16 For an understanding of early Muslim perceptions of "betrayal" see Boland (1971); Dahm (1969), pp. 297–98; and H. Endang Saifuddin Anshari, *Piagam Jakarta 22 Juni 1945 dan Sejarah Konsensus Nasional Antara Nasionalis Islami dan Nasionalis "Sekuler" Tentang Dasar Negara Republik Indonesia 1945–1959* [The Jakarta Charter, June 22, 1945 and the National Consensus Between Islamic Nationalists and "Secular" Nationalists Regarding the Basis of the Republic of Indonesia, 1945–1959] (Jakarta: Rajawali, 1986).

17 Abdul Haris Nasution (1972), p. 63.

18 Boland (1971), pp. 52–53, noted that the elections of 1955 "resulted in great disappointment for the Islamic parties" as they had falsely assumed that all Muslims would vote on the basis of their faith. On the elections of 1955 the classic source is Herbert Feith, *Decline of Constitutional Democracy in Indonesia* (Ithaca: Cornell University Press, 1962), pp. 424–440.

19 See, for example, Deliar Noer, *The Modernist Muslim Movement in Indonesia, 1900–1942* (Singapore: Oxford University Press, 1973); and Boland (1971). However, the unsuitability of terms like "modernist" and "traditional" for describing the contemporary Indonesian Islamic movement is pointed out by Greg Barton, "The Impact of Islamic Neo-Modernism on Indonesian Islamic Thought: the Emergence of a New Pluralism," in David Bourchier and John Legge, eds, *Democracy in Indonesia: 1950s and 1990s* (Clayton, Victoria: Centre of Southeast Asian Studies, Monash University, 1994).

20 Fred von der Mehden, *Religion and Modernization in Southeast Asia* (Syracuse: Syracuse University Press, 1986), p. 184.

21 The definition of *aliran* is taken from Clifford Geertz, "The Javanese Village," in G. William Skinner, ed., *Local, Ethnic, and National Loyalties in Village Indonesia* (Ithaca: Cornell University Modern Indonesian Project, 1959), p. 37.

22 The Constituent Assembly is commonly referred to in Indonesia as the "*Konstituante*". Hereafter the term will be used without emphasis.

23 Indonesia has had three constitutions. The 1945 Constitution, which calls for an extremely powerful presidency, was replaced in 1949 by a Constitution for the "United States of Indonesia" which stipulated a loose federation; this was replaced in 1950 by a document that established a parliamentary form of government. The Constitution of 1950 was said to be provisional with a permanent constitution to be devised by an elected Constituent Assembly.

24 See Adnan Buyung Nasution (1992), pp. 51–118; and especially Sukarno's original conception in the "*Lahirnya* Pancasila" speech in Sukarno (1964).

25 J.D. Legge, *Sukarno, A Political Biography* (Harmondsworth, Middlesex: Penguin Books Ltd., 1972), pp. 251–252.

26 Sukarno, cited in Feith (1962), p. 281. West Irian was formally incorporated as Indonesia's twenty-sixth province in 1969.

27 On the *Darul Islam* revolts see Boland (1971), pp. 54–74 and C. van Dijk, *Rebellion Under the Banner of Islam; the Darul Islam in Indonesia* (The Hague: Martinus Nijhoff, 1981).

28 ABRI officers interviewed by the author in 1992 and 1993 often mentioned the *Darul Islam* revolts to explain the need for the armed forces to guard against such threats to the state. Djohan Effendi has argued that Muslims themselves are partially to blame for being depicted as threatening to the state by the military and others because Muslims in the 1950s "narrow-mindedly" saw Pancasila as a threat to Islam. See Effendi, "The Contribution of the Islamic Parties to the Decline of Democracy in the 1950s," paper, Conference on Indonesian Democracy, Monash University, December 18, 1992.

29 The PKI's support of Pancasila is noteworthy. It was clearly a political tactic to side with mainstream, nationalist thinking. The Belief in God principle was seemingly incompatible with communist ideology. Indeed, after 1965 the "atheistic" nature of communism was highlighted by the armed forces, Muslims, and others to depict the PKI as "anti-Pancasila" and thereby "un-Indonesian." The PKI's acceptance of Pancasila was later depicted as treacherous manipulation. Studies of the PKI include Rex Mortimer, *Indonesian Communism Under Sukarno: Ideology and Politics 1959–1965* (Ithaca: Cornell University Press, 1974); and Donald Hindley, *The Communist Party of Indonesia, 1951–1963* (Berkeley: University of California Press, 1966).

30 Adnan Buyung Nasution (1992), p. 421.

31 See David Bourchier, "Totalitarianism and the 'National Personality': Recent Controversy about the Philosophical Basis of the Indonesian State," in James Schiller, ed., *Indonesian Political Culture: Asking the Right Questions* (Athens, Ohio: Ohio University Center for Southeast Asian Studies, forthcoming); Marsillam Simanjuntak "Unsur Hegelian Dalam Pandangan Negara Integralistik [Hegelian Elements in the Integralistic View of the State]," (MA Thesis, University of Indonesia, Faculty of Law, 1989); and Adnan Buyung Nasution (1992), pp. 90–103.

32 On General Nasution's key role in the dissolution of the Konstituante and the return to the Constitution of 1945 see C.L.M. Penders and Ulf Sundhaussen, *Abdul Haris Nasution, A Political Biography* (St. Lucia, Queensland: University of Queensland Press, 1985). It is important to note the crucial military role in the dissolution of the Konstituante. In order to combat the *Darul Islam* and other separatist rebellions in the 1950s, the military consistently expanded its authority, particularly after the declaration of martial law in 1957.

33 Adnan Buyung Nasution's analysis of the debates of the Konstituante (Nasution, 1992) contests the myth of the "failure" of the Assembly. Rather, Nasution argues that the Konstituante was made to fail by Sukarno and the armed forces. He shows that there were grounds to expect an eventual compromise consensus on major issues before the delegates. This is significant because ABRI and New Order supporters often say that the "inability" of the Konstituante and the parliament in the 1950s to agree on anything was indicative of the inappropriateness of multi-party democracy for Indonesia.

34 For description and analysis of the period of Guided Democracy and the role of the communist party, see Daniel Lev, *The Transition to Guided Democracy, Indonesian Politics 1957–59* (Ithaca: Cornell University Modern Indonesia Project, 1966); Ruth McVey, "Indonesian Communism Under Guided Democracy" in A.D. Barnett, ed., *Communist Strategies in Asia, A Comparative Analysis of Government and Parties* (New York: Praeger, 1963); and Harold Crouch, *The Army and Politics in Indonesia* (Ithaca: Cornell University Press, 1978), pp. 43–96.

35 Sukarno, "Let us Bury the Parties" in Herbert Feith and Lance Castles, eds, *Indonesian Political Thinking 1945–1965* (Ithaca: Cornell University Press, 1970), p. 81–83.

36 On the Japanese establishment of an Indonesian defense force, known as the PETA (Defenders of the Fatherland), see Anderson, *Java in a Time of Revolution* (Ithaca: Cornell University Press, 1972); and Guy Pauker, "The Role of the Military in Indonesia," in J.J. Johnson, ed., *The Role of the Military in Underdeveloped Countries* (Princeton: Princeton University Press, 1962), pp. 187–192.

37 Known as ABRI (Armed Forces of the Republic of Indonesia) after military reorganization under the New Order.

38 The successful conclusion to the revolutionary struggle for full independence was, in reality, a complex combination of negotiations, military actions, and international pressure (especially American) on the Dutch to give up its colonial ambitions in light of the building cold war in Europe. See Salim Said, *The Genesis of Power: General Sudirman and the Indonesian Military in Politics, 1945–1949* (Singapore: Institute of Southeast Asian Studies, 1992), p. 93–94.

39 On the PKI's involvement in what became known as the "Madiun Affair," a standard account is George Kahin, *Nationalism and*

Revolution in Indonesia (Ithaca: Cornell University Press, 1952), pp. 284–303.

40 PRRI (*Pemerintah Revolusioner Republik Indonesia*, or the Revolutionary Government of the Republic of Indonesia, was a rebel movement based in West Sumatra. It was allied with *Permesta*, a Sulawesi-based rebellion. Both were defeated by the central government in military campaigns, 1958–1959.

41 International political pressure, diplomacy, and Indonesian military action eventually convinced the Dutch to give up West Irian. For ABRI, however, the West Irian campaign reinforced military perception of itself as the pre-eminent defender of the national interest.

42 Crouch (1978), p. 33.

43 Ibid., p. 24.

44 See Ulf Sundhaussen, *The Road To Power: Indonesian Military Politics 1945–67* (Kuala Lumpur: Oxford University Press, 1982).

45 The best studies of Golkar are David Reeve, *Golkar of Indonesia: An Alternative to the Party System* (Singapore: Oxford University Press, 1985); and Leo Suryadinata, *Military Ascendancy and Political Culture: A Study of Indonesia's Golkar* (Athens, Ohio: Ohio University Monograph Series in International Studies, 1989).

46 For interpretations of the controversial events of September 30/October 1, 1965 which set in motion the end of Sukarno's reign and the beginning of the New Order the most balanced explanation is found in Crouch (1978), pp. 97–134. Other interpretations of the coup attempt are found in Benedict Anderson and Ruth McVey, *A Preliminary Analysis of the October 1, 1965 Coup in Indonesia* (Ithaca: Cornell University, Modern Indonesia Project, 1971); Justus van der Kroef, "Origins of the 1965 Coup in Indonesia: Probabilities and Alternatives," *Journal of Southeast Asian Studies* vol. 3, no. 2 (September 1972), pp. 277–298; the Indonesian Armed Forces' version is Nugroho Notosusanto and Ismael Saleh, *The Coup Attempt of the "September 30th Movement" in Indonesia* (Jakarta: Pembimbing Masa, 1968).

47 For Soeharto's own account of his assumption of power in his autobiography *My Thoughts, Words, and Deeds: An Autobiography*, as told to G. Dwipayana and Ramadhan K.H., English translation by Sumadi (Jakarta: PT. Citra Lamtoro Gung Persada, 1991), pp. 99–171.

48 The most comprehensive work on these events is Robert Cribb, ed., *The Indonesian Killings 1965–1966: Studies From Java and Bali*, Monash Papers on Southeast Asia, no. 21 (Clayton, Victoria: Centre for Southeast Asian Studies, Monash University, 1990).

49 Admiral Sudomo, former commander of KOPKAMTIB (Operations Command to Restore Order and Security, set up under the New Order) stated that between 450,000 and 500,000 people were killed. See "Setelah Wawancara Sudomo," [After the Sudomo Interview], *Tempo*, July 10, 1976, p. 7.

50 M.C. Ricklefs wrote that nearly all these early supporters of the New Order saw the new regime as far preferable to either a return to the chaos of the Sukarno era or an Islamic state. See Ricklefs, *A History of Indonesia* (Bloomington: Indiana University Press, 1981), p. 278.

51 In Indonesian: *Majelis Permusyawaratan Rakyat Sementara.*

52 See *Ketetapan Majelis Permusyawaratan Rakyat Sementara Republik Indonesia* [Decision of the Provisional People's Consultative Assembly], *no. XX/MPRS/1966.*

53 Ibid. See also the account of the proceedings and achievements of the MPRS by its Speaker, General Abdul Haris Nasution (1972), p. 6.

54 See *Pidato Presiden Republik Indonesia dan Menutama Bidang Politik Pada Peringatan Hari Lahirnya Pancasila* [Speech of the President of the Republic of Indonesia and the Senior Minister for Political Affairs on the Remembrance of the Birth of Pancasila] June 1, 1967 (Jakarta: Department of Information, Republic of Indonesia and PT Gunung Agung, 1967). Hereafter citations of these speeches will be as "Malik (1967)" or "Soeharto (1967)."

55 In official New Order histories of the 1950s parliamentary party politics are portrayed as leading to chaos and incompatible with Indonesian political culture. For an analysis of how the 1950s are represented in the New Order see David Bourchier, "The 1950s in New Order Ideology and Politics," in Bourchier and Legge (1994) pp. 50–62.

56 Soeharto (1967), p. 11.

57 Malik (1967), p. 15.

58 Ibid., pp. 17–19.

59 Ibid., p. 18.

60 On the role of ABRI in the New Order, see also Ali Moertopo (1972). For analysis of the New Order's Development Ideology, see Mohtar Mas'oed, "The State Reorganization of Society under the New Order," *Prisma*, no. 47 (September 1989), pp. 3–33.

61 The classic study of the parliamentary democracy period of the 1950s is Feith (1962).

62 Marsillam Simanjuntak, interview, April 7, 1993. Jamie Mackie also makes this point in "Economic Growth and Depoliticization," in James W. Morley, ed., *Driven By Growth: Political Change in the Asia-Pacific Region*, (Armonk, New York: M.E. Sharpe, 1993), pp. 75–76.

63 See Michael Vatikiotis, "Pastoral Politics," *FEER*, October 5, 1989, p. 30. Early New Order supporters such as Harry Tjan Silalahi, who headed the Catholic students' organization and later the Catholic Party, argued that intellectuals did not support deposing Sukarno only to see political Islam (which, it was feared might not guarantee minority religious rights) become the dominant post-PKI/Sukarno power. Interview, January 12, 1992.

64 Jusuf Wanandi, interview July 1, 1992. See also Hamish McDonald, *Suharto's Indonesia* (Blackburn, Victoria: Fontana, 1980), p. 99.

65 For the significance of Ali Moertopo's role see David Jenkins, *Suharto and His Generals: Indonesian Military Politics, 1975–1983* (Ithaca: Cornell University Modern Indonesia Project, 1984), *passim*. Indonesian political scientist Mochtar Pabottingi argues that Ali Moertopo was perhaps the most important political and ideological strategist in the New Order. See Pabottingi, "Indonesia: Historicizing the New Order's Legitimacy Dilemma," in Muthiah Alagappa, ed., *Political Legitimacy in Southeast Asia: Quest for Moral Authority* (Stanford: Stanford University Press, 1995).

66 J.A.C. Mackie, "The Golkar Victory and party-Aliran Alignments," in Oey Hong Lee, ed., *Indonesia After the 1971 Elections* (London: Oxford University Press, 1974), p. 66.

67 Ali Moertopo, *The Acceleration and Modernization of 25 Years' Development* (Jakarta: CSIS, 1972), pp. 85–86. This collection of Ali Moertopo's thoughts is a remarkable exposition on the political thinking of the New Order. Moertopo shows how the New Order's political, ideological, and economic planning was exceptionally long-term.

68 See the transcript "President Soeharto's Message In Gathering with the KPNI (Indonesian National Youth Committee) on July 19, 1982" (unpublished).

69 Moertopo, *Acceleration and Modernization* (1972), p. 45.

70 Ibid., pp. 23 and 45. Clear explanations of ABRI ideology and its "dual function" can be found in Crouch (1978), Sundhaussen (1982), Jenkins (1984), and Suryadinata (1989).

71 Imaduddin Abdul Rahim, a founding member of ICMI (interview, April 16, 1993) and Din Syamsuddin (interview, April 29, 1993), the leader of the youth wing of the *Muhammadiyah*, both speak of the "trauma" of Islam in the early New Order years. Syamsuddin, however, is too young to have directly experienced those events. See Chapter 3.

72 Sidney Jones, "The Contraction and Expansion of the 'Umat' and the Role of the *Nahdlatul Ulama* in Indonesia," *Indonesia* no. 38 (October 1984), p. 9.

73 The formal legislative bodies of government include two representative houses. The DPR, or "House of Representatives," consists of 500 members, 400 of whom are selected in general elections every five years. 100 seats are reserved for ABRI and are appointed by the President. The DPR meets several times each year to approve government-initiated legislation. The MPR, or People's Consultative Assembly, consists of all members of the DPR plus 500 additional members appointed by the President. The 1,000-member MPR meets once every five years to elect the President and Vice President, to approve an accounting by the President of his previous five-year term, and to approve the five-year plan and "The Broad Outlines of State Policy," or GBHN. Although the Constitution stipulates that the MPR is supreme repository of the people's sovereignty, in practice it has little authority over government and does not initiate legislation.

74 This MPR decision is popularly known as P-4, after its Indonesian title *Pedoman Penghayatan dan Pengamalan Pancasila* [Guide to the Comprehension and Practice of Pancasila].

75 See, in translation, the full text of the MPR Decree: *P-4: The Guide to the Living and Practice of Pancasila and GBHN: The Broad Outlines of the State Policy* (Jakarta: CSIS, 1978).

76 For details on the political motivation of the regime and political values the government sought to inculcate through the courses see, for example: Morfit (1981), Gunn (1979), Diarsi (1992), and Douglas E. Ramage, "The Political Function of Pancasila" (MA Thesis, University of South Carolina, 1987). For the best example of government ideological education materials (P-4), see Professor Padmo Wahjono, *Bahan-Bahan Pedoman Penghayatan dan Pengamalan Pancasila* [Materials for the Guide to the Comprehension and Practice of Pancasila] (Jakarta: Aksara Baru, 1984).

77 Although it was part of the forcibly unified coalition of Islamic parties, the NU still acted as an independent organization.

78 Sidney Jones (October 1984), p. 11.

79 Jenkins (1984), p. 159.

80 See Soeharto's remarks in "Amanat Tambahan Presiden Soeharto Pada Pembukaan Rapat Pimpinan ABRI 1980" [Addition to President Soeharto's Speech at the Opening of the 1980 ABRI Commanders' Meeting], *Kompas*, April 8, 1980.

81 Jenkins (1984), p. 158. Abdurrahman Wahid strongly rejects the notion that the NU action in 1978 was in any way directed against Pancasila. Indeed, of all the major groups in the Islamic movement, NU has generally been the most accommodating towards Pancasila. See Chapter 2.

82 Soeharto's remarks cited in "Banyak Isyu Dilemparkan Untuk Menyingkirkan Presiden Soeharto" [Many Issues are Raised in order to Sideline President Soeharto], *Kompas*, April 17, 1980.

83 See, for example, "Sasaran Pidato Presiden di Cijantung Adalah P-3" [The Target of the President's Speech in Cijantung was PPP], *Merdeka*, July 28, 1980.

84 Text of the original Statement of Concern printed in the daily *Pelita*, July 16, 1980.

85 The Petition of Fifty still exists today as a private forum for discussion and debate and is led by Ali Sadikin. It periodically issues statements and press releases critical of various aspects of national policy and politics.

86 See for example, *Melihat Kembali: Pernyataan Keprihatinan – 5 Mei 1980* [Looking Again at the May 5, 1980 Statement of Concern] (Jakarta: Kelompok Kerja Petisi Limapuluh [Petition of Fifty Working Group], 1991).

87 See, for example, "Komentar Sekitar Anggota 'Petisi 50' Ikut Pemilu 1982" [Commentary Surrounding the Members of the Petition of 50 is Part of the 1982 Election], *Sinar Harapan*, April 27, 1981.

88 I am indebted to Dr. Damardjati Supadjar in the Department of Philosophy at Gajah Mada University, Yogyakarta, for his

explanation of the relationship between Javanese beliefs and Pancasila. Interview, October 8, 1992.

89 On the distinctly "Javanese" character to Soeharto's political behavior see, for example, Susumu Awanohara, "Suharto's Kingdom," *FEER*, August 9, 1984, pp. 32–36. David Jenkins also writes that Soeharto's obsession with Pancasila is linked to his projection of "the aura of a traditional Javanese king." Jenkins saw Soeharto (in 1983/84) as becoming "more feudalistic, more mystical." Jenkins (1984), pp. 158–159.

90 See the transcript of "President Soeharto's Message In Gathering with the KPNI (Indonesian National Youth Committee)," July 19, 1982.

91 One of the government's leading ideologists, Dr. Soerjanto Poespowardojo, argues that if Pancasila is too narrowly interpreted in an Islamic sense, then the "followers of Javanese mystical beliefs, who are religious people," will have nowhere to go and Pancasila will no longer speak to them. Interview, July 8, 1992.

92 Soeharto's remarks, cited in *Antara*, August 16, 1982.

93 Sjafruddin Prawiranegara, "Pancasila as the Sole Foundation," *Indonesia* vol. 38 (October 1984), p. 80.

94 Susumu Awanohara argues that Soeharto responded to Sjafruddin's "inflammatory" letter. See "Firming Up a Philosophy," *FEER*, August 11, 1983, p. 37.

95 "Presiden Berhalal bi Halal Dengan Perwira Senior ABRI di Tapos Bogor: Asas Tunggal Perlu Untuk Stabilitas" [President (has an Islamic social gathering) With Senior ABRI Officers at Tapos (Soeharto's Ranch), Bogor: The Sole Foundation is Needed for Stability], *Sinar Harapan*, July 18, 1983.

96 Lincoln Kaye, "Legislating Harmony," *FEER*, June 13, 1985, p. 14.

97 R. William Liddle, "Why Suharto Tries to Bring Islam to Heel," *Asian Wall Street Journal Weekly*, March 12, 1984, p. 11.

98 Cited in an interview with Adam Malik by Derek Davies and Susumu Awanohara, "Javanese Dilemma," *FEER*, May 21, 1982, p. 35.

99 Susumu Awanohara, "The New Call To Prayer," *FEER*, January 24, 1985, p. 26.

100 Awanohara, "The New Call To Prayer," *FEER*, January 24, 1985, p. 26.

101 Munawir Sjadzali, interview, April 12, 1993.

102 On the riots and their connection to Pancasila, see for example, Susumu Awanohara, "A First Warning Shot: Muslim Riots in Jakarta Reveal Tensions over the State Ideology," *FEER*, September 27, 1984; and "Pangab Minta Masyarakat Waspada Terhadap Segala Bentuk Gangguan Keamanan" [Commander of the Armed Forces Asks the People to be Vigilant Against any form of Disturbance to Public Safety], *Antara*, September 13, 1984.

103 See the explanation given by then Commander of ABRI, General L.B. Moerdani in "Penjelasan Panglima ABRI Jenderal L.B. Moerdani di Depan Rakergab DPR-RI Tentang Peristiwa Tanjung

Priok" [Explanation by General Moerdani to the Parliamentary Commission Concerning the Tanjung Priok Incident], reprinted in *Kiblat* no. 10 (October 1984). In this statement Moerdani explains that the rioters were incited by people exploiting "SARA" (ethnic, religious, racial and class) issues.

104 Abdurrahman Wahid, interview, May 3, 1993.

105 Susumu Awanohara, "A Matter of Principles," *FEER*, October 25, 1985.

106 See "Tiga Ledakan di Ibukota, Pangab: ABRI Bertanggungjawab Atas Keselamatan Semua Warga Negara" [Three Explosions in the Capital, ABRI Commander: ABRI is Responsible for the Safety of all Citizens], *Kompas*, October 5, 1984; and Susumu Awanohara, "Bombs in Chinatown," *FEER*, October 18, 1984.

107 See, for example, "H.R. Dharsono Ditahan: Dituduh Melakukan Tindak Pidana Subversi" [Dharsono Arrested: Charged with Carrying Out Subversive Action], *Sinar Harapan*, November 19, 1984; and Susumu Awanohara, "Clampdown on the 50," *FEER*, November 22, 1984.

108 Abdurrahman Wahid, "Kasus Tanjung Priok Tragedi Yang Tak Perlu" [The Case of Tanjung Priok: An Unnecessary Tragedy], *Pelita*, September 15, 1984.

109 Adam Schwarz, "Pause for New Growth," *FEER*, April 18, 1991, pp. 33–47; On deregulation, see Hadi Soesastro, "The Political Economy of Deregulation in Indonesia," *Asian Survey*, vol. 29, no. 9 (September 1989), pp. 853–869.

110 *The East Asian Miracle: Economic Growth and Public Policy* (Washington, D.C.: World Bank, 1993); See also Sjharir, "Groping Through the Dark in Indonesia," *Asian Wall Street Journal*, April 29, 1993, p. 6; and Philip Shenon, "As Indonesia Crushes its Critics, It Raises Millions Out of Poverty," *New York Times*, August 27, 1993.

111 Sri Bintang Pamungkas, interview, April 1, 1993.

112 Alfian, interview, February 20, 1992. Alfian was also the Director of Political Studies at the Indonesian Academy of Sciences (LIPI) until his death in November 1992.

113 See Bourchier (forthcoming); Franz Magnis Suseno, interview, March 21, 1992.

114 "22 Wajah Baru Dalam Cabinet Baru" [22 New Faces in the New Cabinet], *Republika*, March 18, 1993. On the economic line-up in the new Cabinet, see Henry Sender, "New Boys' Challenge," *FEER*, April 1, 1993, pp. 72–77.

115 For accounts of the business activities of the President's family, see Adam Schwarz, "All is Relative," *FEER*, April 30, 1992, pp. 54–58; and Jay Branegan, "Empire of the Sons – and Daughter," *Time* (Asia Pacific edition), February 3, 1992, pp. 10–13.

116 On the political economy of ABRI see Richard Robison, *Indonesia: The Rise of Capital* (Sydney: Allen & Unwin, 1986), pp. 250–270.

117 Adi Sasono, a NGO activist and leading member of ICMI, interview, March 3, 1993.

118 NU formally withdrew from politics in December 1984 in order to concentrate on social, educational, and cultural development. See Chapter 3.

119 A former leader of the HMI (Islamic Students Association) in the 1960s, Nurcholish provoked heated controversy in the Islamic community in the 1970s by explicitly calling for a de-linking of Islamic politics and religion in his now-famous "Islam Yes, Islamic Party No" speech.

120 On the recent changes in Indonesian Islam as seen by analysis of major Indonesian Islamic thinkers, see Barton in Bourchier and Legge (1994); Greg Barton, "Neo-Modernism – A Vital Synthesis of Traditionalist and Modernist Islamic Thought in Indonesia," paper, Islam and the Challenge of Modernization Conference held in conjunction with the 29th Congress of *Nahdlatul Ulama*, Tasikmalaya, West Java, December 1–5, 1994; Howard M. Federspiel, *Muslim Intellectuals and National Development in Indonesia* (New York: Nova Science Publishers, Inc., 1992). See also Nurcholish Madjid, *Islam Kemodernan dan Keindonesiaan* [Modernist and Indonesianized Islam] (Jakarta: Mizan, 1987).

121 Michael Vatikiotis, *Indonesian Politics Under Suharto: Order, Development and Pressure for Change* (London: Routledge, 1993), p. 139.

2 ABDURRAHMAN WAHID AND *NAHDLATUL ULAMA*

1 Interviews, June 18 and June 24, 1992.

2 Carol Gluck, *Japan's Modern Myths: Ideology in the Late Mëji Period* (Princeton, Princeton University Press, 1985), p. 8.

3 Members of NU are aware of their organization's unique status in internationally comparative terms. For example, Muchlisin, a leading *Mubaliq* [Islamic preacher] in Central Java, noted with pride that "not even in Saudi Arabia do they have a mass Muslim organization such as NU. The government there will not allow it." Interview, October 28, 1992 in Semarang, Central Java. Similarly, although some NU members may not agree with or understand Wahid's complex views, they are still proud of the international attention he receives, according to Syamsuddin Anwar, head of the *Syuriah* [Religious Law Council of NU] for Central Java. Interview, October 29, 1992.

4 In the Indonesian press Abdurrahman Wahid is consistently and misleadingly referred to as "the President" of the WCRP. He is, however, an elected member of the Presidential Board, of which there are 28 "presidents." The position is none the less a significant example of Wahid's international stature and reputation.

5 See, for example, "Intellectuals Establish Forum to Bolster Democracy in Indonesia," *Jakarta Post*, April 4, 1991; and Adam Schwarz, "A Worrying Word: New Group Aims to Promote Values of Democracy," *FEER*, April 25, 1991, p. 23.

6 Wahid's contribution to contemporary political debate occurs through his writings published in several dailies, frequent interviews, and regular public lectures. Almost all of Wahid's public commentary is reported in the written mass media.

7 Ichlasul Amal, Dean of Faculty of Social Sciences and Politics, Gajah Mada University, Yogyakarta. Interview, October 7, 1992.

8 At the 27th NU Congress at Situbondo in 1984 Wahid was not elected, but appointed by a senior group of *kiai*. Wahid's position as General Chairman, along with other important organizational posts, was worked out, in part, through intensive consultation between various NU factions prior to the Congress. At the 1989 28th NU Congress in Krapyak, Central Java, formal, secret ballot elections were held only at the nominating stage for Chairman. Wahid's potential challengers did not receive the requisite forty votes to qualify for the final round of voting for NU Chairman and so Wahid was elected by acclamation. The 29th NU Congress in Tasikmalaya in 1994 was characterized by a stiff challenge to Wahid's leadership in the final round of voting for Chairman. However, Wahid was re-elected to a third five-year term by a relatively narrow margin. Wahid's victory in 1994 was widely perceived in Indonesia as a victory for democracy because many observers believed the 1994 NU Congress election was also characterized by government interference designed to depose Wahid. Personal observations, December 1994.

9 On the 1984 NU Congress see, for example, Manggi Habir, "Ulamas Change Course," *FEER*, January 10, 1985, pp. 37–39. On the 1989 NU Congress, see Martin van Bruinessen, "The 28th Congress of the *Nahdlatul Ulama*: Power Struggle and Social Concerns," *Archipel 41* (Paris, 1991), pp. 185–200. For an excellent treatment of the 1994 Congress see Greg Fealy, "The 1994 *Nahdlatul Ulama* Congress and Aftermath: Gus Dur, *Suksesi*, and the Battle for Control of NU," in *Inside Indonesia* (forthcoming, 1995).

10 Abdurrahman Wahid, interview, September 17, 1994.

11 The December 1994 NU Congress and the re-election of Wahid is significant for several reasons. First, it demonstrates that Wahid remains the single most supported NU leader despite his controversial behavior within the organization and his visit to Israel. Second, Wahid's independence, advocacy of secular democracy, and critical comments on the authoritarian nature of the Indonesian regime generated some government interference at the NU Congress designed to engineer his defeat. That Wahid prevailed over this government intervention was widely perceived within NU and in much of the Jakarta press as evidence of the political independence of Wahid and NU. I was an observer at the Congress in Tasikmalaya, West Java and it was clear that many NU delegates believed that certain factions within the government were trying to depose Wahid and replace him with a less critical, regime-friendly NU leadership. It is important to note that the government was not wholly opposed to Wahid's re-election. Senior NU leaders close

to Wahid argued that only those government officials and ABRI officers sympathetic to ICMI and Habibie (see Chapters 3 and 4) sought to replace Wahid while other regime factions preferred to remain neutral or were supportive of Wahid. Confidential interviews, December 1994. There was also genuine internal NU opposition to Wahid for of a variety of reasons, including perceptions that he is a poor administrator and neglectful of NU's branches outside Java.

12 Greg Barton, "The Impact of Neo-Modernism on Indonesian Islamic Thought: the Emergence of a New Pluralism," in Bourchier and Legge (1994), p. 148.

13 Mochtar Lubis, interview, March 30, 1992.

14 Roeslan Abdulgani, "Kejenuhan" [Saturation], *Tempo*, January 15, 1992.

15 In the scholarly literature, see for example, Harry J. Benda, *The Crescent and the Rising Sun: Indonesian Islam under Japanese Occupation* (The Hague: W. Van Hoeve Ltd., 1958); Herbert Feith *The Decline of Constitutional Democracy in Indonesia* (Ithaca: Cornell University Press, 1962); B.J. Boland (1971); Greg Fealy and Greg Barton, eds, *Nahdlatul Ulama: Traditional Islam and Modernity* (Clayton, Victoria: Centre of Southeast Asian Studies, Monash University, 1995); Martin van Bruinessen, *NU: Tradisi, Relasi-Relasi Kuasa [dan] Pencarian Wacana Baru* [NU: Tradition, Power Relations and the Search for a New Discourse] (Yogyakarta: LKiS, 1994); and Andrée Feillard, "Traditionalist Islam and the State in Indonesia: Flexibility, Legitimacy, and Renewal," paper, Conference on Islam and the Social Construction of Identities: Comparative Perspectives on Southeast Asian Muslims, University of Hawaii, August 4–6, 1993. See also Ellyasa K.H. Dharwis, ed., *Gus Dur, NU, dan Masyarakat Sipil* [Abdurrahman Wahid, NU and Civil Society] (Yogyakarta: LKiS, 1994); and H.M. Said Budairy, ed., *Nahdlatul Ulama Dari Berbagai Sudut Pandang* [NU from Various Viewpoints] (Jakarta: LAKPESDAM, 1994).

16 See Adam Schwarz, "Charismatic Enigma," *FEER*, November 12, 1992, p. 34.

17 Quotation from the Ramon Magsaysay Foundation's Award Citation presented to Abdurrahman Wahid in August 1993.

18 Amir Santoso, interview, November 4, 1992. Santoso was Chair of the Department of Political Science at the University of Indonesia. See also "Ismail Sunny: Selama Ada NU, Gus Dur Sektarian Juga" [As Long as there is NU, Wahid is also Sectarian], *Detik*, November 2, 1992, p. 9.

19 Adi Sasono, interview, March 3, 1993.

20 Mochtar Buchori, "NU: A Bulwark of Indonesian Democracy?" in *Jakarta Post*, December 7, 1994.

21 H.M. Muchlisin, interview, October 28, 1992.

22 Abdurrahman Wahid, interviews, June 15, June 23, and September 17, 1994.

23 Franz Magnis Suseno, interview, June 21, 1994.

24 There is no biography of Abdurrahman Wahid. Biographical information was obtained through interviews and from articles on NU. I am particularly indebted to Djohan Effendi, Senior Researcher in the Indonesian Ministry of Religion, and to Australian scholars Greg Fealy (Monash University) and Greg Barton (Deakin University) for providing a great deal of background information on NU, Abdurrahman Wahid, and Islamic thought.

25 Hashim Wahid, interview, May 3, 1993. "*Orang awam*" are "the common people" while "*muslim kaki lima*" refers to poor people who sell from three-wheeled carts.

26 Djohan Effendi, a leading Islamic scholar, is Senior Researcher in the Department of Religion; Nurcholish Madjid is among the most prominent Indonesian Islamic scholars and heads a private Islamic institute, Yayasan Paramadina. The late Ahmad Wahib was a young, broad-minded modernist thinker in the late 1960s.

27 Barton in Bourchier and Legge (1994), pp. 144–147. See also Abdurrahman Wahid, "Islam, Politics, and Democracy in the 1950s and 1990s," in Bourchier and Legge (1994), pp. 151–155.

28 Barton in Bourchier and Legge (1994), p. 147.

29 See, for example, the statement by Wahid Hasyim in 1945 that only with the "indissoluble unity of the nation" could the healthy position of Islam be guaranteed. Cited in Benda (1958), p. 189.

30 Achmad Buchori Masruri, interview, October 29, 1992.

31 Wahid's remarks are reprinted as "Langkah Strategis Menjadi Pertimbangan NU" [Strategic Approach Becomes a Consideration for NU], *Aula* (NU Journal), July 1992, p. 26.

32 One of the leaders of ICMI argued that nationalism is not a sufficient basis for Indonesian unity and integration. Imaduddin argued that such a unifying base can only be Islam. Interview, April 16, 1993.

33 The relationship between NU and ABRI has significant implications for our understanding of the cross-cutting ideological alliances that are, perhaps unwittingly, being created in Indonesia today. See also Chapter 4.

34 Wahid, "Langkah Strategis – ," *Aula*, July 1992, p. 26. Emphasis added.

35 Imaduddin Abdul Rahim, interview, April 16, 1993.

36 On NU's acceptance of Pancasila during the *asas tunggal* debates, see Sidney Jones, "The Contraction and Expansion of the 'Umat' and the Role of *Nahdlatul Ulama* in Indonesia," *Indonesia*, no. 38, (October 1984); Einar M. Sitompul, *Nahdlatul Ulama dan Pancasila* [NU and Pancasila], (Jakarta: Pustaka Sinar Harapan, 1991); Arief Mudatsir, "From Situbondo Towards a New NU – A First Note," *Prisma*, no. 35 (March 1985), pp. 167–177; and Abdurrahman Wahid, "The Islamic Masses in the Life of State and Nation," *Prisma*, no. 35 (March 1985), pp. 3–10.

37 Recall that NU had been singled out by Soeharto in 1980 for being anti-Pancasila. On the 1983 declaration of support for Pancasila, see for example "Mengapa NU Menerima Pancasila Sebagai Asas"

[Why NU Accepted Pancasila as Its Sole Principle], *Suara Karya*, January 3, 1984.

38 NU nationalist credentials and its stated position that an Islamic state was not necessary in Indonesia can be traced back to as early as 1935 (see Sitompul, 1991) and in an explicit statement by Achmad Siddiq in the Konstituante in 1957. See Wahid's citation of Siddiq's speech in "The 1992 Election: A Devastating Political Earthquake?" in Harold Crouch and Hal Hill, eds., *Indonesian Assessment 1992: Political Perspectives on the 1990s* (Canberra: Australian National University, 1992), p. 125. However, it is also true that some NU members of the Konstituante did argue for an Islamic state.

39 See, for example, Abdurrahman Wahid, "Pancasila dan Kondisi Obyektif Kehidupan Beragama" [Pancasila and the Objective Conditions of Religious Life], *Kompas*, September 26, 1985; "Abdurrahman Wahid Tentang Pancasila dan Agama" [Abdurrahman Wahid On Pancasila and Religion], *Sinar Harapan*, March 15, 1985; and Manggi Habir, "Ulamas Change Course," *FEER*, January 10, 1985, pp. 36–39.

40 Sidney Jones, "The Contraction and Expansion – " Indonesia, no. 38 (October 1984), p. 17.

41 Munawir Sjadzali, Minister of Religion (1983–1993). Interview, April 12, 1993.

42 See Martin van Bruinessen (1991), p. 186. Van Bruinessen provides an excellent account of both the internal NU politics in the late 1980s as well as the changing relationship between NU and the Soeharto government.

43 See Sitompul (1991); and Arief Mudatsir, "From Situbondo Towards a New NU–A First Note," *Prisma*, no. 35, (March 1985), p. 161. See also the official NU statement, *Khittah Nahdlatul Ulama* (Jakarta: Pusat Besar Nahdlatul Ulama, 1985).

44 Barton in Bourchier and Legge (1994), p. 147. See also Greg Fealy and Greg Barton eds, *Nahdlatul Ulama: Traditional Islam and Modernity* (Clayton, Victoria: Centre of Southeast Asian Studies, Monash University, 1995).

45 Abdurrahman Wahid, interview, June 18, 1992. See also the interview with Wahid, "We Want to Reform Society," *Asiaweek*, March 20, 1992, p. 37.

46 See, for example, Leo Suryadinata, *Military Ascendancy and Political Culture: A Study of Indonesia's Golkar* (Athens, Ohio: Ohio University Monograph Series in International Studies, 1989).

47 Abdurrahman Wahid, interviews June 18 and June 24, 1992.

48 Hereafter referred to without added emphasis.

49 See "Rapat Akbar NU Aman, Tertib, Lancar" [NU's Rapat Akbar: Safe, Orderly, Smooth], *Kompas*, March 2, 1992; and "Only 150,000 Come to NU Gathering," *Jakarta Post*, March 2, 1992. However, Abdurrahman Wahid argues that nearly 500,000 NU followers came to the stadium. Only those gathered directly in front of the main podium numbered approximately 150,000. Wahid also says that the

armed forces prevented many thousands more from coming to Jakarta for the rally. Interview, September 17, 1994.

50 Excellent coverage of the Rapat Akbar is found in many of Jakarta's dailies and national news weeklies. See, for example, "Gus Dur dan Massa di Parkir Timur" [Wahid and the Masses in the East Parking Lot], *Tempo*, March 7, 1992, pp. 23–26; and cover story in *Editor*, "Warga NU Mana Kiblatmu" [NU Members: Where is Your *Kiblat* (the directional orientation to Mecca)], March 7, 1992, pp. 11–31.

51 See "NU: RI Yang Berdasar Pancasila dan UUD 1945, Bentuk Final Negara Kami" [NU: Republic of Indonesia Based on Pancasila and the Constitution of 1945 is the Final Form of Our Nation], *Suara Karya*, March 2, 1992; and "Nilai Pancasila Belum Sepenuhnya Diamalkan" [Values of Pancasila are not yet Fully Realized], *Suara Pembaruan*, March 1, 1992, p. 1.

52 On Wahid's initial plan for up to two million people to attend the Rapat Akbar, see his interview "Saya Ini Makelar Akhirat" [I am the Broker of the Hereafter], *Matra*, March 1992, p. 13.

53 Muhammad Ryaas Rasyid, "State Formation, Party System and the Prospect for Democracy in Indonesia: The Case of Golkar, 1967–1993," Ph.D. Dissertation, University of Hawaii, 1994, p. 293.

54 In late 1991 NU was split over several contentious issues including a controversy over NU acceptance of funds derived from a state-sponsored lottery. Because such funds were gained from a form of gambling, they were *haram* [forbidden] under Islamic teachings. Wahid had been politically wounded in this controversy because he professed ignorance as to whether NU accepted lottery monies. Additionally, there was a bitter internal NU leadership fight concerning the *Rois Am*, the titular religious leader of NU. (Wahid as General Chairman is leader of the organization on a day-to-day basis.)

55 Abdurrahman Wahid, interview, June 18, 1992.

56 Ibid.

57 Ibid.

58 Ibid.

59 Ibid. Aswab Mahasin argued that Soeharto fully understood Wahid's strategy. Interview, April 3, 1993. Therefore, it is possible for that reason Soeharto sought to ensure that the number of people attending the rally was as low as possible.

60 Abdurrahman Wahid, interview, June 24, 1992.

61 Ibid.

62 Mahasin is the founding editor of the scholarly journal, *Prisma* and former director of LP3ES, the Institute for Economic and Social Research, Education and Information. He is currently Deputy Director of the Foundation for Sustainable Development.

63 Aswab Mahasin, "Suksesi dan Posisi Gus Dur di Sudut Yang Runcing" [Succession and the Position of Abdurrahman Wahid in a Tight Corner], *Media Indonesia*, April 20, 1992, p. 1; and interview, April 3, 1993.

64 Personal observation, 29th Congress of *Nahdlatul Ulama*, Tasikmalaya, West Java, December 1, 1994.
65 Abdurrahman Wahid, interview, May 3, 1993.
66 Adam Schwarz, "Charismatic Enigma," *FEER*, November 12, 1992.
67 Personal observation, 29th Congress of *Nahdlatul Ulama*, Tasikmalaya, West Java, December 3, 1994. See also the transcript of Abdurrahman Wahid's remarks in *Suara Pembaruan*, December 11, 1994.
68 J. Soedjati Djiwandono, a member of the Board of Directors of CSIS and Head of Research and Development for the daily *Suara Karya*, interview, January 13, 1992.
69 Political scientist Mohtar Mas'oed at Gajah Mada University in Yogyakarta argued that the President's *haj* was widely perceived by Muslims (the "masses") as proof of Soeharto's Islamic bonafides and devotion to the *umat*. Interview, October 6, 1992.
70 On the founding of ICMI, see for example, "Presiden Soeharto: Tepat Waktu, Prakarsa Cendekiawan Muslim Bahas Pembangunan Abad XXI" [Soeharto: Appropriate Time for a Muslim Intellectual Initiative to Discuss Development in the 21st Century], *Kompas*, December 7, 1990; "Cendekiawan Muslim: Melangkah dari Malang," [Muslim Intellectuals: Striding out from Malang] and "Momentum ICMI dan Munculnya Habibie" [ICMI's Momentum and the Emergence of Habibie], *Tempo*, December 9, 1990.
71 See, for example, the arguments of Sri Bintang Pamungkas in "Pak Try Kurang Cocok" [Try Sutrisno Is Inappropriate], *Detik*, March 10, 1993, p. 8 and Dawam Rahardjo in "Pak Try Sulit Ditermina Presiden" [Difficult for the President to Accept Try Sutrisno], *Detik*, March 10, 1993, p. 12.
72 Abdurrahman Wahid, interview, June 18, 1992.
73 Abdurrahman Wahid, interview, June 24, 1992. Emphasis added.
74 Abdurrahman Wahid, October 15, 1992.
75 Abdurrahman Wahid, ibid.; and interviews, May 3, 1993, and June 15, 1994.
76 The perceptions of prominent ABRI leaders on these questions, particularly ICMI, will be examined in detail in Chapter 4.
77 Abdurrahman Wahid, interview, June 18, 1992.
78 Wahid's support for the New Order's de-confessionalization process is also evident in Wahid, "Islam, Politics and Democracy in the 1950s and 1990s," in Bourchier and Legge (1994).
79 Abdurrahman Wahid, interview, May 3, 1993.
80 After sending the letter to President Soeharto, Wahid reportedly sent copies to newspaper editors. A copy of the letter was provided to the author by an editor of one of Jakarta's dailies. Note that Wahid's letter to Soeharto refers to the "68th" anniversary of NU, which is correct by NU's Islamic calendar calculations. NU was established in 1926, however. To avoid confusion the Rapat Akbar is identified in the study as its "66th" anniversary.
81 Wahid's letter, p.1.
82 Ibid., p.2. Emphasis added.

83 Ibid.
84 Abdurrahman Wahid, interviews, October 15, 1992 and May 3, 1993.
85 Matori Abdul Djalil, interview, July 4, 1994.
86 On this point I am indebted to Greg Fealy, a historian at Monash University who spent much of 1991–1992 with Abdurrahman Wahid conducting research on NU politics from the 1950s to early 1960s.
87 Indeed, some members of ICMI such as Sri Bintang Pamungkas, a prominent member of the PPP in the DPR, freely admit this is part of ICMI's strategy. This is considered in depth in Chapter 3.
88 Abdurrahman Wahid, interview, May 3, 1993.
89 According to Wahid, on several occasions members of the inner Soeharto group, including Colonel Prabowo, Soeharto's son-in-law, have come to warn him to halt his criticisms of the President and to withdraw from the democratization movement. Interviews, June 24 and October 15, 1992.
90 The government's nearly automatic aversion to any potentially influential independent political activity is illustrated by persistent government attempts throughout 1994 and into 1995 to sow discord in the Indonesian Democratic Party (PDI). Since December 1993 the PDI has been led by the popular, charismatic and astute Megawati Sukarnoputri. The government seeks to weaken the party internally so that Megawati's personal popularity will not transform the PDI into a more independent political party capable of effectively challenging Golkar in the 1997 general elections.
91 See Wahid's letter to Soeharto and Wahid's interview, June 18, 1992 and Buchori Masruri (General Chairman of NU for Central Java), interview, October 29, 1992.
92 Abdurrahman Wahid, interview, September 17, 1994.
93 Abdurrahman Wahid, "Islam and Pancasila: Development of a Religious Political Doctrine in Indonesia," paper submitted to the panel "Religious Beliefs: The Transmission and Development of Doctrine," Conference of The Assembly of the World's Religions, Seoul, Korea, August 25, 1990; and interview, June 24, 1992.
94 Abdurrahman Wahid, interview, October 15, 1992.
95 See for example "Langkah Nonpolitik dari Politik *Nahdlatul Ulama*" [Non-political Movements in the Politics of *Nahdlatul Ulama*], *Kompas*, March 20, 1992.
96 Interviews with senior ABRI officers, June and July 1994. See Chapter 4.
97 Abdurrahman Wahid, September 17, 1994; Other NU leaders and followers made the same argument, including Achmad Buchori Masruri, Chairman of NU for Central Java, October 29, 1992; and Matori Abdul Djalil, NU stalwart and Secretary General of the PPP, July 4, 1994.
98 Abdurrahman Wahid, interview, June 18, 1992.
99 Abdurrahman Wahid, interviews, September 17, 1994 and December 10, 1994.
100 "The NU Rally," *Jakarta Post*, March 2, 1992.

3 THE INDONESIAN MUSLIM INTELLECTUALS' ASSOCIATION (ICMI)

1 Interview, October 7, 1992, Yogyakarta. Amien Rais, a political scientist at Gajah Mada University in Yogyakarta, is Chairman of the Executive Board of *Muhammadiyah* and a member of ICMI's *Dewan Pakar* [Board of Expert Advisors].

2 Interview, March 3, 1993. Adi Sasono is a well-known NGO activist, member of ICMI's Board of Experts, and is on the editorial board of the daily *Republika*.

3 For example, at the time of ICMI's founding, Dawam Rahardjo commented that he "didn't know since when Habibie started to pray." Dawam Rahardjo quoted in "Momentum ICMI, dan Munculnya Habibie" [ICMI's Momentum and the Emergence of Habibie], *Tempo*, December 8, 1990.

4 See for example, Greg Barton in Bourchier and Legge (1994) and Howard M. Federspiel *Muslim Intellectuals and National Development in Indonesia* (New York: Nova Science Publishers, 1992). Goenawan Mohamad, the founding editor of *Tempo* and a leading social critic, sees Madjid, along with Abdurrahman Wahid and the late Achmad Wahib, as the most "revolutionary" new thinkers in Indonesian Islam. Interview, May 4, 1993.

5 Nurcholish Madjid, interview, July 11, 1994.

6 Nasir Tamara, interview, April 5, 1993. Tamara (Ph.D. Sorbonne) is an editor with *Republika*. He was a journalist who was one of the only foreigners to accompany the Ayatollah Khomeini on his return to Tehran from Paris in 1979. Tamara was a reporter for *Sinar Harapan* and student in Paris at the time and later wrote a book on the Iranian Revolution. Tamara says that "having seen Islamic revolution and an Islamic state, I would not want this for my country."

7 Interview, April 16, 1993. For explanation of Imaduddin's key role in establishing ICMI, see his interview in *Detik*, "Negara Kita Bisa Disebut Negara Islam" [Our Nation Can Be Considered an Islamic Nation], April 1–7, 1993, pp. 20–21. Imaduddin, who holds a Ph.D. in Human Resource Management, is a former university Muslim activist and former Deputy Head of the World Assembly of Muslim Youth (1973–1980). He was imprisoned for 17 months (1978–1979) under the New Order without trial. Imaduddin is also the founder of the famous Salman Mosque on the grounds of the Bandung Institute of Technology.

8 Nasir Tamara, interview, April 5, 1993.

9 Munawir Sjadzali, interview, April 13, 1993.

10 Robert W. Hefner, "Islam, State, and Civil Society: ICMI and the Struggle for the Indonesian Middle Class," *Indonesia*, vol. 56 (October 1993).

11 Nasir Tamara, interview, April 5, 1993; Dewi Fortuna Anwar, interview, June 29, 1994; and Sri Bintang Pamungkas, interview, April 1, 1993.

12 Nurcholish Madjid (interview June 25, 1992) and Din Syamsuddin (interview, April 29, 1993) both suggest that because Muslim energies cannot be directed towards formal political behavior, this may have had the effect of encouraging cultural and spiritual development of Islam.
13 Nurcholish Madjid, interview, June 25, 1992. Emphasis added.
14 Nurcholish Madjid, interview, June 25, 1992.
15 Din Syamsuddin, interview, April 29, 1993.
16 Nurcholish Madjid, interview, June 25, 1992.
17 Amir Santoso, interview, November 4, 1992.
18 Soeharto, *My Thoughts, Words, and Deeds: An Autobiography*, as told to G. Dwipayana and Ramadhan K.H., English translation by Sumadi (Jakarta: PT. Citra Lamtoro Gung Persada, 1991), p. 352.
19 Discussion of the betrayal of the nationalists over the omission of the Jakarta Charter was still part of the discourse during the *asas tunggal* debates in the early 1980s. See, for example, H. Endang Saifuddin Anshari, *Piagam Jakarta 22 Juni 1945 dan Sejarah Konsensus Nasional Antara Nasionalis Islami dan Nasionalis "Sekuler" Tentang Dasar Negara Republik Indonesia 1945–1959* [The Jakarta Charter, June 22, 1945 and the National Consensus Between Islamic Nationalists and "Secular" Nationalists Regarding the Basis of the Republic of Indonesia, 1945–1959] (Jakarta: Rajwali, 1986).
20 Amien Rais, interview, October 7, 1992.
21 This is an oversimplification of the sophisticated analyses of Indonesian Islam by the Dutch scholar Snouck Hurgronje. On his contributions see Harry J. Benda, *The Crescent and the Rising Sun: Indonesian Islam Under Japanese Occupation* (The Hague: W. Van Hoeve Ltd., 1958) especially Part One, "The Colonial Legacy."
22 Munawir Sjadzali, interview, April 12, 1993.
23 This represents the thinking of President Soeharto, according to Munawir Sjadzali. He asserts on this matter he was very close to Soeharto and frequently privy to his thoughts and feelings on the issues of *asas tunggal* and Pancasila. Interviews, April 12 and 13, 1993.
24 See Soeharto's autobiography (1991) on P-4, pp. 288–290 and on the *asas tunggal*, pp. 351–353.
25 Munawir Sjadzali, interview, April 13, 1993.
26 Harry Tjan Silalahi, interview, January 16, 1992.
27 Mohtar Mas'oed, interview, October 6, 1992.
28 Nurcholish Madjid says that "Soeharto is very sincere in his religious life, but maybe because of the Javanese aspect of his life, he perceives this kind of thing as private." Interview, June 25, 1992.
29 Although widely known that he was not the ABRI choice for Vice President, the MPR eventually did agree by acclamation to elevate Sudharmono to be Soeharto's deputy. Although a general, Sudharmono was a military lawyer, bureaucrat, Golkar head, and close confident of Soeharto. He was not highly regarded by the armed forces as representative of ABRI interests.

30 For example, at the NU Congress in 1989, Soeharto addressed the gathered *ulama* [Muslim scholars] and lavished praise on the organization's acceptance of Pancasila. See Harry Bhaskara, "Soeharto Hails NU's Resolve to Shun Politics," *Jakarta Post*, November 27, 1989 and Michael Vatikiotis, "Call to the Faithful: Government seeks to woo Muslim electorate," *FEER*, December 14, 1989, p.34.

31 On the religious courts law see *Himpunan Perundang-undangan dan Peraturan Peradilan Agama* [Compilation of Legislation and Regulations on Religious Judicature] compiled by Abdul Gani Abdullah (Jakarta: PT Intermasa, 1991). For Wahid's critique of these laws, see his "Religious Beliefs: The Transmission and Development of Doctrine," *Jakarta Post*, September 7, 1991.

32 Munawir Sjadzali, interviews, April 12 and 13, 1993.

33 Interviews, Abdurrahman Wahid, June 18 and 24, 1992. See also Wahid, "Religious Beliefs," *Jakarta Post*, September 7, 1991.

34 Munawir Sjadzali, interview, April 12, 1993.

35 Abdurrahman Wahid, interview, June 24, 1992.

36 Adnan Buyung Nasution, interview, April 15, 1993.

37 Several Christian intellectuals who voiced these concerns emphasized that they are hesitant to state such fears publicly because they will then be identified as "anti-Muslim."

38 Amien Rais, quoted in *Tempo*, October 27, 1990.

39 On the "*Monitor* Affair," see the offending article: "Ini Dia: 50 Tokoh Yang Dikagumi Pembaca Kita" [Here They Are: 50 Figures Admired By Our Readers], *Monitor*, IV, no. 255, October 15, 1990. For in-depth coverage see the cover stories in the weeklies *Editor*, IV, no. 7, October 27, 1990, *Tempo*, October 27, 1990, and *Tempo*, November 3, 1990.

40 Abdurrahman Wahid, cited in *Tempo*, October 27, 1990. Interviews, June 18 and June 24, 1992.

41 On the founding of ICMI, see "Cendekiawan Muslim: Melangkah dari Malang" [Muslim Intellectuals: Striding Out from Malang], and accompanying articles in *Tempo*, December 8, 1990 and "Menggalang Ukhuwah" [Supporting a Fraternity of Believers], and accompanying articles in *Editor*, February 16, 1991.

42 Abdurrahman Wahid, interviews, June 24 and October 15, 1992.

43 Munawir Sjadzali's remarks originally appeared in the daily *Pelita*, July 8, 1992. They were later translated into English and Arabic and published by the Department of Religious Affairs as *Muslims' Interests are Better Served in the Absence of Muslim Parties* (Jakarta, 1992).

44 Confidential interview, April 1993.

45 See Djohan Effendi, "The Contribution of the Islamic Parties to the Decline of Democracy in the 1950s," paper, Conference on Indonesian Democracy, Monash University, December 18, 1992.

46 Soetjipto Wirosardjono, interview, April 2, 1993. See also, "ICMI Sets Up Foundation for Moslem Education," *Jakarta Post*, August 19, 1992, p. 2; and "Moslem Intellectuals Start Aid Projects in Slum Areas," *Jakarta Post*, April 14, 1992. Some of ICMI's plans and goals

are laid out in "Mencari 15 Juta Anggota" [Looking for 15 Million Members], *Tempo*, December 14, 1991.

47 Imaduddin, interview, April 16, 1993 and Sri Bintang Pamungkas, interview, April 1, 1993.

48 Dewi Fortuna Anwar, interview, June 29, 1994.

49 Adi Sasono, interview, March 3, 1993 and Nasir Tamara, interview, April 5, 1993.

50 At the Democracy Conference at Monash University (December 17–21, 1992) Soetjipto argued that the "ideal of ICMI is to get all Islamic organizations to sit together and to organize together." Moreover, he said that he views ICMI as a movement to "overcome" sectarianism, not to foster it. Similar views expressed in interview, April 2, 1993.

51 A popular Yogyakarta-based intellectual and frequent contributor to *Tempo* and other publications.

52 Soetjipto Wirosardjono, interview, April 2, 1993.

53 Nasir Tamara, interview, April 5, 1993.

54 Din Syamsuddin, interview, April 29, 1993. He does not condone such perceptions. However, he insists that such views are, in fact, "real." He argues that a positive benefit of ICMI is that it acts to moderate some Muslims' feelings of bitterness.

55 See "Habibie Takes Credit for Government, Moslem Relations," *Jakarta Post*, February 1, 1994. For other statements by Habibie on ICMI's non-political nature, see for example: "B.J. Habibie: ICMI Dibentuk Bukan Untuk Islamisasi" [Habibie: ICMI Not Established for Islamization], *Merdeka*, December 8, 1992; "Habibie: Saya Tak Tahu Apa Itu *Masyumi*" [Habibie: I Don't Know What *Masyumi* Is], *Merdeka*, November 30, 1992; and "B.J. Habibie: ICMI Bukan Partai Politik" [Habibie: ICMI is Not a Political Party], quoted by *Antara*, October 26, 1992.

56 This study will not discuss in detail Habibie's personal political ambitions or strategies. What is most relevant here is the thinking of the ICMI activist members who see ICMI as a way to Islamize the state. They are willing to be used for Habibie's possible political ambitions in order to work through ICMI towards their broader Islamizing objectives.

57 Confidential interview, April 1993.

58 Sri Bintang Pamungkas, interview, April 1, 1993.

59 Amir Santoso, interview, November 4, 1992.

60 Aswab Mahasin, interviews, April 3, 1993 and July 5, 1994.

61 See Effendi, conference paper (1992); Aswab Mahasin, interview April 3, 1993; and Abdurrahman Wahid, interviews, June 18, June 24, and October 15, 1992.

62 Adi Sasono, interview, March 3, 1993. See also the *Formulir Pemesanan Saham* [Share Order Form] issued by the Abdi Bangsa Foundation.

63 Soetjipto Wirosardjono, interview, April 2, 1993.

64 Ibid.

65 Din Syamsuddin, interview, April 29, 1993.

66 "Mencari 15 Juta Anggota" [Looking for 15 Million Members], *Tempo*, December 14, 1991.
67 Imaduddin, interview, April 16, 1993.
68 See "Pak Try Sulit Diterima Presiden" [Difficult for the President to Accept Try Sutrisno], *Detik*, March 10, 1993, p. 12.
69 Adi Sasono, interview, March 3, 1993.
70 Ibid.
71 Imaduddin, interview, April 16, 1993.
72 Amir Santoso, November 4, 1992.
73 Imaduddin, ibid,; and Adi Sasono, interview March 3, 1993. See Chapter 5 for detailed considerations of the concerns of secular nationalists, non-Islamic proponents of democratization, and Christian minorities.
74 See the interview of Rais, "Yang Berharap Banyak Akan Kecewa" [Those With High Hopes will be Disappointed], *Detik*, March 3, 1993.
75 Aswab Mahasin, interview, July 5, 1994.
76 Sri Bintang Pamungkas, interview, July 5, 1994.
77 Amien Rais, interview, October 7, 1992.
78 See for example the interview with Imaduddin in *Detik*, April 1, 1993; Din Syamsuddin, interview, June 27, 1994; and confidential interviews, June 1994.
79 See interview with Imaduddin, "Negara Kita Bisa Disebut Negara Islam" [Our Nation Can be Considered an Islamic Nation], *Detik*, April 1–7, 1993, pp. 20–21.
80 Amien Rais, interview, October 7, 1992.
81 The notion that Soeharto is now "forgiven" for allowing Christian Indonesians to influence New Order policy up through the 1980s was a frequent not-for-attribution comment by ICMI supporters (interviews, October and November 1992, March and April, 1993 and June and July 1994).
82 While it is true that a number of intellectuals associated with CSIS are Catholic, it is misleading to identify CSIS as a "Catholic" institution. Numerous leading CSIS figures are Muslim, including Daud Yusuf, the current head of CSIS.
83 Lieutenant General H.B. Mantiri, interview, July 8, 1994.
84 Abdurrahman Wahid, interview, June 24, 1992.
85 See Margot Cohen, "Eton of the East," *FEER*, July 22, 1993, p. 20.
86 Soetjipto Wirosardjono, interview, April 2, 1993.
87 See for example the favorable comments about Malaysia's NEP in the interview with Amien Rais in *Detik*, March 3, 1993, pp. 8–9. The NEP is the official Malaysian government plan to expand the non-Chinese, ethnic Malay, portion of the national wealth.
88 Amir Santoso, interview, November 4, 1992.
89 Sri Bintang Pamungkas, interview, April 1, 1993. See also interview with Bintang in *Forum Keadilan*, "Status Quo Ada Batasnya" [The Status Quo Has Its Limits], no. 25, April 1, 1993, pp. 14–16.
90 Nasir Tamara, Adi Sasono, Imaduddin, and Soetjipto Wirosardjono all voiced this view.

91 Adam Schwarz, *A Nation in Waiting: Indonesia in the 1990s*, (Sydney: Allen & Unwin and Boulder: Westview Press, 1994). Citation from draft manuscript (dated June 22, 1993) chapter 3, p. 56.
92 Sri Bintang Pamungkas, interview, July 5, 1994.
93 Ibid.
94 Imaduddin, interview, April 16, 1993.
95 Sri Bintang Pamungkas, interviews, April 1, 1993 and July 5, 1994.
96 Sri Bintang Pamungkas, April 1, 1993; Adi Sasono, March 3, 1993 and Imaduddin, April 16, 1993.
97 Amir Santoso, interview, November 4, 1992.
98 Aswab Mahasin, interview, April 3, 1993.
99 Imaduddin, interview, April 16, 1993.
100 For example, see the reference above to Amien Rais' refusal to concede that Soeharto had any role in the "Christianization" of government. Amien Rais, interview, October 7, 1992.
101 Adi Sasono, interview, March 3, 1993.
102 Sri Bintang Pamungkas, interview, July 5, 1994.
103 Adi Sasono, interview, March 3, 1993.
104 See "Amien Rais: Yang Berharap Banyak akan Kecewa" [Amien Rais: Those with High Hopes will be Disappointed], *Detik*, March 3, 1993, pp. 8–9.
105 Recall that "succession politics" tends to dominate much of the political discourse in Indonesia in recent years. Thus, it is not surprising that Islamic groups, along with the military and others, have considered options on how to deal with the post-Soeharto era in ways which best reflect their interests.
106 Amien Rais in *Detik*, March 3, 1993, p. 9.
107 Din Syamsuddin, interview, June 27, 1994.
108 Confidential interview, June 1994.
109 See "Call for National Debate on Suharto's Successor," *Straits Times Weekly Edition*, December 18, 1993.
110 Imaduddin, interview, April 16, 1993.
111 Sembiring's statement was in reaction to Habibie's influential role in the selection of a new Golkar chairman in October 1993. Sembiring's comments reported in *Detik*, October 27, 1993, *Editor*, November 11, 1993, and *Tempo*, November 6, 1993.
112 For Siswono's critique of ICMI, see "Mencari 'Hantu' Sektarian" [Looking for the Sectarian "Ghost"], *Forum Keadilan*, June 9, 1994.
113 The author's conversations with many Indonesian Chinese, as well as *pribumi* non-Muslims indicate that they worry about the emergence of a political environment which scapegoats "racial minorities." The targets of Amien Rais, for example, are the rich Chinese-owned business conglomerates, but there is a perception among ordinary middle-class Indonesian Chinese that the only vulnerable and visible targets of Muslim frustration will be their homes, shop-houses, and small-scale businesses if elite manipulation of racial animosity were to erupt in street violence. Margot Cohen writing in *FEER* observed that Islamic revival in Indonesia is widely

perceived to have an "undercurrent of anti-Chinese sentiment." See "Eton of the East," *FEER*, July 22, 1993, pp. 20–22.

114 Munawir Sjadzali, interview, April 13, 1993. For Rudini's views, see "Mendagri Rudini: ICMI Tak Perlu Dicurigai" [Rudini: No Need to Be Suspicious of ICMI], *Media Indonesia*, December 6, 1992.

115 Sri Bintang Pamungkas, interview, April 1, 1993.

116 Imaduddin, interview, April 16, 1993.

117 Amien Rais, interview, October 7, 1992.

118 Amir Santoso, interview, November 4, 1992.

119 Ibid.; and Nasir Tamara, interview, April 5, 1993.

120 Sri Bintang Pamungkas, "Status Quo Ada Batasnya," p. 16. Compare, for example, to the MPRS Decision no. XX/1966.

121 Sri Bintang Pamungkas, interview, April 1, 1993. See also the interviews "Status Quo Ada Batasnya," pp. 14–16; and "Pak Try Kurang Cocok" [General Try is Inappropriate], *Detik*, March 10 1993, p. 9.

122 Mubyarto, interview, October 27, 1992.

123 "Creating Equity Among Groups Difficult," *Jakarta Post*, April 16, 1992.

124 Soetjipto Wirosardjono, interview, April 2, 1993; and Din Syamsuddin, February 19, 1993.

125 Imaduddin, interview, April 16, 1993.

126 Amien Rais cited in "Islam's Role in Nationalism Debated," *Jakarta Post*, June 7, 1994.

127 Interview, Achmad Buchori Masruri, October 29, 1992.

128 Mohtar Mas'oed, interview, October 5, 1992. Mas'oed is a Muslim intellectual whose lack of active participation in ICMI has been criticized by some intellectuals who have opted for ICMI activism.

129 For example, Amir Santoso (interview, November 4, 1992), Din Syamsuddin (interview, April 29, 1993), and Soetjipto Wirosardjono (interview, April 2, 1993), all endorsed the concept of a district system.

130 The following discussion draws heavily on the author's first-hand observations and interviews in Jakarta at the time of the banning. See also *Human Rights in Indonesia and East Timor: The Limits of Openness* (New York: Human Rights Watch/Asia, September 1994).

131 See the cover story, "Habibie dan Kapal itu" [Habibie and those Ships], *Tempo*, June 11, 1994.

132 Nasir Tamara, interview, July 5, 1994.

133 Confidential interviews, June and July 1994.

134 "Pangab: Jangan Terjebak Isu Politik Yang Berlabel Agama" [Chief of Staff: Don't Be Caught Up in Political Issues With Religious Labels], *Suara Karya*, February 28, 1994; "Pangab Harapkan Umat Islam Mengingatkan Toleransi" [Chief of Staff Hopes Muslim Community Remembers Tolerance], *Suara Karya*, February 17, 1994. For the criticism of Bintang Pamungkas see "Kassospol ABRI: Ada Yang Bangga Bila Jelekkan Bangsa Sendiri" [Head of ABRI's Socio-Political Division: Some are Proud if they Denigrate their own Country], *Republika*, September 21, 1994. Confidential sources

speculated that Hartono may have been referring to Sri Bintang Pamungkas in this statement.

135 This observation is based on the author's interviews in 1991–1994 with a wide range of active and retired ABRI officers from most service branches.

136 The organization referred to by Imaduddin is *Persatuan Inteligensia Kristen Indonesia* [Association of Indonesian Christian Intellectuals, or PIKI].

137 See "Ismail Sunny: Selama ada NU, Gus Dur Sektarian Juga" [Ismail Sunny: As Long as there is NU, Abdurrahman Wahid is also Sectarian], *Detik*, November 2, 1992, p. 9.

138 See, for example, the comments by Ismail Sunny in *Detik*, November 2, 1992, p. 9.

139 "Try Sutrisno: Islam Bukan Ancaman" [Islam is not a Threat], *Republika*, January 30, 1993, p. 1.

140 Soetjipto Wirosardjono, interview, April 2, 1993; and Nasir Tamara, interview, April 5, 1993.

141 Air Vice Marshal Teddy Rusdy, interview, November 11, 1992; and Brigadier General (retired) Roekmini, June 28, 1994.

142 Buchori Masruri, interview, October 29, 1992.

143 Matori Abdul Djalil, interview, July 4, 1994.

144 Abdurrahman Wahid, interview, October 15, 1992.

145 Nasir Tamara, interview, April 5, 1993.

146 Soetjipto Wirosardjono, interview, April 2, 1993.

147 "Mencari 'Hantu' Sektarian" [Looking for the Sectarian "Ghost"], *Forum Keadilan*, June 9, 1994.

148 Imaduddin, interview, April 16, 1993.

149 Soetjipto Wirosardjono, interview, April 2, 1993.

150 Mohtar Mas'oed, interview, October 6, 1992; Din Syamsuddin, interview, April 29, 1993.

151 Confidential interview, April, 1993. Such comments indicate that senior members of the government are also worried about what Soeharto has created. They tend to agree with his *rapprochement* with Islam, but also suggest they hold grave misgivings that the process has begun to politicize Islam – to "re-confessionalize" politics. Views like this also suggest possible misgivings in Golkar about ICMI.

152 Adnan Buyung Nasution, interviews, April 15, 1993 and July 7, 1994.

153 For Soeharto's remarks see "Suharto: Preserve Cohesion – Religion Based Groups Urged to Work in Unity," *Straits Times Weekly Edition*, August 13, 1994; "Presiden Minta ABRI Waspadai Usaha Ganti Pancasila" [President Urges ABRI Vigilance Against Efforts to Replace Pancasila], *Kompas*, January 24, 1994; "Presiden Soeharto pada ICMI: Dijaga, Agar Tak Muncul Sistem Alternatif Terhadap Pancasila" [Soeharto to ICMI: Be On Guard so that Alternative Systems to Pancasila do not Emerge], *Pelita*, December 8, 1992, p. 1.

154 "Presiden Soeharto: Munculnya Sektarianisme dan Primordialisme

Harus Dicegah" [President Soeharto: The Emergence of Sectarianism and Primordialism Must be Blocked], *Kompas*, December 6, 1991.

155 Admiral Sunardi, interview, November 11, 1992.

156 Ismail Hasan Metareum, interview, November 19, 1992.

157 Radius Prawiro, former Senior Coordinating Economic Minister; Sumarlin, former Finance Minister, and Adrianus Mooy, former Governor of the Bank of Indonesia. The powerful Bank of Indonesia is now under Soedradjad Djiwandono, a Catholic.

158 Hadi Soesastro, interview, July 11, 1994.

4 THE INDONESIAN ARMED FORCES

1 Try Sutrisno was Chief of Staff of the Indonesian Armed Forces from 1988 to 1993 and has been Vice President since March 1993. His remarks are from an interview on the "Foreign Correspondent" television news program on the Australian Broadcasting Network, July 4, 1992. This was a rebroadcast of the BBC's "Assignment" program.

2 Sunardi, interview, November 10, 1992. Sunardi was Advisor for International Affairs to former Defense Minister General (retired) Benny Moerdani and holds the same position for current Defense Minister General (retired) Edy Sudrajat.

3 General Abdul Haris Nasution is one of the founders of the Indonesian Army. He was Army Chief of Staff and Defense Minister under Sukarno and is credited with conceptualizing the *dwifungsi* doctrine. He has since accused Soeharto of betraying the ideals of the New Order and deviating from the intent of *dwifungsi*, which he says was never meant to justify the undemocratic structure built over the past two decades. Interview, July 22, 1992. The best source on Nasution is C.L.M. Penders and Ulf Sundhaussen, *Abdul Haris Nasution, A Political Biography* (St. Lucia, Queensland: University of Queensland Press, 1985).

4 SESKOAD: *Sekolah Staf dan Komando – Angkatan Darat*, or Indonesian Army Staff and Command School. See Charles Donald McFetridge, "SESKOAD – Training the Elite," in *Indonesia*, no. 36 (October 1983), pp. 87–98.

5 Active duty officers often spoke only on a confidential basis. This is not surprising for individuals whose careers and other ambitions may still be at stake.

6 William R. Liddle, *Politics and Culture in Indonesia* (Ann Arbor; Center for Political Studies, Institute for Social Research, University of Michigan, 1988), p. 20.

7 See Ulf Sundhaussen, "The Inner Contraction of the Suharto Regime: A Starting Point for a Withdrawal to the Barracks," in Bourchier and Legge (1994), pp. 272–285.

8 Lieutenant General Harsudiyono Hartas, interview, April 28, 1993, Air Vice Marshal Teddy Rusdy, interview November 11, 1992, and Vice Admiral Sunardi, interviews November 10, 1992 and June 28,

1994 all emphasized this point. General (retired) Nasution, although critical of ABRI for being far too deeply involved in politics, is firmly committed to *dwifungsi* as an essential doctrine. Interview, July 22, 1992.

9 See "Tidak Dikenal Beda Antara ABRI dan Sipil" [No Recognition of Distinctions Between Military and Civilians], *Merdeka*, April 9, 1990.

10 Abdul Kadir Besar was a long-time political assistant to former Chief of Staff (and formulator of the *dwifungsi* doctrine) Abdul Haris Nasution. Besar was General Secretary of the MPRS (1967–1972) and Deputy Commander of SESKOAD (1976–1979). He has also served as special assistant in the Coordinating Ministry for Security and Political Affairs, and advisor in the powerful office of the State Secretariat. He is author of numerous internal ABRI ideological educational materials, is founder of the Pancasila University in Jakarta, and continues to lecture at the senior military staff and command colleges. Interviews, August 4, August 25, and October 27, 1992.

11 Abdul Kadir Besar, interview, October 27, 1992.

12 In official terminology Indonesia is also a "*Negara Kekeluargaan*," or "familial state." See General Try Sutrisno's description of Indonesia as a "family-like state" in his remarks cited on the first page of this chapter.

13 On the constitutional debates see Adnan Buyung Nasution, *The Aspiration for Constitutional Government in Indonesia: A Socio-Legal Study of the Indonesian Konstituante, 1956–1959* (Jakarta: Sinar Harapan, 1992).

14 For recent studies of integralistic thinking and its revival, see Marsillam Simanjuntak (1989); David Bourchier, "Totalitarianism and the 'National Personality': Recent Controversy about the Philosophical Basis of the Indonesian State," in Schiller (forthcoming); and Franz Magnis Suseno, "Sekitar Faham Negara Integralistik" [Understanding Integralistic Thinking], paper, Jakarta, March 21, 1990 (no publication information given).

15 Abdul Kadir Besar, interviews, August 25 and October 27, 1992. For a comprehensive rendering of Kadir Besar's explanations of integralism and ABRI ideology see *Dwifungsi ABRI (Konsep 1979)*, Department of Defense, Army Headquarters, 1979. This unpublished paper is representative of integralistic thinking and how it was taught at SESKOAD. See also Abdul Kadir Besar, *Demokrasi Pancasila dan Pengaturan Penyelenggaraan Demokrasi Politik* [Pancasila Democracy and the Regulation and Implementation of Political Democracy], Jakarta, 1991 (no publication information given).

16 Abdul Kadir Besar, interviews, August 25 and October 27, 1992.

17 Harsudiyono Hartas, interview, April 28, 1993 and Teddy Rusdy, interview, November 11, 1992. Hartas was for five years (until May 1993) the powerful ABRI Chief of Staff for Social and Political Affairs. He now serves on the Supreme Advisory Council (DPA).

18 Benny Moerdani, interview, April 24, 1993.

19 Cited in interview with Brigadier General Hendropriyono in *Tempo*, April 10, 1993, p. 27.

20 For example, retired General Soemitro passionately defended ABRI's pre-eminent role in national life "based on the *Sapta Marga*." Interview, June 15, 1992.

21 Abdul Kadir Besar, interview, October 27, 1992.

22 Harsudiyono Hartas, interview, April 28, 1993.

23 See "Debatkan Paham Kenegaraan Integralistik" [Debate on the Understanding of the Integralistic State], *Republika*, May 19, 1993.

24 In addition to Moerdani (April 24, 1993) and Sunardi (November 10, 1992), this general view was also stressed by the Chief of General Staff, Lieutenant General Mantiri (July 8, 1994), Hartas (April 28, 1993); former Minister of Information and Air Vice Marshal Budiardjo (November 12, 1992); former Speaker of the Parliament and retired Lieutenant General Kharis Suhud (April 16, 1993); former Governor of the National Defense Institute (Lemhanas) retired Major General Soebiyakto (November 10, 1992); former ambassador to the United States, retired Lieutenant General Hasnan Habib (October 26, 1992); and retired General Soemitro (June 15, 1992).

25 Mohtar Mas'oed, interview, October 5, 1992.

26 See, for example Soeharto's comments in "ABRI Tidak Pernah Rakus dengan Kedudukannya di DPR" [ABRI Has Never been Greedy Regarding its Status in the DPR], *Kompas*, February 17, 1992, p. 1; "ABRI Lebih Dorong Demokrasi, Harapan Reaktualisasi Dwifungsi" [ABRI Pushes Democracy, Hopes for a Reactualization of its Dual Function], *Kompas*, January 28, 1993, p. 1; and Moerdani, interview, April 24, 1993.

27 Marsillam Simanjuntak, interview, August 3, 1992. Many democrats and intellectuals such as Marsillam and Mochtar Lubis (a renowned author and social critic, interview, March 30, 1992) became disillusioned when democratization did not materialize under the ABRI-supported New Order.

28 Examples of open expression of ABRI as an obstacle to democracy can be seen in analysis by two scholars. Burhan Magenda, political scientist at the University of Indonesia, said that although ABRI provided the stability necessary for development, its presence also hindered democratization. See "Industrialization, ABRI's Presence Hinders Democracy," *Jakarta Post*, August 8, 1992. Professor Selo Soemardjan argued that the public is becoming increasing critical of both the government and the military. See, "Masyarakat Makin Kritis Terhadap Pemerintah Dan ABRI" [People Becoming Increasingly Critical towards Government and ABRI], *Suara Karya*, April 1, 1992, p. 1.

29 Bourchier, "Totalitarianism and the 'National Personality' " (forthcoming).

30 "Moerdani Vows to Crush Attempts to Replace Pancasila," *Jakarta Post*, September 11, 1991.

31 "Edy Wants People Alert Against Opportunists," *Jakarta Post*, December 26, 1991, p. 2; "Ancaman Disintegrasi Sudah Mulai Muncul" [Threat of Disintegration Begins to Emerge], *Republika*, February 22, 1993, p. 10; An excellent example of general ABRI explanation of threats to Pancasila is found in the military daily *Angkatan Bersenjata*'s editorial "Demokrasi Liberal Tidak Cocok Dengan Kita" [Liberal Democracy is not Appropriate for Us], January 12, 1993.
32 See comments by Hartas in "Kassospol ABRI: Pemasyarakatan Demokrasi Pancasila Makan Waktu" [ABRI's Chief of Staff for Social and Political Affairs: Socialization of Pancasila Democracy Takes Time], *Kompas*, February 26, 1993.
33 Harsudiyono Hartas, interview, April 28, 1993.
34 Teddy Rusdy, interview, November 11, 1992.
35 Teddy Rusdy, interview, November 11, 1992.
36 On the security approach debate see "Mendagri: Pendekatan Keamanan tidak Mungkin Lagi Diterapkan" [Interior Minister: Security Approach will no longer be Applied], *Kompas*, December 9, 1991, p. 1; "Jenderal Try Sutrisno: Security Approach Jangan Dikomentari" [General Sutrisno: Don't Comment on the Security Approach], *Kompas*, December 11, 1991, p. 1.
37 Roekmini, interviews, October 1, 1992 and June 28, 1994. Roekmini was a leading proponent of increased "openness" in Indonesian politics as an ABRI parliamentarian from 1989–1992. According to *Tempo*, Roekmini was dropped from the ranks of ABRI parliamentarians because she was perceived as being too strong an advocate of "openness." See "Vokalis yang Turun Panggung" [The Vocal Ones Leave the Stage], *Tempo*, September 14, 1991; and Kharis Suhud, interview, April 19, 1993.
38 Nurcholish Madjid, interview, June 25, 1992.
39 Sudibyo is a Senior Fellow at the Center for Strategic and International Studies, Jakarta. Interview, June 22, 1992.
40 Interview with Try Sutrisno in "Islam Bukan Ancaman" [Islam is Not a Threat], *Republika*, January 30, 1993, p. 1.
41 Abdurrahman Wahid, interview, June 24, 1992.
42 See, for example, Martin van Bruinessen, "The 28th Congress of the *Nahdlatul Ulama*: Power Struggle and Social Concerns," *Archipel* 41 (Paris, 1991), pp. 185–200.
43 Adi Sasono, interview, March 3, 1993. Sasono added, however, that Try Sutrisno is also clearly committed to the Soeharto government.
44 Nurcholish Madjid, interview, June 25, 1992 and former Minister of Religion, Munawir Sjadzali, interviews, April 12 and 13, 1993.
45 Franz Magnis Suseno, interviews, March 21 and June 15, 1992.
46 Lieutenant General Harsudiyono Hartas, interview April 28, 1993; Benny Moerdani, interview April 24, 1993; and Brigadier General Roekmini, June 28, 1994. Ismail Sunny, a law Professor and ICMI supporter, identified Try Sutrisno as being favorably disposed towards ICMI. See "Ismail Sunny: Selama Ada NU, Gus Dur

Sektarian Juga" [As Long as there is NU, Abdurrahman Wahid is also Sectarian], *Detik*, November 2, 1992, p. 9.

47 Abdurrahman Wahid, interviews, June 18, 1992 and May 3, 1993.

48 See for example Wahid's comments in interview "Abdurrahman Wahid: Saya Presiden Taxi Saja deh" [Wahid: I'm Just a President Taxi (a play on words in which Wahid referred to a Jakarta taxi company when asked if he wanted to be President)], *Detik*, November 2, 1992. In this interview, Wahid claims that "I know ABRI's way of thinking" and that ABRI does not approve of ICMI.

49 Abdurrahman Wahid, interview, June 18, 1992.

50 Abdurrahman Wahid, interview, October 15, 1992.

51 Aswab Mahasin, interview, July 5, 1994.

52 Abdurrahman Wahid, interviews, September 17, 1994 and December 10, 1994.

53 Soemitro, interview, June 15, 1992.

54 Confidential interview, April 1993.

55 Hasnan Habib, interview, October 26, 1992.

56 Abdurrahman Wahid, interview, June 18, 1992 (emphasis added).

57 Abdurrahman Wahid, interview, December 10, 1994.

58 Abdurrahman Wahid, interview, June 18, 1992 (emphasis added).

59 Abdurrahman Wahid, interview, June 18, 1992.

60 Harsudiyono Hartas, interview, April 28, 1993.

61 Benny Moerdani, interview, April 24, 1993.

62 For details on the church dispute and military and government intervention in it, see chapter 7, "Religion, Politics and Torture in North Sumatra," in *The Limits of Openness* (New York: Human Rights Watch/Asia, 1994).

63 Harsudiyono Hartas, interview, April 28, 1993, and Sunardi, interview, November 10, 1992.

64 Known as "36 *Butir*" [the 36 Points]. See the section entitled "Nilai-Nilai dan Norma-Norma Yang Terkandung Dalam Pedoman Penghayatan dan Pengamalan Pancasila" [Values and Norms Contained in the Guide to the Comprehension and Practice of Pancasila] in MPR Decision no. II/MPR/1978. Cited in *Bahan Penataran Pendidikan Moral Pancasila Sesuai Dengan Ketetapan MPR no. II/MPR/1978* [Upgrading Materials for Pancasila Moral Education, In Accordance with MPR Decision no. II, 1978] (Jakarta: Pancasila Moral Education Team, Directorate General for Primary and Secondary Education, Department of Education and Culture, 1980), pp. 10–11.

65 Harsudiyono Hartas, interview, April 28, 1993.

66 Lieutenant General H.B. Mantiri, interview, July 8, 1994.

67 Confidential interviews, April 1993 and June 1994. Given the sensitivity of this subject it is not surprising that comments referring to Muslim/non-Muslim tension within ABRI are unattributable. These perceptions are significant in that they suggest that the growing Islamization of society in general may be reflected in ABRI, as Nurcholish Madjid contends. Although one officer argued that some officers exploit religion to advance their positions, he emphasized

that this does not threaten ABRI unity. Several officers insisted off-the-record that the former ABRI Commander, Edy Sudrajat (Minister of Defense since March 1993) views ICMI as a "step backward" in Indonesia's political development.

68 Teddy Rusdy, November 11, 1992. This argument was made by numerous senior officers, most of them Muslims.

69 Harsudiyono Hartas, interview, April 28, 1993.

70 For example, see Try Sutrisno's commentary on the first page of this chapter.

71 Harsudiyono Hartas, interview, April 28, 1993. Ali Moertopo, the key New Order political strategist, created the concept known as the "floating mass" under which the people would not be politically active in the five-year periods between general elections. To ensure the de-politicization of society, political parties were prohibited from organizing at the sub-district and village levels. See Ali Moertopo, *Strategi Pembangunan Nasional*, (Jakarta: CSIS, 1981).

72 Brigadier General Roekmini, interview, June 28, 1994.

73 Confidential interview, June 1994.

74 Nasir Tamara, interview, July 5, 1994, and Din Syamsuddin, June 27, 1994.

75 This paragraph is drawn from views of numerous officers, including the following: Harsudiyono Hartas (April 28, 1993), Sunardi (November 11, 1992), Teddy Rusdy (November 10, 1992), Soebiyakto (November 10, 1992), Kharis Suhud (April 19, 1993), Benny Moerdani (April 24, 1993) as well as several off-the-record interviews.

76 For a reiteration of this analysis, see Harold Crouch, "Democratic Prospects in Indonesia," in Bourchier and Legge (1994), p. 121:

> the President has been forced to look beyond the ranks of the military for political support. Reversing his earlier attitude to political Islam which was regarded as the main threat to the regime until the mid-1980s, Soeharto is now wooing the Muslim community. Muslim courts have been given wider powers, Islamic classes have to be provided in Christian schools, . . . a new mass organization for Islamic "intellectuals" [ICMI] has been established, and the Soeharto family went on the *haj*.

77 Confidential interview, April 1993. Published reports, however, allude to ABRI's nomination of Try Sutrisno for Vice President "as an important bid by the military to assert its independence [of Soeharto]." See Suhaini Aznam, "The Guessing Game," *FEER*, March 4, 1993, p. 19.

78 Confidential interview, November 1992.

79 It must be remembered that the ICMI activists identified by ABRI as "radicals" are for the most part highly educated, urban, modernist Muslim intellectuals. In the Indonesian context, they are not radicals in the sense that they advocate anything definitively "out-of-bounds" in the Pancasila state. Yet concepts such as "Islamic

society" constitute a grey area. That is, while Muslim intellectuals insist this does not imply an Islamic state, ABRI asserts that it is camouflage for Islamic government. The political reality is that there is suspicion that even though everyone accepts Pancasila, some Muslims still "might" advocate ideas inconsistent with ABRI conceptions of Pancasila and acceptable political behavior.

80 This is similar to Wahid's analysis that the "idealist" group in ICMI, typified by Nurcholish Madjid and Aswab Mahasin, would become disenchanted with ICMI. As noted in Chapter 3, Mahasin withdrew from active participation because he perceived ICMI to be acting like a political pressure group, while Nurcholish continues to stir emotional reactions from within the Islamic community because of his progressive theology, exemplified by the controversy generated after his lecture suggesting that Islam is a "borderless" religion. See Chapter 6 and *Detik*, November 3, 1992.

81 Munawir Sjadzali, interviews, April 12 and 13, 1993.

82 Harsudiyono Hartas, interview, April 28, 1993.

83 Benny Moerdani, interview, April 24, 1993.

84 Soebiyakto, interview, November 10, 1992.

85 In analyses by scholars and commentators, officers identified as having tied their careers most closely to Soeharto's political fortunes, especially Generals Wismoyo, Tanjung, Hartono and Colonel Prabowo (both Wismoyo and Prabowo are relatives of Soeharto), are seen as supportive of ICMI. There is no evidence, however, that they reject ABRI thinking on Islamic politics in general.

86 See the Asia Watch Report *Violence in Lampung, Indonesia* (March 1989).

87 Cited in the *Jakarta Post*, December 26, 1991, p. 2.

88 Confidential interview, July 1994.

89 "Ancaman Disintegrasi Sudah Mulai Muncul" [Threats of Disintegration Have Already Begun to Emerge], *Republika*, February 22, 1993, p. 10. See also, "Try Worries about Emergence of Western-influenced Groups," *Jakarta Post*, April 13, 1992, p. 10.

90 Forum Democracy is the organization established under the leadership of Abdurrahman Wahid in March 1991. Its purpose is to stimulate national discussion on democratization and associated issues. Its members include prominent Muslim, as well as Christian intellectuals – theologians, journalists, publishers, NGO leaders, and academics. It has not formed branch offices and has made no efforts to become a party-like organization although it has caused some government and ABRI leaders to look upon the group with suspicion. See Chapter 5 for full treatment of Forum Democracy.

91 See the interview with Brigadier General Hendropriyono in *Tempo*, April 10, 1993, p. 27.

92 In a similar vein, Hartas said that Forum Democracy would not be forbidden as long as it did not agitate the masses or cause unrest. See Hartas' comments on Forum Democracy in "Tidak Ada Larangan bagi Forum Demokrasi" [No Prohibition against Forum

Democracy], *Kompas*, April 25, 1992; and in "Forum Told to Avoid Agitation," *Jakarta Post*, April 25, 1992.

93 Kwik Kian Gie, interview, July 13, 1992, and Abdurrahman Wahid, October 15, 1992.

94 For Try Sutrisno's views on the purpose of the election, see "Change of Leadership Sought," *Jakarta Post*, April 11, 1992; For reference to the Forum Democracy and Abdurrahman Wahid position on the need for elections to produce social change, see the *Jakarta Post* editorial "Great Expectations," April 27, 1992.

95 Hasnan Habib, interview, October 26, 1992.

96 Soemitro, interview, June 15, 1992.

97 See interview with Try Sutrisno in *Republika,* January 30, 1993, p.1.

98 Hasnan Habib, interview, October 26, 1992 and Brigadier General Sudibyo (retired).

99 Soebiyakto, interview, November 10, 1992.

100 Soemitro, interview, June 15, 1992. Islamic intellectuals such as Amien Rais, acknowledged that the "scariest thing is to be called an enemy of Pancasila." Interview, October 7, 1992.

101 Soemitro, interview, June 15, 1992. See also Max Lane, *"Openness," Political Discontent and Succession in Indonesia: Political Developments in Indonesia, 1989–91* (Nathan, Queensland: Centre for the Study of Australia–Asia Relations, Griffith University, 1991) for review of Soemitro's contributions to the "openness" debate.

102 There has been widespread speculation that ABRI faction members who advocated "openness" were dropped from the 1992 election and appointment lists because of their advocacy of openness.

103 Samsuddin's remarks in the weekly *Editor*, September 8, 1990, p. 24.

104 Roekmini, interview, October 1, 1992. For Roekmini's views, see also "Outgoing Legislator Satisfied with her Terms," *Jakarta Post*, April 10, 1992; "Dewan Belum Berfungsi Penuh" [Parliament Not Yet Fully Functioning] in the Yogyakarta daily, *Kedaulatan Rakyat*, October 7, 1992, p. 1. In this article Roekmini is quoted as saying that President Soeharto is responsible for the openness debate and her respect for Soeharto is especially because of his description of Pancasila as an open ideology. "Openness" only goes so far, however. In typical Soeharto fashion, after dropping Roekmini from the ABRI DPR faction, she was rewarded with promotion from Colonel to Brigadier General, becoming only the second woman in Indonesia to reach this rank.

105 Harold Crouch, "Democratic Prospects in Indonesia," in Bourchier and Legge (1994), p. 122.

106 Soemitro, interview, June 15, 1992.

107 See, for example, *The Limits of Openness* (1994).

108 Roekmini, interview, June 28, 1994. See also "Armed Forces Legislators Regret Media Ban," *Jakarta Post*, July 11, 1994.

109 Lieutenant General Mantiri, interview, July 8, 1994.

110 Harsudiyono Hartas, interview, April 28, 1993 and Abdul Kadir Besar, August 25, 1992.

111 Soemitro, interview, June 15, 1992.
112 Soebiyakto's warning against capitalism is noted in "Capitalist System Applicable in Indonesia, Economist says," *Jakarta Post*, March 14, 1992 and in interview, November 10, 1992.
113 "Moerdani Urges Limits on Wealth," *Jakarta Post*, March 4, 1992.
114 Roeslan Abdulgani, interview, August 6, 1992.
115 There has been a persistent line of argument in some ABRI circles during the New Order that the armed forces should withdraw from actively supporting particular political parties and to support a more "open" political system. For example, see David Jenkins, *Suharto and his Generals: Indonesian Military Politics, 1975–1983* (Ithaca: Cornell University Modern Indonesia Project, 1984).
116 This should not imply that ABRI would be prepared to see Golkar lose an election. In fact, ABRI prefers to lead Golkar and in April 1993 Hartas, among other officers, was suggested by Minister of Defense Edy Sudrajat as an acceptable ABRI candidate for the new chairmanship of Golkar in 1993.
117 Harsudiyono Hartas' interview is in "Tidak Ada Anak Tiri" [There is no Step-Child], *Tempo*, June 13, 1992, p. 32.
118 For these remarks see "Demokrasi tak kenal Kemutlakan Golongan" [Democracy Does Not Recognize Group Domination], *Kompas*, April 25, 1992, p. 13.
119 Imaduddin, Adi Sasono, and others specifically cite Habibie as their major sponsor and protector and speak openly of using him to institutionalize ICMI. See Chapter 3.
120 Confidential interview, June 1994.
121 From ABRI there is also an reservoir of goodwill and appreciation of Wahid's unique abilities to connect with the masses in a nationally constructive fashion. This was aptly illustrated in December 1992 when the armed forces asked Wahid to forgo his long-planned trip to Australia to present a paper at the Monash University Conference on Indonesian Democracy. Wahid was asked to instead go to East Java in order to calm public anxiety arising from a rash of attacks (stonings, burnings and vandalism) on churches in the province. Wahid stated that "my duty is clear, I will always fight for the de-confessionalized state" when explaining his role in appealing for calm – at ABRI's request – in East Java. Interview, May 3, 1993.

5 SECULAR NATIONALISTS

1 Remarks made by Y.B. Mangunwijaya, a Jesuit priest from Central Java renowned for his advocacy of poverty alleviation, human rights, and democracy, at the Monash University Conference on Indonesian Democracy, December 21, 1992.
2 Adnan Buyung Nasution, interview, April 15, 1993. As noted elsewhere in the study, Nasution is one of Indonesia's leading constitutional scholars and human rights advocates.
3 Abdurrahman Wahid, interview, September 17, 1994.

4 Recall the comments of Major General Hendropriyono, the Jakarta Commander, who argued that Forum Democracy and the Petition of Fifty were "diseases" and challenged the "tolerance" of the authorities. See *Tempo*, April 10, 1993, p. 27.

5 The group was formed during a two-day meeting at Cibeureum, a mountain resort south of Jakarta, on March 16–17, 1991. The establishment of the group was announced publicly on April 3 at a Jakarta news conference held by Abdurrahman Wahid, Marsillam Simanjuntak, and others. The Indonesian *Forum Demokrasi* will be referred to hereafter as Forum Democracy.

6 See the editorial "Forum Abdurrahman Wahid," *Pelita*, April 11, 1991.

7 Marsillam Simanjuntak, interview, April 7, 1993.

8 On the establishment of Forum Democracy and Wahid's explanation of the significance of the *Monitor* case, see "Di Tengah Masyarakat Muncul Kecenderungan Sikap Sektarian" [In the Midst of Society Emerge Tendencies towards Sectarian Attitudes], *Pelita*, April 4, 1991.

9 See "Kindling a Democratic Culture: Interview with Abdurrahman Wahid," *Inside Indonesia* (Australia), October 1991, p. 5. Wahid expressed this view on many occasions in interviews with the author, June 18, 24, October 15, 1992 and May 3, 1993.

10 See interview with Abdurrahman Wahid in *Suara Karya*, April 9, 1991.

11 See "Forum Demokrasi Untuk Hilangkan Rasa Saling Curiga-Mencurigai" [Forum Democracy To Eliminate Feelings of Mutual Suspicion], *Suara Pembaruan*, April 4, 1991. On Forum Democracy as supportive of Pancasila see also "Intellectuals Establish Forum to Bolster Democracy in Indonesia," *Jakarta Post*, April 4, 1991.

12 Abdurrahman Wahid, interviews, June 18 and 24, 1992. See also his suggestion that the behavior of some Muslims is undemocratic in *Kompas*, October 14, 1991.

13 Cited in Adam Schwarz, "A Worrying Word," *FEER*, April 25, 1991, p. 23.

14 Abdurrahman Wahid in *FEER*, April 25, 1991; Adnan Buyung Nasution, April 15, 1993 and Aswab Mahasin, July 5, 1994.

15 Aswab Mahasin, interview, July 5, 1994.

16 Confidential interview, April 1993.

17 On Wahid's concern regarding the growth of anti-Chinese attitudes in society see his interview in *Inside Indonesia*, (October, 1991), p. 5. Adam Schwarz (*FEER*, April 25, 1991, p. 23) also reports that a reason for the establishment of Forum Democracy was to counter "increased resentment" towards Chinese Indonesians.

18 Major General Hari Sabarno, cited in "ABRI Officer Says Openness Cause of Indonesia's Dilemma," *Jakarta Post*, July 8, 1994.

19 See "Forum Abdurrahman Wahid," *Pelita*, April 11, 1991. This is a common approach. Members of the Indonesian elite often praise the establishment of formal democratic "structure" under the New

Order, complete with general elections and a partially representative parliament. The most common criticism is that these "democratic structures" are not functioning properly. For example, this is the line of criticism taken up by Soerjadi, then Chairman of the Indonesian Democratic Party (interview, November 6, 1992); Ismail Hasan Metareum, Chairman of the United Development Party (interview, November 19, 1992); and Marzuki Darusman of Golkar (interview, July 16, 1992).

20 For Sudomo's comments see "Forum Demokrasi Aneh" [Forum Democracy is Strange], *Angkatan Bersenjata*, April 6, 1991. The official position of ABRI was laid out in "Nurhadi: Forum Demokrasi Bisa Jadi Politik Praktis: Maksud Baik Gus Dur Dkk Sebaiknya Melalui Wadah Yang Sudah Ada" [Nurhadi: Forum Could Become Political Practitioner: Wahid's Good Intentions are Better Served via Existing Institutions], *Suara Pembaruan*, April 6, 1991. Also note the concern that the Forum could influence the masses. This is a constant worry of ABRI leaders – that any new (or existing) social movement could exert influence over the masses and thereby agitate for political change. See for example the comments by Major General Hendropriyono who warned both the Petition of Fifty and Forum Democracy not to stir up the masses. See *Tempo*, April 10, 1993, p. 27.

21 Arief Budiman's comments are cited in "Government Urged Not to Worry about Motives of Forum Demokrasi," *Jakarta Post*, April 8, 1991. In October 1994 Arief was dismissed from Satya Wacana University for allegedly "embarrassing" his university by criticizing what he considered to be undemocratic procedures concerning selection of university officials. Arief reports that he intends to challenge his dismissal in court.

22 Interview with Abdurrahman Wahid in the monthly *Matra*, March 1992, p. 19.

23 See "Forum Demokrasi Untuk Hilangkan Rasa Saling Curiga-Mencurigai" [Forum Democracy to Eliminate Feelings of Mutual Suspicion], *Suara Pembaruan*, April 4, 1991.

24 For Wahid's denial that Forum Democracy will become a political activist group see his interview in *Suara Karya*, April 9, 1991.

25 The way in which Forum meetings or activities were disrupted nicely illustrates the imperatives of Indonesian political culture. For example, authorities rarely "refuse" to give permission for, in this case, gatherings by intellectuals. Direct rejection of requests, both in personal or political contexts is to be avoided. According to Wahid, in the case of one Forum meeting, for example, only two or three low ranking non-commissioned police officers arrived and informed Wahid that the meeting lacked appropriate official police permits. As Wahid spoke with the NCOs, who were also reluctant to be seen to "force" a man of stature and respect like Wahid to disband the meeting, the gathering continued on around them. Although there was no heavy-handed police activity, authorities none the less managed to convey a message of "disapproval" to

Forum organizers. Wahid, interview, June 24, 1992.

26 General Try Sutrisno's comments cited in "Change of Leadership Sought," *Jakarta Post*, April 11, 1992.

27 Marsillam Simanjuntak, "Democratization in the 1990s: Coming to Terms with Gradualism," in Bourchier and Legge (1994), p. 311.

28 See the statement issued by Forum Democracy *Mufakat Cibeureum II* [Second Cibeureum Consensus], dated February 23, 1992 and signed by Abdurrahman Wahid as "head of the working group of Forum Democracy."

29 ICMI never formally endorsed Soeharto for another term. However, its preference for his continuance in office is clearly reflected in the "same person, different policy" strategy outlined by Amien Rais in his interview in *Detik*, March 3, 1993 and in the author's interviews with numerous ICMI activists.

30 For Hartas' firm warnings to the Forum see "Tidak Ada Larangan bagi Forum Demokrasi" [No Prohibition for Forum Democracy], *Kompas*, April 25, 1992; "Forum told to Avoid Agitation," *Jakarta Post*, April 25, 1992; and "Forum Demokrasi Siap Dialog Konsep Demokrasi Politik" [Forum Democracy Ready for Dialogue on the Concept of Political Democracy], *Suara Karya*, April 27, 1992.

31 Teddy Rusdy, interview, November 11, 1992. See Chapter 4.

32 Hendropriyono cited in *Tempo*, April 10, 1993.

33 For Wahid's response see "Forum Demokrasi Siap Dialog Konsep Demokrasi Politik," *Suara Karya*, April 27, 1992.

34 "Police Criticized for Abruptly Banning Forum Gathering," *Jakarta Post*, April 21, 1992.

35 "Abdurrahman Barred from Speaking in Public," *Jakarta Post*, April 27, 1992; "Soeharto wants Sudomo to Monitor Forum Demokrasi," *Jakarta Post*, April 30, 1992.

36 Abdurrahman Wahid, interviews, June 18 and 24, 1992. See also "Forum Demokrasi Siap Dialog Konsep Demokrasi Politik," *Suara Karya*, April 27, 1992.

37 See "Tentu Saja, Demokrasi Kita Mengacu Kepada Undang-Undang Dasar 1945" [Of Course Our Democracy Refers to the 1945 Constitution], *Kompas*, April 29, 1992.

38 Here Wahid distinguishes between the Preamble to the Constitution of 1945 which contains the Pancasila principles and the Constitution itself.

39 Abdurrahman Wahid, interview, June 24, 1992.

40 Ibid.

41 For Adi Sasono's views, see "Sektarianisme Bukan Masalah Utama Pengembangan Kehidupan Demokrasi – Abdurrahman Wahid Dinilai Mengada-ada" [Sectarianism not the Primary Issue in Development of Democratic Life – Wahid seen as Fabricating], *Pelita*, April 15, 1991.

42 Abdurrahman Wahid, interview, September 17, 1994.

43 Wahid laid out his concept of secular democratic society in two

interviews – June 15, 1994 and September 17, 1994, and in his presentation "Democracy, Religion and Human Rights in Southeast Asia," at the East–West Center, Honolulu, September 16, 1994.

44 The following section is based on interviews with Adnan Buyung Nasution (April 15, 1993 and July 8, 1994), Marsillam Simanjuntak (August 3, 1992 and April 7, 1993), and T. Mulya Lubis (April 2, 1993).

45 Adnan Buyung Nasution, interview, April 15, 1993.

46 Imaduddin Abdul Rahim, interview, April 16, 1993. See Chapter 3.

47 See "Ancaman Disintegrasi Sudah Mulai Muncul" [Threats of Disintegration Begin to Emerge], *Republika*, February 22, 1993, p. 10.

48 Confidential interview, July 1994.

49 Adnan Buyung Nasution, interview, April 15, 1993.

50 "Police Break Up Hunger Strike, Arrest 41," *Jakarta Post*, July 8, 1994. See also LBH's "Open Letter Concerning the Incident of Police Action Entering LBH Grounds and Carrying out Arrests of LBH Guests." (Jakarta: LBH, July 7, 1994.)

51 T. Mulya Lubis, interview, April 2, 1993.

52 Adnan Buyung Nasution, interview, July 8, 1994 (original emphasis).

53 Adam Schwarz, *A Nation in Waiting: Soeharto's Indonesia in the 1990s* (Sydney: Allen & Unwin, and Boulder: Westview Press, 1994). Citation from draft chapter "The Race that Counts," p. 13 (dated June 22, 1993).

54 See Margot Cohen, "Eden of the East," *FEER*, July 27, 1993 and Adam Schwarz, "A Worrying Word," *FEER*, April 25, 1991. Schwarz reported that one of the motivating reasons behind the establishment of Forum Democracy was perception of "increased resentment towards Indonesia's ethnic Chinese minority." A generalized level of fearful anxiety was also perceived by the author in middle-class Indonesian Chinese neighborhoods.

55 See *The Limits of Tolerance* (New York: Human Rights Watch/Asia, 1994), pp. 57–76. Also based on first hand accounts provided to the author in June 1994.

56 Excellent analysis of recent political and economic implications of Indonesian Chinese business activity is in Adam Schwarz, *A Nation in Waiting: Indonesia in the 1990s*, especially his chapter "The Race that Counts."

57 See "Dangerous to Link Race and Wealth, says Buddhist Leader," *Straits Times* (Singapore), October 10, 1991, p. 14.

58 Adam Schwarz (1994), draft chapter, "The Race that Counts," p. 5.

59 Amien Rais, a leading ICMI member and head of *Muhammadiyah*, implied that Indonesian Chinese Christian domination of the economy was the reason for higher poverty rates among Muslims. Interview, October 7, 1992.

60 The author is indebted to Dr. J. Soedjati Djiwandono, a political scientist and head of research for the daily *Suara Karya*, for his analysis on the manipulation of the Chinese in contemporary politics.

61 See Richard S. Howard, "Tridharma: Indonesian Chinese Religion in Transition," MA thesis, University of Illinois at Urbana–Champaign, 1991.

62 See Michael Vatikiotis, "Pastoral Politics," *FEER*, October 5, 1989, p. 30. Vatikiotis also cites an Indonesian priest's observation that "the Catholic Church is indeed grateful to the government for ensuring that religious cleavages ar not as worrisome as they are say in Malaysia or Sri Lanka."

63 On the Javanese content to Pancasila see, for example, the discussion of Soeharto's Javanese interpretation of the ideology in Chapter 1.

64 Franz Magnis Suseno, interviews, March 21, 1992 and June 21, 1994. Harry Tjan Silalahi also argues that the strength of Pancasila as a unifying ideology is found in the culturally imbued tolerance of Javanese religion. Interview, January 16, 1992.

65 Mochtar Lubis, interview, March 30, 1992; and Goenawan Mohamad, interview, February 5, 1992.

66 See "Strong Personalities: Interview with Father Mangunwijaya," *Inside Indonesia*, October 1990, pp. 9–10 and commentary by Mangunwijaya on the author's paper "Pancasila Discourse in Soeharto's Late New Order," Monash University Conference on Indonesian Democracy, December 21, 1992.

67 The following paragraphs are based on Eka Darmaputera's views in "Kondisi Kepribadian dan Integritas Bangsa: Persoalan dan Pemecahannya" [The Condition of the Identity and Integrity of the Nation: Problem and Resolution], paper presented to a PDI seminar, dated only "March 1992" and hereafter cited as "PDI Paper." The PDI discussion was held in Jakarta on March 3, 1992. See the report of the meeting, including an account of Darmaputera's presentation in "Bahaya Yang Mengancam Pancasila Sering Tak Disadari" [Dangers Which Threaten Pancasila not often Recognized], *Suara Karya*, March 6, 1992, p. 1.

68 Eka Darmaputera, interview, February 4, 1992.

69 Darmaputera (PDI paper, 1992), p. 2.

70 Darmaputera (PDI Paper, 1992), p. 5–6 and interview, February 4, 1992.

71 The Dili "Incident" refers to the November 12, 1991 killings of at least 100 East Timorese demonstrators in the East Timor capital, Dili. The Timorese were killed by ABRI forces during a demonstration in commemoration of a young Timorese killed earlier by security forces. These killings refocused global attention on East Timor, leading to a cut-off of aid from several western donor governments and severe criticism of Indonesian policy in East Timor from the Netherlands, Portugal, and other countries. See *East Timor: The November 12 Massacre and its Aftermath*, Asia Watch, December 1991.

72 See the interview with Belo in "Kami Ingin Lebih Bebas" [We Want to be More Free], *Matra*, August 1992, pp. 13–23.

73 Belo, *Matra*, August, 1992, p. 18. Jakarta authorities consistently

reject suggestions that East Timor be granted autonomous status.

74 Belo, *Matra*, August 1992, pp. 19–20.

75 Belo, *Matra*, August 1992, p. 21 (emphasis added).

76 This section is not intended as a comprehensive treatment of Golkar's role or influence in Indonesian politics. Its purpose is limited to examination of individual Golkar members' participation in Pancasila-related discourse. Good studies of Golkar include David Reeve, *Golkar of Indonesia: An Alternative to the Party System* (Singapore: Oxford University Press, 1985) and Leo Suryadinata, *Military Ascendancy and Political Culture: A Study of Indonesia's Golkar* (Athens, Ohio: Ohio University, Monograph Series in International Studies, 1989). More general works on contemporary Indonesia that contain good analyses of Golkar include Michael Vatikiotis, *Indonesian Politics under Suharto: Order, Development and Pressure for Change* (London: Routledge, 1993) and Adam Schwarz, *A Nation in Waiting: Indonesia in the 1990s* (Sydney: Allan & Unwin, 1994).

77 Rachman Tolleng, interview, May 3, 1993.

78 Jusuf Wanandi, interview, July 1, 1992.

79 See the interview with Sarwono Kusumaatmadja in *Detik*, November 30, 1992, p. 23.

80 Sarwono, interview in *Detik*, November 30, 1992, p. 22.

81 Sarwono, interview in *Detik*, November 30, 1992, p. 23. This is merely a glimpse of Sarwono's thinking on ABRI. But it indicates his perception that forces for political change must have ABRI on their side. ICMI activists argue that Islam alone is sufficient to generate political change.

82 R. William Liddle, "Can all good things go together? Democracy, Growth, and Unity in a post-Suharto Indonesia," in Bourchier and Legge (1994), p. 299.

83 Marzuki Darusman, interview, July 16, 1992. See also the long interview with Marzuki: "Saya Ingin Jadi Presiden" [I Want to be President], *Matra*, September 1991, pp. 13–23.

84 Marzuki Darusman, interview, July 16, 1992.

85 See Marzuki Darusman, "Membongkar Kultur Status Quo" [Dismantling the Culture of the Status Quo], *Editor*, June 2, 1994, pp. 24–25.

86 Marzuki Darusman, *Editor*, June 2, 1994, p. 25.

87 Like the preceding Golkar section, this treatment of the PDI is limited to how political discourse linked to Pancasila is part of a PDI voice.

88 See "Saatnya Diakui PPP, PDI Sebagai Oposisi" [Time to Acknowledge PPP and PDI as Opposition], *Media Indonesia*, November 30, 1992.

89 See "Opposition has No Place in Indonesia: PDI Leader," *Jakarta Post*, December 7, 1992.

90 Soerjadi, interview, November 6, 1992.

91 Kwik Kian Gie, interview, July 13, 1992.

92 Ibid.
93 Ibid.
94 Abdurrahman Wahid, interview, December 10, 1994.

6 CONCLUSION: THE MEANING OF PANCASILA DISCOURSE

1 Editorial entitled "Reevaluating Tradition" which endorsed the support of "openness" by then Speaker of the House, Kharis Suhud. *Jakarta Post*, November 6, 1991.
2 Abdurrahman Wahid, "Islam, Politics and Democracy in the 1950s and 1990s," in Bourchier and Legge (1994), p. 152.
3 Carol Gluck, *Japan's Modern Myths: Ideology in the Late Meiji Period* (Princeton: Princeton University Press, 1985), p. 3.
4 Eka Darmaputera, paper presentation to a PDI seminar, March 1992.
5 Lieutenant General Mantiri, interview, July 8, 1994.
6 Soeharto, Butir-Butir Budaya Jawa [Grains of Javanese Culture] (Jakarta: Hardiyanti Rukmana, 1987). Analysis of Soeharto's remarks at the Javanese language congress is contained in Jai Singh Yadav, " 'Butir-Butir Budaya Jawa' [Grains of Javanese Culture] Teaches Love of Mankind," *Jakarta Post*, December 16, 1991.
7 Munawir Sjadzali, interviews, April 12 and 13, 1993.
8 See Chapter 3. Sri Bintang Pamungkas, Adi Sasono, Nasir Tamara, and Imaduddin all differentiated between the activists as "real ICMI" and the Habibie bureaucrats who are not perceived as genuine proponents of a Muslim perspective.
9 Transmigration refers to long-standing Indonesian government efforts to move people from densely populated areas of the archipelago, especially Java, to other less populated islands.
10 Abdurrahman Wahid, interview, May 3, 1993.
11 "Kritik Setelah Mendapat Restu" [Criticism Follows Blessing], *Editor*, June 2, 1994, p. 24.
12 Michael Vatikiotis, "Preferred Candidate," *FEER*, August 31, 1989, p. 10.
13 On Aceh and the government allegation that security disturbances there were caused by Islamic extremists see Michael Vatikiotis, "Security Blanket: Big Military Operation to Suppress Rebels in Aceh," *FEER*, October 11, 1990, p. 22; and Vatikiotis, "Troubled Province," *FEER*, January 24, 1991, pp. 20–21.
14 See for example, "Preacher Charged with Subversion," *Jakarta Post*, January 12, 1992, p. 3 and "Moslem Extremist Gets Eight-Year Jail Term," *Jakarta Post*, June 2, 1992, p. 2.
15 See Margot Cohen, "Religious Feuds Rattle the New Order," *Asian Wall Street Journal*, December 14, 1992.
16 See "Pandangan Kritis Cendekiawan Diperlukan dalam Pembangunan" [Intellectuals' Critical Perspective Needed in Development], *Pelita*, December 6, 1991; "Presiden Soeharto Pada ICMI: Dijaga, Agar Tak Muncul Sistem Alternatif Terhadap Pancasila" [President

Soeharto to ICMI: Guard Against Emergence of Alternative Systems to Pancasila], *Pelita*, December 8, 1992.

17 See Minister of Religion Tarmizi Taher's comments in "Religious Tolerance Crucial to Maintain Peace," *Jakarta Post*, June 15, 1994.

18 See for example, Soeharto's statements in "Pancasila Jamin Keutuhan Hidup Antarumat Beragama" [Pancasila Guarantees the Integrity of Inter-Religious Life], *Kompas*, March 16, 1992; "Presiden Soeharto: Kesadaran Beragama Tidak Boleh Memundur" [President Soeharto: Religious Consciousness Must Not Recede], *Kompas*, February 2, 1992; "Republic of Indonesia Pledges to Promote Religious Harmony: Soeharto," *Jakarta Post*, March 17, 1992.

19 "No Official Religion in Indonesia: Soeharto," *Jakarta Post*, April 10, 1992.

20 Soeharto's comments are found in the *Straits Times Weekly Edition*, August 13, 1994 and *Kompas*, January 24, 1994.

21 Soeharto's remarks on a state television news broadcast, April 24, 1993.

22 See the interview with Munawir Sjadzali in *Detik*, April 23–29, 1993, pp. 21–22.

23 Abdurrahman Wahid, interview, December 10, 1994.

24 Aswab Mahasin, interview, July 5, 1994.

25 Abdurrahman Wahid, interview, October 15, 1992.

26 Franz Magnis Suseno, interview, April 3, 1993.

27 See, for example, the journal *Ulumul Qur'ān*, Vol. IV, no. 1, February 1993. On Nurcholish Madjid's initial lecture, see "Islam Yang Hanif Itu Borderless" [The Tolerant/Universal Islam is Borderless], *Detik*, November 3, 1992 and "Spiritualisme Yes, Agama Formal No" [Spiritualism Yes, Formal Religion No], *Detik*, November 30, 1992, pp. 22–23.

28 Goenawan Mohamad, interview, May 4, 1993.

29 Some prominent ICMI members strongly reject such conspiracy thinking. For example, Sri Bintang Pamungkas argues that the *Tempo* articles on Habibie's role in the ship purchase raised legitimate issues and were healthy indications of open public debate. Bintang argues that by blaming Christians or ABRI for the June 1994 press bannings, Muslims ignore Soeharto's ultimate responsibility. Interview, July 5, 1994.

30 "Fundamentalism" is also visible among Christians. The author has personally encountered evangelical Indonesian Christians who exaggerate fears of Islam and aggressively proselytize Christianity in ways that not surprisingly offend Muslim sensitivities.

31 Sarwono Kusumaatmadja, interview, November 11, 1992.

32 See for example, Ghassan Salame, "Islam and the West," *Foreign Policy*, no. 90 (Spring 1993), pp. 22–37; Leon T. Hadar, "What Green Peril?" and Judith Miller, "The Challenge of Radical Islam," both in *Foreign Affairs*, Vol. 72, no. 2 (Spring 1993).

33 Judith Miller, "The Challenge of Radical Islam," *Foreign Affairs* (Vol. 72, no. 2), p. 53.

34 Salame, "Islam and the West," *Foreign Policy* (Spring 1993), p. 26.
35 Ibid.
36 Abdurrahman Wahid, interview, October 15, 1992.
37 Harry Benda, p. iii, cited in Donald E. Weatherbee, *Ideology in Indonesia: Sukarno's Indonesian Revolution* (Yale University: Southeast Asia Monograph Series no. 8, 1966).

References

Abdulgani, Roeslan. *Pancasila: The Prime Mover of the Indonesian Revolution*. Jakarta: Prapanca, 1958.

Anam, Choirul. *Pertumbuhan dan Perkembangan Nahdlatul Ulama*. Jatayu Sala, 1985.

Anderson, Benedict. *Mythology and the Tolerance of the Javanese*. Ithaca: Modern Indonesian Project, Cornell University, 1965.

—. *Java in a Time of Revolution*. Ithaca: Cornell University Press, 1972.

Anderson, Benedict and Ruth McVey. *A Preliminary Analysis of the October 1, 1965 Coup in Indonesia*. Ithaca: Cornell University Modern Indonesia Project, 1971.

Anshari, H. Endang Saifuddin. *Piagam Jakarta 22 June 1945 dan Sejarah Konsensus Nasional Antara Nasionalis Islami dan Nasionalis "Sekuler" Tentang Dasar Negara Republik Indonesia 1945–1959*. Jakarta: Rajawali, 1986.

Apter, David. "Introduction." In *Ideology and Discontent*, ed. David Apter. New York: Free Press of Glencoe, 1964.

Barton, Greg. "The Impact of Neo-Modernism on Indonesian Islamic Thought: The Emergence of a New Pluralism." In Bourchier and Legge, eds. *Democracy in Indonesia: 1950s and 1990s*. Clayton, Victoria: Centre of Southeast Asian Studies, Monash University, 1994.

—. "Neo-Modernism – a Vital Synthesis of Traditionalist and Modernist Islamic Thought in Indonesia," paper, Conference on Islam and the Challenge of Modernization held in conjunction with the 29th Congress of *Nahdlatul Ulama*, Tasikmalaya, West Java, December 1–5, 1994.

Benda, Harry J. *The Crescent and the Rising Sun: Indonesian Islam Under Japanese Occupation*. The Hague: W. Van Hoeve Ltd., 1958.

—. "Prefatory Note." In *Ideology in Indonesia: Sukarno's Indonesian Revolution*, Donald E. Weatherbee. Yale University: Southeast Asia Monograph Series no. 8, 1966.

Besar, Abdul Kadir. *Demokrasi Pancasila dan Pengaturan Penyelenggaraan Demokrasi Politik*. Jakarta, 1991. No publication information given.

Boland, B.J. *The Struggle of Islam in Modern Indonesia*. The Hague:

Martinus Nijhoff, 1971. Slightly revised reprint, 1982.

Bourchier, David. "The 1950s in New Order Ideology and Politics." In Bourchier and Legge, eds, 1994.

—. "Totalitarianism and the 'National Personality': Recent Controversy about the Philosophical Basis of the Indonesian State." In James Schiller, ed. *Indonesian Political Culture: Asking the Right Questions*. Athens, Ohio: Ohio University Center for Southeast Asian Studies, forthcoming.

Bourchier, David and John Legge, eds. *Democracy in Indonesia: 1950s and 1990s*. Clayton, Victoria: Centre of Southeast Asian Studies, Monash University, 1994.

Bowen, John R. "On the Political Construction of Tradition: Gotong-Royong in Indonesia." *Journal of Asian Studies* 45 (1986): 545–561.

Bresnan, John. *Managing Indonesia: The Modern Political Economy*. New York: Columbia University Press, 1993.

Budairy, Said H.M., ed. *Nahdlatul Ulama Dari Berbagai Sudut Pandang*. Jakarta: LAKPESDAM, 1994.

Budiman, Arief, ed. *State and Civil Society in Indonesia*. Clayton, Victoria: Centre for Southeast Asian Studies, Monash University, 1990.

Cribb, Robert, ed. *The Indonesian Killings 1965–1966: Studies From Java and Bali*. Clayton, Victoria: Centre for Southeast Asian Studies, Monash University, 1990.

—. *The Army and Politics in Indonesia*. Ithaca: Cornell University Press, 1978.

Crouch, Harold. "Democratic Prospects in Indonesia." In Bourchier and Legge, eds. 1994.

Crouch, Harold and Hal Hill, eds. *Indonesian Assessment 1992: Political Perspectives on the 1990s*. Canberra: Australian National University, 1992.

Dahm, Bernhard. *Sukarno and the Struggle for Indonesian Independence*. Ithaca: Cornell University Press, 1969.

—. *History of Indonesia in the Twentieth Century*. London: Pall Mall Press, 1971.

Darmaputera, Eka. *Pancasila and the Search for Identity and Modernity in Indonesian Society: A Cultural and Ethical Analysis*. Leiden: E.J. Brill, 1988.

—. "Kondisi Kepribadian dan Integritas Bangsa: Persoalan dan Pemecahannya." Paper presented at a PDI-organized seminar, Jakarta, March 3, 1992.

Dharwis, Ellyasa K.H., ed. *Gus Dur, NU dan Masyarakat Sipil*. Yogyakarta: LKiS, 1994.

Diarsi, Myra. "The New Order State Hegemony: Analysis of Dominant Ideology in Primary School Textbooks." Seminar on State Ideology, Yayasan SPES, Jakarta, March 18, 1992.

Dipoyudo, Kiri. *Membangun Atas Dasar Pancasila*. Jakarta: Center for Strategic and International Studies, 1990.

Douglas, Stephen A. *Political Socialization and Student Activism in Indonesia*. Urbana: University of Illinois Press, 1970.

Driyakara, S.J. "Pancasila dan Religi." In *Prasaran-Prasaran pada*

Seminar Pancasila I. Yogyakarta: Pancasila Seminar Committee, 1959.

East Timor: The November 12 Massacre and its Aftermath. New York: Asia Watch, December 1991.

Effendi, Djohan. "The Contribution of the Islamic Parties to the Decline of Democracy in the 1950s." Conference on Indonesian Democracy, Monash University, December 18, 1992.

Emmerson, Donald K. *Indonesia's Elite: Political Culture and Cultural Politics*. Ithaca: Cornell University Press, 1976.

—. "Understanding the New Order: Bureaucratic Pluralism in Indonesia." *Asian Survey* 23, no. 11 (November 1983): 1220–1241.

Fealy, Greg. "Wahab Hasbullah, Traditionalism and the Political Development of *Nahdlatul Ulama*." In Fealy and Barton, *Nahdlatul Ulama: Traditional Islam and Modernity*. Clayton, Victoria: Centre of Southeast Asian Studies, Monash University, 1995.

—. "The 1994 *Nahdlatul Ulama* Congress and Aftermath: Gus Dur, *Suksesi*, and the Battle for Control of NU," in *Inside Indonesia* (March 1995).

Fealy, Greg and Greg Barton, eds. *Nahdlatul Ulama: Traditional Islam and Modernity*. Clayton, Victoria: Centre of Southeast Asian Studies, Monash University, 1995.

Federspiel, Howard M. "The Position and Role of Islam in Suharto's Indonesian New Order at the 21st Year Mark." 1988 Annual Meeting of the Southeast Conference, Association for Asian Studies, University of North Carolina at Charlotte, January 15, 1988.

—. *Muslim Intellectuals and National Development in Indonesia*. New York: Nova Science Publishers, 1992.

—. *Popular Indonesian Literature of the Qur'ān*. Ithaca: Cornell Modern Indonesia Project, 1994.

Feillard, Andrée. "Traditionalist Islam and the State in Indonesia: Flexibility, Legitimacy and Renewal," Conference on Islam and the Social Construction of Identities: Comparative Perspectives on Southeast Asian Muslims, University of Hawaii, August 4–6, 1993.

Feith, Herbert. *The Decline of Constitutional Democracy in Indonesia*. Ithaca: Cornell University Press, 1962.

Feith, Herbert and Lance Castles, eds. *Indonesian Political Thinking 1945–1965*. Ithaca: Cornell University Press, 1970.

Geertz, Clifford. "The Javanese Village." In *Local, Ethnic, and National Loyalties in Village Indonesia*, ed. G. William Skinner. Ithaca: Cornell University Modern Indonesia Project, 1959.

—. *The Religion of Java*. Glencoe, Illinois: The Free Press, 1960.

—. "Ideology as a Cultural System." In *Ideology and Discontent*, ed. David Apter. New York: Free Press of Glencoe, 1964.

Gluck, Carol. *Japan's Modern Myths: Ideology in the Late Meiji Period*. Princeton: Princeton University Press, 1985.

Gunn, Geoffrey L. "Ideology and the Concept of Government in the Indonesian New Order." *Asian Survey* XIV, no. 8 (August 1979): 751–769.

Hader, Leon T. "What Green Peril." *Foreign Affairs* Vol. 72, no. 2 (Spring

1993): 27–42.
Hatta, Mohammed. *Memoir*. Jakarta: Tintamas, 1978.
Hefner, Robert. "Islam, State, and Civil Society: ICMI and the Struggle for the Indonesian Middle Class." *Indonesia* vol. 56, (October 1993).
Hindley, Donald. *The Communist Party of Indonesia, 1951–1963*. Berkeley: University of California Press, 1966.
Hooker, M.B., ed. *Islam in Southeast Asia*. Leiden: E.J. Brill, 1983.
Howard, Richard S. "*Tridharma: Indonesian Chinese Religion in Transition*." MA thesis. Urbana: University of Illinois, 1992.
Human Rights in Indonesia and East Timor: The Limits of Openness. New York: Human Rights Watch/Asia, September 1994.
Jackson, Karl D. and Lucian W. Pye, eds. *Political Power and Communication in Indonesia*. Berkeley: University of California Press, 1978.
Jenkins, David. *Suharto and his Generals: Indonesian Military Politics, 1975–1983*. Ithaca: Cornell University Modern Indonesia Project, 1984.
Jones, Sidney. "The Contraction and Expansion of the 'Umat' and the Role of *Nahdlatul Ulama* in Indonesia." *Indonesia*, no. 38 (October 1984).
Kahin, George McT. *Nationalism and Revolution in Indonesia*. Ithaca: Cornell University Press, 1952.
"Kami Ingin Lebih Bebas." *Matra* (August 1992): 13–23. (Interview with Bishop Carlos Belo).
"Kindling a Democratic Culture: Interview with Abdurrahman Wahid." *Inside Indonesia* (October 1991).
King, Dwight. "Indonesia's New Order as a Bureaucratic Polity, a Neo-Patrimonial Regime, or a Bureaucratic-Authoritarian Regime – What Difference Does it Make?" In *Interpreting Indonesian Politics: 13 Contributions to the Debate*, eds. Benedict Anderson and Audrey Kahin. Ithaca: Cornell Modern Indonesia Project, 1982.
Lane, Max. *"Openness," Political Discontent and Succession in Indonesia: Political Developments in Indonesia, 1989–91*. Nathan, Queensland: Centre for the Study of Australia–Asia Relations, Griffith University, 1991.
Lee, Oey Hong. *The Sukarno Controversies of 1980–81*. Occasional Paper no. 4. University of Hull: Centre for Southeast Asian Studies, 1982.
Legge, J.D. *Sukarno, A Political Biography*. Harmondsworth, Middlesex: Penguin Books, 1972.
Leigh, Barbara. "Making the Indonesian State: The Role of School Texts." *Review of Indonesian and Malaysian Affairs* 25, no. 1 (Winter 1991).
Lev, Daniel. *The Transition to Guided Democracy, Indonesian Politics, 1957–1959*. Ithaca: Cornell University Modern Indonesia Project, 1966.
Liddle, R. William. *Politics and Culture in Indonesia*. Ann Arbor: Center for Political Studies, Institute for Social Research, University of Michigan, 1988.
—. "Indonesia's Democratic Past and Future." *Comparative Politics* (July

1992): 443–462.

—. "Indonesia's Threefold Crisis." *Journal of Democracy* 3, no. 4 (October 1992).

—. "Can all good things go together? Democracy, Growth, and Unity in post-Suharto Indonesia." In Bourchier and Legge, eds. 1994.

—. "Improvising Political Cultural Change: Three Indonesian Cases." In James Schiller, ed. *Indonesian Political Culture: Asking the Right Questions*. Athens, Ohio: Ohio University Center for Southeast Asian Studies, forthcoming.

McDonald, Hamish. *Suharto's Indonesia*. Blackburn, Victoria: Fontana, 1980.

McFetridge, Charles Donald. "SESKOAD – Training the Elite." *Indonesia*, no. 36 (October 1983): 87–98.

Mackie, J.A.C. "The Golkar Victory and Party-Aliran Alignments." In *Indonesia After the 1971 Elections*, ed. Oey Hong Lee. London: Oxford University Press, 1974.

Mackie, Jamie. "Economic Growth and Depoliticization." In *Driven by Growth: Political Change in the Asia-Pacific Region*, ed. James W. Morely. Armonk, New York: M.E. Sharpe, 1993.

McVey, Ruth. "Indonesian Communism Under Guided Democracy." In *Communist Strategies in Asia, A Comparative Analysis of Government and Parties*, ed. A.D. Barnett. New York: Praeger, 1963.

Madjid, Nurcholish. *Islam Kemodernan dan Keindonesiaan*. Jakarta: Mizan, 1987.

Mas'oed, Mohtar. "The State Reorganization of Society Under the New Order." *Prisma*, no. 47 (September 1989): 3–33.

Melihat Kembali: Pernyataan Keprihatinan – 5 Mei 1980. Jakarta: Kelompok Kerja Petisi Limapuluh, 1991.

Miller, Judith. "The Challenge of Radical Islam." *Foreign Affairs* Vol. 12, no. 2 (Spring 1993): 43–56.

Moertopo, Ali. *The Acceleration and Modernization of 25 Years' Development*. Jakarta: Yayasan Proklamasi, Center for Strategic and International Studies, 1972.

—. "Some Basic Considerations in 25 Years Development." *Indonesian Quarterly* 1, no. 1 (October 1972).

—. *Strategi Pembangunan Nasional*. Jakarta: Center for Strategic and International Studies, 1981.

Morfit, Michael. "Pancasila: The Indonesian State Ideology." *Asian Survey* XXI, no. 8 (August 1981).

—. "Pancasila Orthodoxy." In *Central Government and Local Development in Indonesia*, ed. Colin MacAndrews. Singapore: Oxford University Press, 1986.

Mortimer, Rex. *Indonesian Communism Under Sukarno: Ideology and Politics, 1959–1965*. Ithaca: Cornell University Press, 1974.

Mudatsir, Arief. "From Situbondo Towards a New NU – A First Note." *Prisma*, no. 35 (March 1985): 167–177.

Mundayat, Aris Arif. "The Rite of 'Tujuhbelasan': Ideological Dissemination Under Soeharto's Regime." Ideology in the New Order

Workshop, Conference on Indonesian Democracy, Monash University, December 21, 1992.

Nasution, Adnan Buyung. *The Aspiration for Constitutional Government in Indonesia: A Socio-Legal Study of the Indonesian Konstituante, 1956–1959*. Jakarta: Sinar Harapan, 1992.

Nasution, Abdul Haris. *Pancasila Democracy Today and Tomorrow*. Jakarta: Provisional People's Consultative Assembly, 1972.

Noer, Deliar *The Modernist Muslim Movement in Indonesia, 1900–1942*. Singapore: Oxford University Press, 1973.

——. *Islam, Pancasila, dan Asas Tunggal*. Jakarta: Yayasan Perkhidmatan, 1983.

Notonagoro. *Pancasila Dasar Filsafat Negara Republik Indonesia*. Yogyakarta: Gadjah Mada University Press, 1951.

Notosusanto, Nugroho. *Proses Perumusan Pancasila Dasar Negara*. Jakarta: Balai Pustaka, 1981.

Notosusanto, Nugroho and Ismael Saleh. *The Coup Attempt of the "September 30th Movement" in Indonesia*. Jakarta: Pembimbing Masa, 1968.

Pabottingi, Mochtar. "Indonesia: Historicizing the New Order's Legitimacy Dilemma." In Muthiah Alagappa, ed. *Political Legitimacy in Southeast Asia: Quest for Moral Authority*. Stanford: Stanford University Press, 1995.

Pandangan Presiden Soeharto Tentang Pancasila. Jakarta: Center for Strategic and International Studies, 1976 and 1984.

Pauker, Guy. "The Role of the Military in Indonesia." In *The Role of the Military in Underdeveloped Countries*, ed. J.J. Johnson. Princeton: Princeton University Press, 1962.

Penders, C.L.M. and Ulf Sundhaussen. *Abdul Haris Nasution, A Political Biography*. St. Lucia, Queensland: University of Queensland Press, 1985.

"Pengamalan Pancasila." *Analisa* 15, no. 8 (August 1986).

Pranarka, A.M.W. *Sejarah Pemikiran Pancasila*. Jakarta: Center for Strategic and International Studies, 1985.

Prawiranegara, Sjafruddin. "Pancasila as the Sole Foundation." *Indonesia*, no. 38 (October 1984): 74–83.

Purdy, Susan Selden. *Legitimation of Power and Authority in a Pluralistic State: Pancasila and Civil Religion in Indonesia*. Ph.D. Dissertation. Columbia University, 1984.

Pye, Lucian W. *Politics, Personality, and Nation Building: Burma's Search for Identity*. New Haven: Yale University Press, 1971.

Ramage, Douglas E. "The Political Function of Pancasila," MA Thesis, University of South Carolina, 1987.

——. "The Political Function of Pancasila Moral Education." 1988 Annual Meeting of the Southeast Conference, Association for Asian Studies, University of North Carolina at Charlotte, January 15, 1988.

——. "Pancasila Discourse in Soeharto's Late New Order," in *Deomocracy in Indonesia: 1950s and 1990s*, David Bourchier and John Legge, eds. Clayton, Victoria: Centre for Southeast Asian Studies, Monash

University, 1994.
—. "Islam, Democratization, and Religious Tolerance: The Political Thought of Abdurrahman Wahid," in *NU: Traditional Islam and Modernity*, Greg Fealy and Greg Barton, eds. Clayton, Victoria: Centre for Southeast Asian Studies, Monash University, 1995.
Raysid, Muhammad Ryaas. *State Formation, Party System and the Prospect for Democracy in Indonesia: The Case of Golkar, 1967–1993.* Ph.D. Dissertation. University of Hawaii, 1994.
Reeve, David. *Golkar of Indonesia: An Alternative to the Party System.* Singapore: Oxford University Press, 1985.
—. "The Corporatist State: The Case of Golkar." In *State and Civil Society in Indonesia*, ed. Arief Budiman. Clayton, Victoria: Centre for Southeast Asian Studies, Monash University, 1990.
Ricklefs, M.C. *A History of Indonesia.* Bloomington: Indiana University Press, 1981.
Robison, Richard. *Indonesia: The Rise of Capital.* Sydney: Allen & Unwin, 1986.
Said, Salim. *The Genesis of Power: General Sudirman and the Indonesian Military in Politics, 1945–1949.* Singapore: Institute of Southeast Asian Studies, 1992.
Salame, Ghassan. "Islam and the West." *Foreign Policy*, no. 90 (Spring 1993): 22–37.
"Saya Ini Makelar Akhirat." *Matra* (March 1992). (Interview with Abdurrahman Wahid.)
"Saya Ingin Jadi Presiden." *Matra* (September 1991): 13–23. (Interview with Marzuki Darusman.)
Schiller, James, ed. *Indonesian Political Culture: Asking the Right Questions.* Athens, Ohio University, Center for Southeast Asian Studies, forthcoming.
Schwarz, Adam. *A Nation in Waiting: Indonesia in the 1990s.* Sydney: Allen & Unwin, and Boulder: Westview Press, 1994.
Scott, James C. *Political Ideology in Malaysia: Reality and the Beliefs of an Elite.* New Haven: Yale University Press, 1968.
—. *Weapons of the Weak: Everyday Forms of Peasant Resistance.* New Haven: Yale University Press, 1985.
Simanjuntak, Marsillam. *Unsur Hegelian Dalam Pandangan Negara Integralistik.* MA Thesis. University of Indonesia, Faculty of Law, 1989.
—. "Democratisation in the 1990s: Coming to Terms with Gradualism?" In Bourchier and Legge, eds. 1994.
Sitompul, Einar M. *Nahdlatul Ulama dan Pancasila.* Jakarta: Pustaka Sinar Harapan, 1991.
Sjadzali, Munawir. *Islam and Governmental System: Teachings, History and Reflection.* Jakarta: Indonesia–Netherlands Cooperation in Islamic Studies, 1991.
—. *Muslims' Interests are Better Served in the Absence of Muslim Parties (the Indonesian Experience).* Jakarta: Ministry of Religious Affairs, 1992.
—. "Aspirasi Umat Islam Terpenuhi Tanpa Partai Islam." *Amanah*, no.

160, August 24– September 6, 1992.
Soebijono, and A.S.S. Tambunan, Hidayat Mukmin, and Roekmini Koesoemo Astoeti. *Dwifungsi ABRI: Perkembangan dan Peranannya dalam Kehidupan Politik di Indonesia*. Yogyakarta: Gajah Mada University Press, 1992.
Soeharto. *Butir-Butir Budaya Jawa*. Jakarta: Hardiyanti Rukmana, 1987.
—. *My Thoughts, Words, and Deeds: An Autobiography*. As told to G. Dwipayana and Ramadhan K.H. English translation by Sumadi. Jakarta: PT. Citra Lamtoro Gung Persada, 1991.
Soesastro, Hadi. "The Political Economy of Deregulation in Indonesia." *Asian Survey* 29, no. 9 (September 1989): 853–869.
"Strong Personalities, Interview with Father Mangunwijaya." *Inside Indonesia* (October 1990): 9–10.
Students Jailed for Puns, Asia Watch Report (March 1993).
Studi Islamika – Indonesian Journal for Islamic Studies, Volumes 1 and 2, 1994.
Sukarno. *Pancasila: The Basis of the State of the Republic of Indonesia*. Jakarta: National Committee for the Commemoration of the Birth of Pancasila, 1964.
—. "Let Us Bury the Parties." In *Indonesian Political Thinking 1945–1965*, eds. Herbert Feith and Lance Castles. Ithaca: Cornell University Press, 1970.
Sundhaussen, Ulf. *The Road to Power: Indonesian Military Politics 1945–1967*. Kuala Lumpur: Oxford University Press, 1982.
—. "Indonesia: Past and Present Encounters with Democracy." In *Democracy in Developing Countries, Volume Three: Asia*, eds. Larry Diamond, Juan J. Linz, and Seymour Martin Lipset, 423–474. Boulder: Lynne Rienner, 1989.
—. "The Inner Contraction of the Suharto Regime: A Starting Point for a Withdrawal to the Barracks." In Bourchier and Legge, eds. 1994.
Suryadinata, Leo. *Military Ascendancy and Political Culture: A Study of Indonesia's Golkar*. Athens, Ohio: Ohio University Monograph Series in International Studies, 1989.
Suseno, Franz Magnis, "Sekitar Faham Negara Integralistik." Jakarta, March 21, 1990. No publication information.
The Indonesian Quarterly: Special Issue on Pancasila. Jakarta: CSIS (October 1987).
The East Asian Miracle: Economic Growth and Public Policy. Washington, D.C.: World Bank, 1993.
van Bruinessen, Martin. "The 28th Congress of the *Nahdlatul Ulama*: Power Struggle and Social Concerns." *Archipel* 41 (Paris, 1991): 185–200.
—. *NU: Tradisi, Relasi-Relasi Kuasa [dan] Pencarian Wacana Baru*. Yogyakarta: LKiS, 1994.
van der Kroef, Justus. "Origins of the 1965 Coup in Indonesia: Probabilities and Alternatives." *Journal of Southeast Asian Studies* Vol. 3, no. 2 (September 1972): 277–298.
van Dijk, C. *Rebellion Under the Banner of Islam: The Darul Islam in*

Indonesia. The Hague: Martinus Nijhoff, 1981.
Van Langenburg, Michael. "Analyzing Indonesia's New Order State: A Keywords Approach." *Review of Indonesian and Malaysian Affairs* (Summer 1986): 1–51.
Vatikiotis, Michael. *Indonesian Politics Under Suharto: Order, Development and Pressure for Change*. London: Routledge, 1993.
Violence in Lampung, Indonesia, Asia Watch Report (March 1989).
von der Mehden, Fred. *Religion and Modernization in Southeast Asia*. Syracuse: Syracuse University Press, 1986.
Wahid, Abdurrahman. "The Islamic Masses in the Life of State and Nation." *Prisma*, no. 35 (March 1985): 3–10.
—. "Islam and Pancasila: Development of a Religious Political Doctrine in Indonesia." Submitted to the panel "Religious Beliefs: The Transmission and Development of Doctrine," Conference of the Assembly of the World's Religions, Seoul, Korea, August 25, 1990. (Wahid did not attend the conference.)
—. "Langkah Strategis Menjadi Pertimbangan NU." *Aula*, July 1992.
—. "The 1992 Election: A Devastating Political Earthquake?" In Crouch and Hill, eds. 1992.
—. "Islam, Politics, and Democracy in the 1950s and 1990s." In Bourchier and Legge, eds. 1994.
Warren, Carol. "Balinese Political Culture and Rhetoric of National Development." In *Creating Indonesian Cultures*, ed. Paul Alexander, 39–54. Sydney: Oceania Publications, 1989.
—. "Rhetoric and Resistance: Political Culture in Bali." *Anthropological Forum* 6, no. 2 (1990): 191–205.
Weatherbee, Donald E. *Ideology in Indonesia: Sukarno's Indonesian Revolution*. Yale University: Southeast Asia Monograph Series no. 8, 1966.
—. "The Consolidation of the Pancasila State." The Asia Society, New York, November 11, 1985.
—. "Indonesia: The Pancasila State." In *Southeast Asian Affairs 1985*, Singapore: Institute of Southeast Asian Studies, 1986.
Yamin, Mohammad H. *Naskah Persiapan Undang-Undang Dasar 1945*. Jakarta: Yayasan Prapanca, 1959.
Zoetmulder, P.J. *The Cultural Background of Indonesian Politics*. Columbia: Institute of International Studies, University of South Carolina, 1967.

MAGAZINES AND JOURNALS

Aula
Analisa
Amanah
Archipel
Asiaweek
Asian Survey
Business Times

Comparative Politics
Editor
Far Eastern Economic Review
Forum Keadilan
Indonesia
The Indonesian Quarterly
Inside Indonesia
Matra
Prisma
Studi Islamika – Indonesian Journal for Islamic Studies
Tempo
Time

NEWSPAPERS

Angkatan Bersenjata
Asian Wall Street Journal
Asian Wall Street Journal Weekly Edition
Detik
International Herald Tribune
Jakarta Post
Kedaulatan Rakyat
Kompas
Media Indonesia
Merdeka
Pelita
New York Times
Republika
Sinar Harapan
Straits Times
Straits Times Weekly Edition
Suara Karya
Suara Pembaruan

NEWS AGENCIES

Antara
Reuters

GOVERNMENT PUBLICATIONS, LAWS, AND OTHER DOCUMENTS

The 1945 Constitution of the Republic of Indonesia. Jakarta: Department of Information, 1972.

Bahan Penataran Pendidikan Moral Pancasila Sesuai Dengan Ketetapan MPR no. II/MPR/1978. Jakarta: Pancasila Moral Education Team, Directorate General for Primary and Secondary Education, Department of Education and Culture, 1980.

Dwifungsi ABRI (Konsep 1979), Department of Defense, Army

Headquarters, 1979.
Ketetapan Majelis Permusyawaratan Rakyat Sementara Republik Indonesia, no. XX/MPRS/1966. Jakarta: MPRS, 1966.
Khittah Nahdlatul Ulama. Jakarta: Pusat Besar Nahdlatul Ulama, 1985.
Kondisi Ketahanan Nasional. Jakarta: National Defense Institute (Lemhanas), 1989.
Himpunan Perundang-undangan dan Peraturan Peradilan Agama. Compiled by Abdul Gani Abdullah. Jakarta: PT Intermasa, 1991.
P-4: The Guide to the Living and Practice of Pancasila and GBHN: The Broad Outlines of the State Policy. Jakarta: Center for Strategic and International Studies, 1978.
Risalah Perundingan [Minutes of the Deliberations], November 1956–June 1959, 17 volumes. Jakarta: Secretariat of the Konstituante, 1956–59.
Sistem Ideologi Pancasila Dalam Rangka Wawasan Nusantara dan Ketahanan Nasional. Jakarta: Alumni Association of the National Defense Institute (Lemhanas), November 1990.
Wahjono, Padmo. *Bahan-Bahan Pedoman Pengayatan dan Pengamalan Pancasila*. Jakarta: Aksara Baru, 1984.

SPEECHES

Effendi, Djohan. "Pembangunan Kehidupan Beragama Dalam Perspektif Negara Pancasila." Presented at the ceremony to mark his promotion to Senior Researcher in the Department of Religion, October 13, 1992.
Pidato Presiden Republik Indonesia dan Menutama Bidang Politik Pada Peringatan Hari Lahirnya Pancasila. Jakarta: Department of Information, Republic of Indonesia and PT Gunung Agung, June 1, 1967.
Soeharto. "President Soeharto's Message in Gathering with the KPNI." Transcript of President Soeharto's speech before the Indonesian National Youth Committee (KPNI), July 17, 1982. Unpublished.

Index

NOTES

1. Most Indonesian names are not inverted e.g. Adi Sasono, not Sosono, Adi.
2. Emboldened references are definitions.
3. Entries for Notes (pages 203–48) are restricted to those where extra detail is given or where authors are quoted.